S. HRG. 105–263

ENCRYPTION, KEY RECOVERY, AND PRIVACY PROTECTION IN THE INFORMATION AGE

HEARING

BEFORE THE

COMMITTEE ON THE JUDICIARY UNITED STATES SENATE

ONE HUNDRED FIFTH CONGRESS

FIRST SESSION

ON

S. 376

A BILL TO AFFIRM THE RIGHTS OF AMERICANS TO USE AND SELL ENCRYPTION PRODUCTS, TO ESTABLISH PRIVACY STANDARDS FOR VOLUNTARY KEY RECOVERY ENCRYPTION SYSTEMS, AND FOR OTHER PURPOSES

S. 909

A BILL TO ENCOURAGE AND FACILITATE THE CREATION OF SECURE PUBLIC NETWORKS FOR COMMUNICATION, COMMERCE, EDUCATION, MEDICINE, AND GOVERNMENT

JULY 9, 1997

Serial No. J–105–31

Printed for the use of the Senate Committee on the Judiciary

U.S. GOVERNMENT PRINTING OFFICE

44–452 CC WASHINGTON : 1997

For sale by the U.S. Government Printing Office
Superintendent of Documents, Congressional Sales Office, Washington, DC 20402
ISBN 0-16-055918-9

SENATE COMMITTEE ON THE JUDICIARY

ORRIN G. HATCH, Utah, *Chairman*

STROM THURMOND, South Carolina
CHARLES E. GRASSLEY, Iowa
ARLEN SPECTER, Pennsylvania
FRED THOMPSON, Tennessee
JON KYL, Arizona
MIKE DEWINE, Ohio
JOHN ASHCROFT, Missouri
SPENCER ABRAHAM, Michigan
JEFF SESSIONS, Alabama

PATRICK J. LEAHY, Vermont
EDWARD M. KENNEDY, Massachusetts
JOSEPH R. BIDEN, JR., Delaware
HERBERT KOHL, Wisconsin
DIANNE FEINSTEIN, California
RUSSELL D. FEINGOLD, Wisconsin
RICHARD J. DURBIN, Illinois
ROBERT G. TORRICELLI, New Jersey

MANUS COONEY, *Chief Counsel and Staff Director*
BRUCE A. COHEN, *Minority Chief Counsel*

CONTENTS

STATEMENTS OF COMMITTEE MEMBERS

CHRONOLOGICAL LIST OF WITNESSES

ALPHABETICAL LIST AND MATERIALS SUBMITTED

APPENDIX

Questions and Answers

Additional Submission for the Record

ENCRYPTION, KEY RECOVERY, AND PRIVACY PROTECTION IN THE INFORMATION AGE

WEDNESDAY, JULY 9, 1997

U.S. SENATE,
COMMITTEE ON THE JUDICIARY,
Washington, DC.

The committee met, pursuant to notice, at 10:07 a.m., in room SD–226, Dirksen Senate Office Building, Hon. Orrin G. Hatch (chairman of the committee) presiding.

Also present: Senators Grassley, Specter, Kyl, Ashcroft, Leahy, and Feinstein.

OPENING STATEMENT OF HON. ORRIN G. HATCH, A U.S. SENATOR FROM THE STATE OF UTAH

The CHAIRMAN. Although encryption has historically been a technology reserved for national security and military applications, the explosive growth of both electronic communications and stored data has enhanced the need to protect business, governmental, and individual communications and information from improper access and use.

A direct deterrent to economic espionage, consumer or commercial theft or fraud, or improper eavesdropping of private information or communications is the encryption of such information. By employing mathematical algorithms which convert electronic information into meaningless text, encryption prevents anyone other than a keyholder who has the algorithm necessary to unscramble or decrypt this information from gaining access to the information.

The importance of meaningful legislation in this area cannot be understated. Consider, for instance, that consumer confidence in a secure network is deemed essential to the development of such things as online commerce, which is projected to grow from last year's $500 million to as much as $12 billion by the year 2000.

The difficulty in evaluating a meaningful encryption policy is that, while its employment does protect the privacy of legitimate business and personal interests, it can also be used for the opposite effect, namely by criminals to hide their communications and operations from lawful court-ordered access. Such illicit use presents a direct threat to law enforcement and national security interests.

Balanced against these concerns, the advent of the Global Information Infrastructure and its applications has heightened the need for information privacy. Such concerns have resulted in a dramatic increase in demand by consumers for security in their electronic communications and stored data. In an effort to address this need, as it has in virtually all other areas in computer software and hardware development, U.S. industry has stepped up to the plate and become the world's leader in research and development of commercial encryption.

A 1996 report of the U.S. National Research Council entitled "Cryptography's Role in Securing the Information Society" confirms the need for robust commercial encryption, wherein it concludes that without strong cryptography to provide security for the Global Information Infrastructure, U.S. national and economic security will be at risk.

Today, Americans throughout this Nation enjoy the ability to use, and industry is free to market, commercial encryption of any strength domestically without restriction. The focus of congressional debate is the export and dissemination of U.S. encryption products abroad and the development of key recovery features that allow law enforcement access to encrypted communications under appropriate circumstances.

The export control issue has been the focus of serious debate both in Government and the public domain, centered primarily on the viability of linking a relaxation of such controls to a key recovery requirement. In the Congress, this debate has closely examined the propriety of such relaxation and why it is or is not important to link these controls to key recovery, without examining the subject of key recovery itself.

On such an important national security and business issue, one would expect the executive branch to lead. Unfortunately, the Clinton administration has been all over the map, floating policy options which range from maintaining the status quo to carving out new exceptions for financial institutions software. In their behalf, I have to say this is a difficult area, and nobody, to my knowledge, to date has come up with all the solutions in this area.

The Administration does now appear to be abandoning attempts to directly link key recovery to export controls. Instead, an effort has been initiated to tie key recovery to "certificate authorities," which are entities responsible for authenticating digital or electronic signatures.

The need for such authorities is recognized as indispensable to the integrity and development of electronic commerce. Such effort to develop a meaningful key recovery infrastructure which allows access under appropriate circumstances to law enforcement and national security is embodied in S. 909, introduced by Senators McCain and Kerrey and reported out of the Commerce Committee in June.

The concept of key recovery at first blush appears rather simple. Like giving an extra set of house keys to your neighbor, it is simply a means of allowing access to decryption information should the need arise. Considerable controversy arises, however, as to whether the development of such a system will create an inherent vulnerability to the security of the Global Information Infrastructure.

Nonetheless, it would appear that the development of some form of key recovery is inevitable. What is not at all clear and serves as a primary basis for this hearing is whether our national encryption policy should be based on a Government-mandated or controlled key recovery scheme, whether the Government should remove itself from this debate and allow for a purely market-driven development of key recovery, or whether there exists a true middle ground whereby Government and industry can work together in a manner that strikes a reasonable compromise between or among these competing interests.

Congress is now acting as a broker for these competing interests. This committee must serve as a forum for open debate in this area, and to work in a bipartisan fashion to devise meaningful legislation which will attempt to promote the interests of American business while working to protect the legitimate concerns of law enforcement and national security.

In closing, it appears that the development of a global key recovery framework is a necessary and inevitable development in the best interests of not only law enforcement, but international commerce as well. While encouraging the implementation of such an infrastructure, it is our responsibility to ensure that U.S. business remains competitive in an increasingly global market. Should this Congress fail to take action on this issue, I am fearful that the end result will be U.S. companies moving production offshore and foreign business interests engaging in greater proliferation of robust encryption in an effort to wrestle control of the international hardware and software markets from U.S. business. The end result of either of these developments is a greater proliferation of encryption abroad, posing a direct threat to our national security, as well as both domestic and international law enforcement.

Before turning to our first panel, I would like to turn to the ranking minority member, Senator Leahy, who has been a leader in Congress in the encryption debate and has steadfastly worked to craft meaningful legislation in this area and with whom it has been a pleasure for me to work. So I appreciate the good intelligence and the effort that he puts forth in this area.

I will allow one other set of remarks. As I understand it, Senator Grassley, you would like to make some short remarks so that you can leave because you have another commitment.

Senator GRASSLEY. Yes.

The CHAIRMAN. Well, we will permit that after the ranking member.

STATEMENT OF HON. PATRICK J. LEAHY, A U.S. SENATOR FROM THE STATE OF VERMONT

Senator LEAHY. Thank you, Mr. Chairman, and I commend your statement. I find myself, as you know, in great agreement with it, and I also note the letter that we have received from the Majority Leader, Senator Lott, expressing some of the same concerns you have raised.

I have worked on this issue of cryptography for many years, from the Intelligence Committee, the Judiciary Committee, Appropriations, and a number of other areas. We know that cryptography is important for our economy and our privacy and our national security. Of course, it becomes even more critical as computers become more frequently used.

Now, much of Washington until now, and Capitol Hill included, has enjoyed standing blessedly clear of the debate on cryptography. We have reveled in our ignorance of this issue, and for many of our colleagues, Mr. Chairman, and actually for many in the Administration, the word "encryption" has been just about as baffling as a bit of computer code. So even as many of us still struggle to understand how encryption works, appreciating the importance of this technology is an imperative as we watch ourselves go into the information age.

Over the years, I have questioned each iteration of the administration's encryption policy and I have made clear that this is not a black-and-white issue. Some have tried to simplify this debate as one in which you are either for law enforcement and national security or you are for Internet freedom. I think characterizing it that way is not productive. It does not help the dialog and it is inaccurate.

Those who want to see the Internet flourish are also people who are concerned about national security. We are all Americans. We are all concerned about good law enforcement—we are all people who want to make sure that we are safe. But as with other new advanced technologies that implicate both law enforcement and civil liberty interests, the solution is only going to come about if you balance all the legitimate interests.

This year, the Administration has finally come around to my view that settling the encryption issue and finding the right solution is best accomplished in the legislative arena and not through a series of sometimes conflicting Executive orders. All of us care deeply about our national security. Nobody wants to make it easier for criminals and terrorists to commit criminal acts. I mean, we can just assume that as a given.

But we should not lose sight of the fact that sometimes the best defense is a strong offense, and we can take affirmative steps to use strong encryption that can aid law enforcement, that can protect national security by limiting the threat of industrial espionage and foreign spying. It can reduce the vulnerability of electronic information to online snoops and breaches of privacy.

Furthermore, if we adopt an encryption policy that protects the global competitiveness of our high-tech industries, that is going to serve our national security interests better in the long run than driving our encryption expertise and the markets overseas, as a short-sighted policy would do.

I chaired a hearing, Mr. Chairman, 4 years ago on the clipper chip proposal. We had Justice Department witnesses who said no legislation was necessary to implement a law enforcement solution to the encryption problem or to clarify obligations or liabilities of keyholders. They said that current export controls must remain in place at 40-bit encryption. They were reluctant to consider anyone other than Government agencies as keyholders. In fact, they were so out of the loop on that that they were convinced that a Government-developed and implemented clipper chip encryption scheme was going to be popular in the marketplace. Well, it turned out to be universally shunned and derided by the marketplace.

In contrast with the situation 4 years ago, the Administration is now looking for a legislative solution, and I commend that. Export controls have been relaxed to permit U.S. firms to sell abroad 56-bit encryption, on condition they promise to develop key recovery systems. Under a new policy, banks and other financial institutions would be able to export encryption of any length, with or without key recovery, for use by customers worldwide.

I mention this only because we wouldn't be this far along, Mr. Chairman, if we hadn't asked some hard questions as we went along. But some things don't change. At the 1994 clipper chip hearing, the Administration could not answer critical questions about how much clipper chip would cost, how exactly foreign governments would get access to the private decryption keys of Americans, and how secure it would be. We have had a lot of experts raise the same questions about the current policy.

Now, what happened before is they pushed forward without internal review. Now, the Administration is pushing forward before even seeing the results from the 10 ongoing key recovery pilot programs that the Government funded at a cost of $7.8 million. You know, have the program and have the study, but don't look for the results.

There was one key recovery bill pending in the Senate. It was there in the last Congress; it has been here for this one, too. This is the Encrypted Communications Privacy Act, which I introduced along with Senator Burns and a number of Senators on both sides of the aisle, pending here as S. 376. I think that there will be a use for a market-driven, user-friendly, cost-effective form of key recovery. Nobody is going to want to have somebody who runs their encryption program get hit by a bus and not be able to get the things back.

Last month, the Commerce Committee reported a bill, introduced 2 days earlier with the backing of the Administration. Well, the Chairman and I have requested sequential referral of S. 909. It creates 15 new Federal crimes. It addresses intellectual property use of encryption. It encompasses several other issues within this Committee's jurisdiction. Many people have raised questions about this bill, notwithstanding the fact that it zipped through in 2 days before anybody actually even saw the final draft.

So I would hope, Mr. Chairman, that you and I will be able to get the cooperation of the Administration and the FBI and the NSA, as well as a number of others who are interested in this, to sit down with us and find a real solution finally to this encryption issue so that the thing just doesn't sit out there in such a nebulous fashion that the Europeans and the Asians decide they will just come in and take the market away.

I will put my whole statement in the record.

The CHAIRMAN. Thank you, Senator. We will put the whole statement in the record.

[The prepared statement of Senator Leahy follows:]

PREPARED STATEMENT OF SENATOR PATRICK LEAHY

I have followed the encryption issue closely for some years now. Cryptography is important for our economy, our privacy and our national security and will only become more critical with our increasing reliance on computers, computer networks and other digital communications and electronic media.

Until now, much of Washington, Capitol Hill included, has enjoyed standing blessedly clear of this debate. For many of my colleagues, and for many in the Administration, the word "encryption" has been just about as baffling as a bit of computer code. Even if many of us still struggle to understand how encryption works, appreciating the importance of this technology is an imperative of our inexorable transition into what we call the Information Age.

Over the years, as I have questioned each iteration of the Administration's encryption policy, I have made clear that this is not a black-and-white issue. Some have tried to simplify this debate as one in which you are either for law enforcement and national security or for Internet freedom. Characterizing the debate in these simplistic terms is neither productive nor accurate. As with other new and advanced technologies that implicate both law enforcement and civil liberties interests, the solution will only be reached by balancing all legitimate interests. This year, the Administration has finally come around to my view that settling the encryption issue and finding the right solution is best accomplished in the legislative arena.

All of us care deeply about our national security, and no one wants to make it any easier for criminals and terrorists to commit criminal acts. We should not lose sight of the fact that oftentimes the best defense is a strong offense. Taking affirmative steps to use strong encryption can aid law enforcement and protect national security by limiting the threat of industrial espionage and foreign spying, and reducing the vulnerability of electronic information to online snoops and breaches of privacy. Furthermore, adopting an encryption policy that protects the global competitiveness of our high-tech industries will serve our national security interests better in the long run than driving encryption expertise and markets overseas.

At a hearing I chaired four years ago on the Clipper Chip proposal, Justice Department witnesses told the Judiciary Subcommittee on Technology and the Law that no legislation was necessary to implement a law enforcement solution to the encryption problem or to clarify obligations or liabilities of key holders. They said that "current export controls must remain in place" at 40-bit encryption. They were reluctant to consider anyone other than government agencies as key holders. They were optimistic that the government-developed and implemented Clipper Chip encryption scheme would be popular in the marketplace because it represented such strong encryption.

Well, Clipper Chip turned out to be a marketplace flop. By contrast to the situation four years ago; now the Administration is actively pursuing a legislative solution. Export controls have been relaxed to permit U.S. firms to sell abroad 56-bit encryption on condition that they promise to develop key recovery systems. Under a new policy, banks and other financial institutions will be able to export encryption of any length, with or without key recovery, for use by their customers world-wide.

I mention these changes in Administration encryption policy both to commend the Administration for the progress made and to caution my colleagues that we must continue to ask hard questions to move this debate forward and get us closer to finding the right solution.

Some things have not changed. At the 1994 Clipper Chip hearing, the Administration witnesses could not answer critical questions about how much Clipper Chip would cost, how exactly foreign governments would get access to the private decryption keys of American citizens and businesses, and how secure the Clipper Chip system would be from abuse, mistakes and misuse.

We have had expert cryptographers raise some of the same questions about the costs and security risks of the key recovery scheme currently being pushed by the Administration. I hope we can begin to get better answers here today.

The Administration pushed forward with Clipper Chip before completing internal reviews thoroughly testing how that system would work when implemented nationally. Now the Administration is pushing forward with a key recovery scheme for the government and the private sector, before even seeing the results from the 10 ongoing key recovery pilot projects the government is funding at a cost of $7.8 million.

Asking hard questions about key recovery encryption should not be misinterpreted as rigid opposition to such systems. There has been one key recovery bill pending in the Senate in the last Congress and for most of this one. That is the "Encrypted Communications Privacy Act," which I introduced with Senator Burns and others colleagues from both sides of the aisle. It is pending before this Committee as S. 376.

Today we are going to hear significant questions raised about the costs, vulnerabilities and feasibility of the key recovery system envisioned by the Administration and reflected in the Commerce Committee bill. I have always believed that there will be a use for a market-driven, user-friendly, cost-effective form of key recovery, so that businesses and individuals can recover encrypted data that is important to them. No business wants to lose access to important confidential financial information because the employee who encrypted it took a holiday or got hit by a bus. At the same time, law enforcement access should be accommodated subject to appropriate procedures to safeguard privacy and civil liberties. That is the thrust of the Leahy-Burns encryption bill.

However, government-dictated recovery systems are radically different in nature. The Administration's insistence on burdensome regulation of key recovery systems, guaranteed access to both encrypted communications and stored files, access to keys by both domestic and foreign law enforcement agencies without court orders, and no notice ever of key disclosures to the owners of those keys, all pose significant obstacles to a market-driven approach to the development of key recovery systems.

Last month, the Commerce Committee reported a bill, S. 909, introduced two days earlier with the backing of the Administration. The Chairman and I have requested sequential referral of this bill, which creates 15 new federal crimes, addresses intellectual property uses of encryption, and encompasses several other issues within this Committee's jurisdiction. I have already heard significant questions raised about provisions in that bill, and I have a few myself. For example, I am concerned about the wisdom of granting the Secretary of Commerce the power to subject American citizens to criminal and civil penalties for violating regulations that we have not seen, and which do not even exist yet.

The Chairman and I would like the cooperation of the Administration, and specifically, the FBI and the NSA, as well as the other interested stakeholders in this debate, to sit down with us and discuss the compromises necessary to find a real solution, at last, to the encryption issue.

The CHAIRMAN. I am going to just yield for a few minutes to Senator Grassley, who has to leave early, and this would ordinarily come out of your 10-minute question time.

Senator Grassley.

STATEMENT OF HON. CHARLES E. GRASSLEY, A U.S. SENATOR FROM THE STATE OF IOWA

Senator GRASSLEY. As chairman of the International Trade Subcommittee, I have to be concerned about our international competitiveness, and just like every other person speaking today, we also have a responsibility to be concerned about our constitutional rights of privacy. Along the latter point, I have opposed some of the Justice Department's overreaching requests to get roving wiretap authority. So I come to this debate mindful of the benefits of encryption and the need to strengthen American industry in the context of our international trade, but I do have some concerns, and I want to raise concerns about local and State law enforcement because we tend in this committee, and maybe rightly so, to talk about the FBI and the Federal Government in general.

Along the latter line, I have sponsored an amendment to last year's economic espionage bill that requires the Sentencing Commission to report to Congress each year on how the Federal criminal justice system is encountering encryption.

But it also impacts local and State law enforcement as well. Working through the National Center on White Collar Crime, my office was the recipient of many, many communications that we requested from local law enforcement about what types of criminals are using encryption and what they are using it for. Sadly, I think it is fair to say that encryption is hindering the investigation and prosecution of child sex offenses, as well as other types of crimes. I want to share just a few examples.

In the Denver area, the Colorado Bureau of Investigation, Agent Chuck Davis, wrote to me that he had investigated a case in which an 11-year-old boy had committed suicide after telling family and friends that he had been sexually molested. When the police searched the boy's room, they found an electronic personal organizer which the boy had just received as an early Christmas present. Family members reported that the boy spent a lot of time during his last few days of life typing information into the organizer.

The police think that they have a suspect based on hearsay evidence from the child's mother, and the police believe that the boy may have left details as to who had molested him in this organizer. Obviously, this evidence would be very helpful. In fact, the organizer is password-encrypted. The police are trying to crack the password, but there are 1.9 million possibilities and the Colorado Bureau doesn't have the capacity to get through to this password.

I first received an E-mail from Agent Davis discussing the case in February 1996. In preparation for this hearing, I contacted Agent Davis to find out the status of the case. Now, over a year later, the case is in a holding pattern because the Colorado police cannot break the password. In my view, this is unacceptable and Congress needs to act.

Doug Ehrlich, a criminologist from my State of Iowa, has reported that he has had a child pornography and child molestation case where an entire computer hard drive was encrypted. In this case, a 16-year-old boy was suspected of molesting a younger sister. This 16-year-old bragged that he had encrypted his hard drive and refused to provide a password. Fortunately, Iowa is one of four States in the country where the State crime lab treats computer evidence as a forensic science problem, so they were able to unscramble the hard drive, where they found incriminating evidence, including child porn downloaded from the Internet. But according to Agent Ehrlich, he wouldn't have been able to make a case if the 16-year-old had used a slightly more sophisticated encryption program.

Now, these are just two examples of where encryption has hindered prosecuting child molesters and child pornographers. Whatever the benefits of encryption, and there are many, any proposal that doesn't deal with situations like these fall short of what the American people have a right to expect from national leaders.

Unfortunately, it seems the supporters of completely uncontrolled encryption aren't willing to make a good-faith effort to take law enforcement needs into account. In his written statement to the committee, one of the witnesses on panel two writes, "The expected misuses of crypto would have to clearly dominate the benefits from the expected uses to justify a widespread key recovery system."

So, in other words, what is really being said here is that some level of unprosecuted crime is the cost for uncontrolled encryption. My question, then, is how would the proponents of this point of view draw the line? How much crime is enough to say that the misuse of encryption clearly dominate the benefits of encryption, such as Government control, is justified?

In the example that I discussed earlier about the 11-year-old boy in Denver, how many child molesters should go free because of encryption? I don't think that uncontrolled encryption should serve as a "get out of jail free" card for criminal elements, but that is the road that we are heading down if we aren't careful.

I think we need a balanced approach to encryption policy that takes law enforcement concerns into account, and I am glad that the committee will be weighing in on this issue, since I have a feeling that other committees in Congress are not set up to take law enforcement needs into account. I especially want to bring this committee's attention to the problems of State and local law enforcement, as well as Federal law enforcement.

Thank you.

The CHAIRMAN. Thank you, Senator Grassley.

We are happy today to have Senator Kerrey here as our first witness. I want to commend Senator Kerrey for his efforts to bring about a meaningful compromise on these very complex issues, as he does in so many areas.

So we are happy to have you here. We welcome you to the committee and we look forward to taking your statement at this time.

Senator KYL. Mr. Chairman, might I just have unanimous consent to insert two statements in the record? The first is my prepared statement. The second is a staff report I asked my Subcommittee on Technology, Terrorism, and Government Information to prepare analyzing, for the benefit of full committee members, the Encryption 'Risks' Report published by the Center for Democracy and Technology and under discussion here today.

The CHAIRMAN. Without objection, we will put all statements in the record.

[Senator Kyl submitted the following materials:]

PREPARED STATEMENT OF SENATOR JON KYL

Mr. Chairman, I appreciate your leadership in bringing this very important and complex issue before our Committee. I believe that what we do or fail to do in fashioning national policies over encryption will have profound implications for personal privacy, the integrity of commerce, law enforcement, and national security.

There are two separate and distinct issues here, each in need of consideration on the merits: First, a domestic infrastructure to support the needs of consumers and public safety in having reliable management of encryption and encrypted transactions, and second, export controls to ensure that high quality U.S. technology does not fall into the wrong hands.

Encryption products are the future for the privacy and security of communications and information. Americans have a right to be secure in the knowledge that their private communications and information remain private, and that they can conduct electronic commercial transactions reasonably safe from fraud or compromise. Security embedded in consumer goods (as well as in information systems) needs to become a common part of how we do business.

But encryption can also be a menace in the hands of criminals, hiding their illicit records and criminal transactions. Because of the importance of electronic surveillance to criminal investigations, law enforcement agencies across the country believe the impact of widely proliferating encryption will be disastrous for them, unless they have a means of lawfully decrypting communications and information of criminal suspects.

If the government does nothing but passively watch as encryption proliferates with no standards to guide it, law enforcement will lose critical investigative capabilities. In all likelihood, they will be forced to turn to more intrusive techniques (microphones in the room or car rather than taps on telephones), which are more invasive of privacy and which put more police officers lives at risk. Criminals (drug dealers, kidnappers, thieves) will enjoy safe havens they do not presently have, and more good citizens will find themselves victims of unsolved crimes. And Congress will not be able to say, we did not know it would be this bad.

Today, pursuant to Court order, law enforcement may conduct electronic surveillance including wiretaps, as well as search files and other documents for evidence of criminal activity. Subject to the limits of our Constitutional guarantees, law enforcement needs to be able to continue to do its job in the information age. This will require a domestic key recovery infrastructure. Law enforcement does not need more intrusive authorities or abilities; it needs merely to be able to continue to use the same investigative techniques presently available, subject to Constitutional protection.

The U.S. needs to establish common standards for accessing encrypted data and comms ("key recovery") to support commercial needs (e.g., companies need to be able to get at their electronic records if the person who encrypted them dies or turns into a vindictive disgruntled employee), consumer transactions (trusted and easy interoperability), and law enforcement. A domestic key recovery infrastructure is the answer to that.

And, on an even more profound level, we need to find ways to bridge the gap that is dividing Americans from one another, between those who care that law enforcement have the tools to be able to do the job we expect it to do, and those who apparently have come to believe that law enforcement is a greater threat to civil liberties than the criminals. A lawless society is no defender of our liberties.

A second, separate and distinct issue—but one that sometimes wrongly gets confused with domestic encryption policy—is what controls properly should cover the export of encryption products, to support national security concerns.

Export controls are the single most important tool we have for protecting sensitive national security interests in this arena. U.S. national security is heavily dependent on being able to collect intelligence by listening in on what adversaries are up to. This intelligence saves lives, wins wars, and preserves the peace. And in an era of information warfare, having superior information systems may be key to military power.

The bottom line is this: Free export of U.S. encryption beyond a certain level would seriously hurt U.S. foreign intelligence capabilities. Any further weakening of export controls would have a deeply debilitating impact on national security. Where it comes to classified national security matters, the American people rightly expect that their elected representatives will quietly but firmly do their job to protect the country. We must not fail in this responsibility.

Encryption products are big business, and growing. There should be little surprise, therefore, in the interest this issue has generated. Whatever legislative remedy may emerge from this debate, we need to ensure that national security and law enforcement concerns are not submerged to commercial expediency.

STAFF REPORT—ANALYSIS OF ENCRYPTION 'RISKS' REPORT

October 1, 1997.

PREFACE

Earlier this year, the Center for Democracy and Technology [1] published a report by a group of people who are historically outspoken on government involvement in encryption policy. That report, called The Risks of Key Recovery, Key Escrow, and Trusted Third-Party Encryption, [2] has been cited in a number of hearings on the encryption issue.

This critique, prepared by the staff of the Judiciary Subcommittee on Technology, Terrorism, and Government Information, provides an analysis of the 'Risks' paper as directed by Subcommittee Chairman Kyl.

INTRODUCTION

The nation needs a balanced encryption policy; one that addresses the legitimate needs of the stakeholders and establishes a solid framework for the U.S. economy of the 21st century. The attributes of a balanced national encryption policy will include:

- Widely-used, robust encryption for the protection of information;
- Law enforcement access to criminal information to protect public safety;
- Export controls on encryption to address national security needs;
- Industry access to global markets.

The technical cornerstone of a national policy is the development of trustworthy key management infrastructures that also support key recovery. Unfortunately, the 'Risks' paper inadequately covers the key management and key recovery topics (both of which are needed for securing public networks and for helping to ensure public safety) since:

(1) Its technical analysis is often incomplete, biased, or contradictory, and

---

[1] The Center for Democracy and Technology is a civil liberties-oriented interest group funded by major contributions from software developers and privacy advocates.

[2] *The Risks of Key Recovery, Key Escrow, and Trusted Third-Party Encryption;* Report by: H. Abelson, R. Anderson, S. Bellovin, J. Benaloh, M. Blaze, W. Diffie, J. Gilmore, P. Neumann, R. Rivest, J. Schiller, B. Schneier, dated 27 May 1997, hereafter known as the 'Risks' paper. Available on World Wide Web at: www.crypto.com/key—study

(2) The encryption issue is treated primarily as a technical one. By ignoring the social consequences and the economic penalties that the nation will face without key management infrastructures and key recovery, the paper fails to be a useful study of the issues.

ANALYSIS

The 'Risks' paper's views are paraphrased below in *italics,* organized by **SECTION HEADINGS** from the report. Comments and notes on those views are in **bold-face**, below the paper's views.

ABSTRACT

The abstract says that the report outlines the technical risks, costs, and implications of key recovery.

The report does not meet the objectives defined in the abstract. The paper is:

- **Incomplete—By omitting the benefits of key recovery and the consequences of excluding key recovery, the true "costs" and "implications" are not presented.**
- **Often a political commentary on the issue—Not a technical examination.**
- **Not a true scientific evaluation of the issues—Data are often mis-characterized or biased in presentation.**

EXECUTIVE SUMMARY

Key recovery is so complex and costly that it is "breathtaking".

Several companies have already addressed the issues that the paper asserts are "too hard" or "costly" and are selling commercial products today to industry users who recognize the value of key recovery.

This section does not state or acknowledge the societal consequences and business costs of a world without key recovery.

GROUP CHARTER

The report is a collaborative effort to study the technical implications of controversial proposals by the United States and other national governments.

The paper strays from the group's "technical" charter; it is often a political commentary on the issue, rather than a technical one. Many arguments are unsubstantiated; others seem borrowed from statements and papers prepared by special interest groups. Regardless of the source, the paper does not provide a scientific evaluation of the issues since data are often mis-characterized or biased in presentation.

Contrary to the statement of the group charter, the report does not address the concerns of "other national governments", an important factor in the encryption debate. It is interesting to note that all countries that are major producers of encryption controls its export. This paper omits or minimizes these facts.

For example, in June 1997 various European participants in the Trans-atlantic Dialogue on Broadcasting and Information Society indicated to all participants, public and private, that if the U.S. were to eliminate export controls [on non-key recovery-based encryption, there would be a strong European reaction, perhaps leading to European import restriction on U.S. encryption products. Interestingly, a number of multinational corporations represented at the meeting indicated that they will only use encryption with key recovery.

1. BACKGROUND

1.1 ENCRYPTION AND THE GLOBAL INFORMATION INFRASTRUCTURE

This section provides a good overview of the benefits of encryption and correctly states that sensitive information is finding its way into electronic form and that encryption can be used to protect it.

This section lists the good things that encryption will be used for, but omits that it can also be used to prevent public safety officers from detecting illegal activities that citizens want to eliminate, such as:

- **Drug traffickers**
- **Radical anti-government militia**
- **Violent criminals**

- **Racist/hate groups**
- **Nuclear & biological weapons smugglers**
- **Child pornographers**
- **Terrorists**

Without the possibility of lawful access to these groups' communications, law enforcement will find itself 'out-gunned' on the Information Highway. This is a serious concern to this nation's—and other nations of the world—public safety officers. Because of these concerns, the National Sheriffs' Association and the International Association of Chiefs of Police (>13,000 members) are on-record as supporting key recovery-based encryption.

[Encryption makes it] "more difficult for law enforcement to conduct certain kinds of surreptitious electronic surveillance".

This greatly understates the impact of encryption on criminal investigations since, without key recovery, it will be virtually impossible to decrypt criminal communications. Electronic surveillance, which is conducted under proper legal authority, is generally used in investigations involving major criminal offenses and even then, on a relatively selective basis. It is a tool of last resort, used when other techniques are likely to fail and/or are too dangerous.

1.2 "KEY RECOVERY": REQUIREMENTS AND PROPOSALS

Provides good definitions of key recovery, escrow, and other terms.

The substance of much of this section is sound, but gratuitous inflammatory words are sometimes used to set the stage for later biased (vs. scientific) presentation of key recovery (e.g., "key recovery will * * * ultimately impose substantial new risks and costs").

1.3 KEY RECOVERABILITY: GOVERNMENT VS. END-USER REQUIREMENTS

This section compares government and user key recovery requirements.

There are a number of misleading statements and important omissions in this section. Examples:

*"Key recovery systems have gained currency due to the desire of government * * * agencies to guarantee access to encrypted information without the knowledge or consent of encryption users.".*

These words seem to imply that key recovery gives the government more power than it is authorized or violates due process. In reality, key recovery simply enables law enforcement agencies to maintain existing authorities and capabilities to keep pace with the technology that law-breakers will be using.

"There is very little overlap between systems that address [the key recovery requirements of the commercial world and the Government]".

Not true. This argument appears to be left-over from the early-1990s when Clipper's escrowed keys were held by the government and were not available to users who have lost their keys. Key recovery systems are being purchased today due to the requirements of the private sector, not just law enforcement, and the systems that have been approved for export can meet the needs of both. Many in the private and public sector want to be able to protect themselves against lost or otherwise unavailable encryption keys, so that continued availability of critical data is assured.

"The key management and key recoverability systems naturally arising in the commercial world do not adapt well to a government's requirements."

A very puzzling (and incorrect) statement since the government has already approved over thirty six commercial key recovery plans, and five companies' export licenses for the sale of commercial key recovery products.

1.3.1 COMMUNICATION TRAFFIC VS. STORED DATA

This section contains a confused presentation on the market demand for key recovery for stored data and for Email.

There is a clear market demand for key recovery for stored data and Email. Some vendors are already marketing the feature (Netscape and PGP, for example). IBM, Apple, Mitsubishi, RSA, America Online, and over 50 other domestic and international companies have joined forces to pursue the key recovery-based encryption market.

This section correctly states that the market demand for key recovery is different for "communication traffic".

This section incorrectly understates the likely demand for key recovery for communication traffic ("there is basically no business model [for key recovery for encrypted communications]"). Today (according to the American Management Association, a trade association of about 10,000 corporations employing ~25% of the American workforce):

- **35% of all American companies electronically monitor workers' telephone calls, voice mail, and the like [for quality assurance, to detect criminal activity, etc.]**
- **81% of financial institutions do so.**
- **10.4% go so far as to tape phone conversations.**
- **16% monitor workers' computers to see what they have on their screen and measure the number of keystrokes.**

Why do they do these things? These corporations have decided that it's a good business practice. Clearly, as encryption is used more to protect communication traffic, the market demand for key recovery for communication traffic will grow. Encryption's use has many benefits, but corporations and governments alike are concerned that it could also be mis-used to conceal criminal activity, and corporations do not want rouge employees to hold them hostage by using encryption as an electronic shredder.

1.3.2 AUTHENTICATION VS. CONFIDENTIALITY KEYS

Implies that the government advocates the escrowing of authentication/signatures keys.

This is a serious mis-representation of the government's position since there is no law enforcement requirement to escrow signature keys. In fact, the federal government actively advocates against this type of escrow.

Implies that signature keys must be escrowed in order to escrow confidentiality keys.

This is another example of the paper using an example that is not representative of the norm. In most key recovery/escrow schemes, the signature key is not escrowed.

1.3.3 INFRASTRUCTURE: LOCAL VS. THIRD-PARTY CONTROL

This section describes why the average encryption user needs key recovery and how it might support him.

In this section the paper describes key recovery as a routine service that users will expect of their data management infrastructure. This differs significantly from earlier assertions that key recovery is too complex and beyond the current competency of the field.

Additionally, the paper uses another 'worst case' example of key recovery schemes while trying to make a stretched point. In reality, there are well over 30 different key recovery schemes that are documented extensively on the Internet.

1.3.4 INFRASTRUCTURE: KEY CERTIFICATION AND DISTRIBUTION VS. KEY RECOVERY

This section briefly describes roles of Certificate Authorities (CAs) but contains many inaccuracies and omissions. As a result, it is an inadequate description of what is necessary to achieve trustworthy encryption used on a large scale.

Required clarifications:

- **CAs need to certify the authenticity of keys used for encryption, not just keys used for signature.**
- **Encryption Key Management Infrastructures (KMIs) provide the services necessary to enable encryption to be used widely and with trust. CAs provide some of those services, and other KMI components provide other services. By downplaying and mis-communicating the role of, and need for, encryption support services, the paper can be confusing to those trying to understand what's necessary to achieve secure global electronic commerce.**

2. RISKS AND COSTS OF KEY RECOVERY

The overarching assertion in this section is that key recovery systems are less secure, more costly, and more difficult to use than systems without key recovery.

The paper uses narrow arguments and fails to prove the general case, primarily because the assertions are not true when the true "risks" and "costs" are considered. In reality, we anticipate that key recovery will be considered well worth the cost by most encryption users and can literally help save lives. What follows are a few examples that help show the kinds

of "costs and risks" that need to be considered by a society that will soon be using encryption widely:

- **Suppose a company suspects—but isn't sure—that a critical, valuable employee in their computer department is communicating (using encryption) sensitive company data to a competitor. How can the company protect the health of its business by discretely monitoring company communications without tipping-off innocent or guilt employees?**
- **Suppose the Social Security Administration encrypts its databases and the encryption key is lost or corrupted. What is the cost to re-survey/reconstruct the data? What is the impact on ('cost') needy citizens who are inappropriately denied benefits (or on others who are inappropriately given them) if government policy makers have to rely on out-dated information when determining how to fund social programs?**
- **Suppose a law enforcement investigation has tapped a kidnapper's phone line (under a court order) and instead of the kidnapper's voice hears "xD}fn345#&(4jkD7,fodfkd9 * * *.". How will this affect law enforcement efforts to free the kidnap victim?**

Because of the failure to address these kinds of "risks and costs", most of section 2 is of limited value—especially the conclusions drawn from it.

"The failure of key recovery mechanisms can jeopardize the proper operation, underlying confidentiality, and ultimate security of encryption systems" [and could] "fail to meet law enforcement demands".

A non-key recovery system also has these associated risks, and will certainly not meet law enforcement requirements in the same way that key recovery-based encryption can.

2.1 NEW VULNERABILITIES AND RISKS

Asserts that key recovery "introduces a new and vulnerable path to the unauthorized recovery of data".

The implication that, by definition, a new path is "vulnerable" is unsubstantiated and contradicts the fact that several vendors have already implemented key recovery securely. It could also be interpreted as casting doubt on public key encryption itself, presumably not one of the intentions of the paper.

Implies that authentication/signatures keys should be escrowed.

The government does not have a need for access to escrowed signature keys. Indeed, the Executive Branch has taken the position that their escrow is inappropriate and undesirable.

2.1.1 NEW PATHS TO PLAINTEXT

Equates "escrow" with "insecure".

This is incorrect. There are many secure, time-tested methods to protect keys that will be escrowed. The paper implies that because a recoverable key is "out of control of the user", it is not secure. Does this mean that citizens should not trust, for example, banks to hold their spare cash?

2.1.2 INSIDER ABUSE

Argues that "key recovery systems are particularly vulnerable to insider abuse".

This is not substantiated in the paper. Key recovery systems, like any system containing valuable data, are built to prevent and detect insider abuse. Most are designed so that it is not possible for a single insider to compromise a key.

2.1.3 NEW TARGETS FOR ATTACK

Argues that a concentration of escrowed keys will be a tempting target to those who have an interest in the keys.

There is some merit to this argument, however, the paper's supporting arguments are misdirected. Instead of noting that there are many known secure, straightforward ways to counter the 'key concentration' concern, the paper seems to dismiss key recovery completely. This is a 'risk aversion' philosophy, as opposed to a more reasonable 'risk management' philosophy. Using the paper's risk aversion philosophy, one might argue against putting your money in the bank, since people are tempted to rob banks ('because that's where the money is'). A more reasonable risk management approach is to build trustworthy banks, and put your money there where you know it will be well-protected.

2.1.4 FORWARD SECRECY

This section defines the term 'forward secrecy' but provides incorrect examples of forward secrecy throughout the rest of the section.

Among cryptographers, forward secrecy usually means that the compromise of one key does not mean that future communications are compromised. Forward secrecy can be assured in a variety of ways.

The paper instead discusses what the authors believe to be the merits of ensuring that an encrypted conversation can never be recovered via key recovery. It is the similar argument used by those who argue for the abolishment of court-ordered wiretaps: that conversations are private and courts shouldn't authorize law enforcement to conduct interceptions. These views seem to be rather extreme; the U.S. Supreme Court has repeatedly affirmed that such court orders are permitted limited by the U.S. Constitution.

2.2 NEW COMPLEXITIES

"The commercial and academic world simply does not have the tools to properly analyze or design the complex systems that arise from key recovery.".

The following companies have either already built products that support key recovery or are members of an alliance (the Key Recovery Alliance) that is doing exactly what the paper says can't be done.

Apple Computer, Inc.
Atalla
Baltimore Technologies
Boeing
Candle Corporation
CertCo
Certicom
Compaq Computer Corp.
Cryptomathic
CygnaCom Solutions, Inc.
Cylink Corp.
DASCOM, Inc.
Data Securities Int'l, Inc.
Digital Equipment Corp.
Digital Secured Networks
Digital Signature Trust Co.
Entrust Technologies
First Data Corp.
Frontier Technologies Corp.
Fort Knox Escrow Services
Fujitsu Ltd.
GemPlus
Gradient Technologies, Inc.
Groupe Bull
Hewlett-Packard
Hitachi
IBM
ICL
Intel
IRE, Inc.
McAfee
Mitsubishi Corp of Japan
Mitsubishi Electric America
Motorola
Mykotronx
Mytec Technologies, Inc.
nCipher
NCR Corp.
NEC
Network Systems Group of StorageTek
Novell, Inc.
Open Horizon, Inc.
Portland Software
Price Waterhouse
PSA
Racal Data Group

Rainbow Technologies
Red Creek Communications
RPK
RSA
SafeNet Trusted Services Corp
Santa Cruz Operations, Inc.
Secure Computing Corp.
Siemens AG
Silicon Graphics, Inc.
SourceFile
Spyrus Sun Microsystems, Inc.
Sterling Commerce
Tandem
Technical Communications Corp (TCC)
Technology, Inc.
Toshiba
Trusted Information Sys., Inc.
Unisys
UPS
Utimaco Safeware AG
VPNet Technologies

*"Most of the key recovery or key escrow proposals * * * have had weaknesses discovered".*

This is misleading. For example, the paper mentions a prototype key escrow system but fails to mention that this "weakness" did not in any way put the user's data at risk of compromise. There is no other data presented in this section to substantiate the assertion that 'most proposals have flaws'.

2.2.1 SCALE & 2.2.2 OPERATIONAL COMPLEXITY

*"Key recovery * * * will require the deployment of a secure infrastructure * * * worldwide interacting and cooperating on an unprecedented scale.".*

This part of the paper blurs key recovery costs with key management infrastructure costs. It greatly overstates key recovery costs and incorrectly downplays the need for key management infrastructures. Key management infrastructures with key recovery will enable encryption to be used widely, securely, and with confidence.

Additionally, these sections use inconsistent, worst-case, or unlikely examples in an attempt to give the impression that the key recovery service that individuals will want—and the nation's public safety officials will need—is too hard to do. In reality, there are over 30 different methods to perform key recovery; vendors and users can select from any of these methods depending on their applications or needs. The facts on key management and key recovery are:

- **They are complex but achievable.**
- **They are necessary for encryption to be used widely and with confidence, for electronic commerce to grow, and for the nation to realize the full potential of the Information Age.**

The better question for the paper to ask is 'How much more will it cost to add key recovery to key management infrastructures?'. The answer is that the additional cost need not be great, and that the benefits will be substantial.

2.2.3 AUTHORIZATION FOR KEY RECOVERY

It will be very difficult to reliably authenticate individuals who are requesting an escrowed key. "Human forms of identification—passports, birth certificates, and the like—are often easily counterfeited.".

Why is it more difficult for key recovery agents to authenticate individuals than for any other organization such as a bank, medical facility, court, business, etc.? How has key recovery decreased the validity of "passports, birth certificates, and the like"?

2.3 NEW COSTS

Key recovery will be expensive.

Not doing key recovery will be more expensive: Valuable data will be lost, and public safety will decrease. For encryption users, key recovery is like

an encryption insurance policy that allows them to get back data when they really need it; for the public, key recovery is like a safety net that will ensure that law enforcement officials are not left behind on the Information Highway.

Contrary to the paper's unsubstantiated assertions that key recovery is enormously expensive is that fact that a vendor who has already developed and marketed key recovery services says that the price of key recovery is approximately one dollar per year. The Defense Department's most recent key recovery system is being operated at a cost of well under twenty cents per key per year.

2.3.1 OPERATIONAL COSTS

"In general, cryptography is an intrinsically inexpensive technology; there is little need for externally-operated 'infrastructure'".

Incorrect. Without an infrastructure to support its secure use, cryptography is not just "inexpensive", it is of little value to, for example, a corporation seeking to conduct electronic commerce.

The authors thoroughly blur key management infrastructures, which are needed for secure, widespread encryption usage, and key recovery, which is one of many potential services of a key management infrastructure.

*"Key recovery requires a complex and poorly understood—and hence expensive and insecure—infrastructure.". "It remains unclear whether the high-risk, high-liability business of * * * key recovery * * * will be economically viable.".*

This is a re-statement of the 'it's too hard so let's not do it' argument. As pointed out earlier, many prominent companies seem to disagree with the above assertion and are already selling or planning to sell key recovery-based products. The Department of Defense has been using secure electronic key management infrastructures for decades. Additionally, the government is currently conducting ten key management pilot projects, in conjunction with private sector participants, that will be used to support the secure use of commercial encryption.

2.3.2 PRODUCT DESIGN COSTS

Key recovery will substantially increase product design costs.

Some vendors offer a key recovery overlay service that minimizes the design cost to add a key recovery feature. Additionally, there are many working examples of it being incorporated into software. Lastly, new hardware products do not require additional hardware just to support key recovery.

2.3.3 END-USER COSTS

"Highly secure communication and storage need require nothing further than the purchase of reputable commercial [encryption] product.".

So long as this argument is accepted and trustworthy key management infrastructures aren't built, one or both of the following will happen, contrary to the nation's interests:

- **Encryption will not be used widely because people won't be able to trust it. Keys will not be trustworthy enough for people to trust encryption to protect their electronic information to the same degree that they trust the protection afforded to paper transactions.**
- **Encryption will be used with a false sense of security.—People will incorrectly assume that encryption with untrustworthy keys provides adequate protection to their electronic information.**

The description of key recovery's impact to the end user is described here, but the "cost" is never described.

Perhaps one of the reasons the cost is not described is the fact that, in most cases, the impact to the end user is very low since he interfaces to the key recovery agent only one time (or very infrequently).

The text in this section seems instead to be focused on concerns over the fact that there's a spare key. In reality, an individual will be very happy knowing there's a spare key when he runs into problems with his primary key. The situation is quite similar to computer passwords and bank PIN numbers: When you forget a password or PIN number, you are very thankful that a trusted individual/organization (e.g., your system administrator or bank) can help you get access to your information or money.

2.4 TRADE-OFFS

Summarizes the types of trade-offs that are available when designing a key recovery system.

This section contributes positively to the technical understanding of the issue but, unfortunately, too often picks worst-case examples and ignores the fact that there are those more than 30 widely known key recovery methods with more under development, many of which can address the concerns that the paper focuses on.

2.4.1 KEY RECOVERY GRANULARITY AND SCOPE

Summarizes the trade-offs in more detail.

While the first part of this section is fair, the last paragraph of this raises red herrings in describing concerns that are routinely and securely addressed today using time-tested methods (e.g., the last paragraph characterizes normal key management issues as "vulnerabilities").

3. CONCLUSIONS

"Key recovery systems are inherently less secure, more costly, and more difficult to use than similar systems without key recovery." "Attempts to force the widespread adoption of key recovery through export controls, import or domestic use restrictions, or international standards should be considered in light of these factors."

The paper's conclusions suffer from the deficiencies of the preceding sections.

The paper's "technical" charter is absent in this section, and the political commentary is prominent.

Ultimately, the paper fails to be a useful study of the issues because of its poor technical analysis, and its failure to address the social consequences and the economic penalties that individuals and society as a whole will face without key management infrastructures and key recovery.

The CHAIRMAN. Senator Kerrey.

STATEMENT OF HON. J. ROBERT KERREY, A U.S. SENATOR FROM THE STATE OF NEBRASKA

Senator KERREY. Thank you very much, Mr. Chairman. While you were saying I was welcome here, your compadre there on your left was shaking his head no.

Senator LEAHY. I just had something caught in my eye, Senator Kerrey. [Laughter.]

The CHAIRMAN. I was wondering if I was making some sort of a mistake, which I am prone to do.

Senator KERREY. Mr. Chairman, I have got a statement that I would ask to be included in the record.

The CHAIRMAN. Without objection.

Senator KERREY. I have also got two documents that might be useful for you and members of this committee. One is questions and answers about the piece of legislation that was passed, as amended, out of the Commerce Committee, the Secure Public Networks Act of 1997. And another is a response to a very widely circulated piece that appeared in the San Jose Mercury News. This is the second time that this newspaper has had something widely circulated. I won't comment on the previous one.

But this response to some of the questions that have been raised—as I said, it has been widely circulated in a "Dear Colleague" letter, as well as introduced in the record on the House side. There are some very helpful things in this column, but there are some inaccurate things in the column as well, and I wanted this committee to have an opportunity, as well as other members, to get an opportunity for some response to it.

The CHAIRMAN. Well, thank you. We will make them part of the record.

[The prepared statement of Senator Kerrey and the information referred to follow:]

PREPARED STATEMENT OF SENATOR J. ROBERT KERREY

Mr. Chairman, and members of the Senate Judiciary Committee, I appreciate the opportunity to testify.

There is a growing consensus that the Congress must act and must act urgently to enhance security on America's computer networks. There are a number of examples of individual security being compromised on-line.

The Internet is a vibrant, exciting and important mode of communications and commerce. Unfortunately, many Americans regard using a credit card on the Internet or transmitting personal data via computer network as risky business. According to Business Week, a small fraction of Americans make on-line purchases. A recent survey found that the biggest deterrent to computer users making purchases on-line was lack of confidence in Internet security.

Concerns about privacy and security are well placed. A popular net browser was found to provide web site operators direct access to users hard drives, a criminal gathered 100,000 credit card numbers from on-line service provider and personal information is gathered then bought and sold on the Internet.

For the Internet to be a successful environment for commerce, government service and personal communications, the security on public networks must be improved.

There is little doubt that encryption technology is an essential tool to enhance security on public networks. The problem is that certain type of encryption technologies, if fully integrated into the communications network would cripple the ability of our law enforcement and national security agencies from protecting Americans from criminal and terrorist attack.

Fortunately, there is a technology which guarantees maximum security, meets a demonstrated market need and does not destroy law enforcement's ability to protect Americans. That technology is key recovery encryption. The advantage is that the private sector wants and needs this technology. A workable system of key recovery is also desperately needed by business to assure that valuable data is not lost with the departure of any employee holding the keys to encrypted company information.

For more than five years the Congress has been struggling with legislation on encryption policy. Senators McCain, Hollings, Kerry and I have put forward legislation which has won the approval of the Senate Commerce Committee to strike that delicate balance between needs of U.S. industry and U.S. national security. This legislation borrowed from all the proposals before the Congress and circulated within the Administration and proposes a much needed middle ground.

Our legislation, the Secure Public Networks Act, is a good faith effort to balance the competing equities and find a workable plan to enhance security on-line.

As this Committee investigates the needs of law enforcement, and business, I urge you to consider the approach taken by our legislation.

The Secure Public Network Act (SPNA) relies on market forces and incentives rather than heavy handed mandates to enhance security on public networks and punishes those who would violate privacy or misuse encryption technology. It creates a basis for deploying the powerful security measures necessary for network commerce, government and communications without compromising the ability to fight crime and terrorism.

Our legislation creates strong privacy protections for network users, preserves the right of private citizens to use encryption, creates market based incentives for the development, and deployment of encryption systems which use key recovery technology, limits government access to decoding keys, and penalizes those who would abuse their authority to violate privacy.

The bill also finds a sensible compromise to the five year debate that has been raging over encryption exports by providing for an immediate liberalization of the rules for the export of encryption products without a license and a process of continuous review of encryption export policies to assure that only a national security finding by the President can block the free export of encryption products that are generally or will be imminently available in foreign markets. The bill also provides for speedy consideration of individual licenses which can permit the sale of encryption products to foreign customers even if the product is stronger than what can be exported without a license. The SPNA makes it easier to export encryption software than current law.

The legislation is also tough on those who would use encryption technology to commit crime, or abuse their authority or position of trust to violate privacy and property rights.

The bill also includes an entirely voluntary system of federal registration for key recovery agents and certificate authorities. These providers of services of trust would be required to meet minimum standards which would give users confidence that their security is being protected when they use a registered agent or authority. Registration and the use of registered agents and authorities are entirely voluntary.

By embracing a market driven approach to the development of key recovery infrastructure, business, law enforcement and national security needs can be carefully balanced while strong encryption is made available to protect the security of users. There is a need and a market demand for key recovery technology.

Rather than using regulatory mandates, the SPNA uses the buying power of the federal government, and market based incentives to encourage the deployment of a network infrastructure which provides users total confidence in the security of their communications without compromising the limited, lawful and legitimate needs of law enforcement and national security. This legislation strikes the balance between commerce and national security which is missing from bills which deal just with encryption exports.

I would like to take a moment to address concerns some have expressed about certain provisions of the SPNA. Regarding government access to keys recovery information, our bill provides no additional authority to law enforcement to access encoded information. Before law enforcement can gain access to decoding keys, they need lawful authority over the coded information. Any law enforcement official who exceeds their lawful authority will be discovered and prosecuted. As to the "linkage" between the use of key recovery and federally registered certificate authorities, no one is required to participate in the federal system. Those who don't want the benefits of the SPNA are free to opt out of the system.

This legislation is fully consistent with the President's Electronic Commerce White Paper and I am confident that it can be the basis of meaningful, productive compromise between the Congress, the industry and the Administration.

There is an urgent need to create security on America's public networks. I applaud the Senate Judiciary Committee, and especially the leadership of Senator Leahy for bringing this matter to the center of the public debate.

Finally, Mr. Chairman, I ask that the text of a letter and an informative question and answer sheet about the SPNA be included in the hearing record.

Thank you, Mr. Chairman.

QUESTIONS AND ANSWERS ON THE SECURE PUBLIC NETWORKS ACT OF 1997

Question. Will the Government hold the encryption keys of all its citizens under the SPNA?

Answer. No. Private sector companies and institutions as well as government agencies will be able to serve as key recovery agents. Government agencies and private companies may decide to be their own key recovery agents or may contract this service out to private key recovery agents.

Question. Does the Secure Public Networks Act force people to use key recovery?

Answer. No. The key management infrastructure which is encouraged by the Secure Public Networks Act is voluntary. Under the SPNA, an American citizen can choose to use key recovery products or can choose to use non-key recovery products. Also, the Secure Public Networks Act permits persons to choose either to operate wholly within or outside the federally registered key management system.

Question. How does the Secure Public Networks Act promote the use of key recovery?

Answer. The SPNA helps promote key recovery by creating a federal government procurement market for key recovery. This policy both expresses confidence in these products and immediately develops a large market for key recovery. The SPNA also has legal incentives for individuals and companies to participate within the federally registered key management infrastructure. It also establishes standards of conduct for all key recovery agents to protect important key recovery information.

Question. Why would an individual or a company want to use a federally registered key recovery agents or certificate authorities?

Answer. By reviewing and registering key recovery agents and certificate authorities, the Commerce Secretary will help ensure the quality, trustworthiness, and security of these institutions. Key recovery agents will hold the information necessary to determine the plaintext. Certificate authorities verify the identity of individuals and companies using encryption keys for communication purposes. The registration process will help assure consumers that these key recovery agents and certificate authorities are upstanding, well managed businesses. The Secretary will also verify that certificate authority and key recovery agent procedures and encryption processes are secure. Consumers who use certificate authorities and key recovery agents will benefit from the reasonable care defense provisions should their use of encryption become an issue in a court case. While we believe this system offers important benefits, consumers are free under the SPNA to opt out of the federally registered system.

Question. How will those institutions which receive federal funds be affected by this Act?

Answer. It depends on the purpose for which the federal funds are provided. If federal funds are to be used to purchase, develop, or build a new encrypted network for the transaction of government business, the recipient of these funds must purchase key recovery products. If Federal funds are provided for the specific purpose of purchasing encryption software or hardware, the recipient of those funds will buy key recovery products. However, those institutions, organizations, or individuals who receive federal funds for purposes other than those stated above are not required to buy key recovery products.

Question. How can we be certain there is a market for key recovery products and that the key management infrastructure will work in practice?

Answer. Key recovery is working in practice. Today, companies such as Trusted Information Systems and IBM are marketing and selling key recovery encryption products. As Netscape CEO Jim Barksdale said in a March 19, 1997 hearing before the Senate Commerce Committee, "(w)e have always said there was a huge demand for key recovery" for stored data. Companies which make up the Key Recovery Alliance, which includes over 60 international computer and telecommunications companies, state the market is moving to key recovery for communications as well.

Further, the federal government is managing a pilot program among government agencies to test how key recovery agents and certificate authorities will interact and how a key management infrastructure can best be implemented. Individual companies both here and abroad have also begun developing their own key management infrastructures.

Question. A report entitled "The Risks of Key Recovery, Key Escrow, and Trusted Third Party System" criticizes the usage of key recovery products as being less secure, more costly, and more difficult to use than similar systems with a recovery feature. Is this analysis correct?

Answer. Key recovery products are as secure and in some cases more secure than non-key recovery products. How any encryption product, be it key recovery or non-key recovery, is implemented plays a significant part in determining the security level of a system.

There are many different key recovery technologies and methods by which to implement these products. The authors of this report picked technologies and implementation methods which produced worst-case scenarios. Their analysis was based on an analysis of a key escrow system in which keys would have to be maintained by a single third party. With new key recovery technologies and protocols, private encryption keys do not have to be maintained by a third party. Also, instead of a single entity holding a key, portions of the key recovery information may be held by many parties. In this "split-key" arrangement, the security provided is in many ways greater than what is provided by non-key recovery products and the security concerns raised in that report are eliminated.

More importantly, the report did not acknowledge the benefits customers receive from using key recovery products. Key recovery products allow users to have access to their data and communications if they have lost their keys. Otherwise, the strength of the encryption products being used today would effectively prevent them from ever decrypting their data or communications should they lose their keys.

Question. Does the Secure Public Networks Act protect the privacy rights of individual citizens?

Answer. Absolutely. SPNA assures that law enforcement will only have access to key recovery information provided they have preexisting authority to the underlying information. A law enforcement official will be required to have the same constitutional authority to acquire, intercept or otherwise be in the possession of encrypted information before key recovery information can be subpoenaed. If today the law enforcement official requires a search warrant to gain access to information or needs a court order for a wire tap, under the SPNA he or she must go through the same processes and meet the same requirements before he or she can have access to key recovery information. The SPNA grants law enforcement officials no additional authority to gain access to property, data, or information.

The SPNA protects against the possibility that access to key recovery information may be abused, both by private individuals with access to key recovery agents or by law enforcement officials acting beyond their legal capacity. That is why the SPNA will make it illegal to obtain or use key recovery information without lawful authority for the purpose of decrypting data or communications. Also, to ensure key recovery information is provided to law enforcement officials only if authority exists for access to the underlying information, the Attorney General will perform periodic audits to ensure subpoenas are issued pursuant to lawful authority.

Question. How can the Secure Public Networks Act help law enforcement if strong non-key recovery encryption is already available?

Answer. Encryption is necessary for greater security on networks. Today, the development of networks in the United States has reached a turning point. If key recovery is accepted widely throughout our networks, there will be less of an effect on law enforcement with no effect on security. Currently, relatively few individuals are using encryption to mask their communications and data. However, in the future, encryption of communications and data storage will become pervasive throughout our telecommunications infrastructure and the process of encryption may become transparent to the user. A person sending an email message or making a cellular phone call will not have to consciously decide to encrypt his communications—the encryption process will be built into the hardware and software he is using.

If key recovery encryption is widely used by legitimate, law abiding citizens and companies, criminal elements will become vulnerable when they communicate with the rest of society. While they may use non-key recovery encryption to communicate within their organizations, criminals will have to use key recovery to talk to hotels, airlines, car rental companies and other legitimate businesses. If key recovery encryption is not accepted by those engaging in legitimate private, commercial, and government communications, law enforcement officials will lose the ability to capture and convict drug dealers, terrorists, child pornographers, and members of organized criminal conspiracies.

Question. Why is key recovery so important to law enforcement?

Answer. While others question law enforcement's need for key recovery, we believe it is essential to ensuring the public safety of all Americans. From 1986 to 1995, federal, state and local law enforcement officials used court sanctioned wiretaps to convict over 20,000 criminals. In a future, non-key recovery encrypted world, American law enforcement officials would not have the same ability to investigate, arrest and convict criminals as they do today. The more than 20,000 prison inmates convicted in today's nonencrypted world would still be committing crimes on the streets of towns and cities across America.

Question. What is 56 bit DES encryption and how strong is it?

Answer. 56 bit DES encryption is a Digital Encryption Standard developed 21 years ago for use by the federal government. There are a total of 72 quadrillion (that's 72,000,000,000,000,000) combinations of numbers that may form the key to a DES message. Recent newspaper stories reported that a group of computer experts had "cracked" the 56 bit DES encryption code. In reality, the computer experts had not found any weakness or backdoor to the DES mathematical algorithm. In what is called a "brute force" attack, a group of computer technicians using tens of thousands of computers took four months to decode a one sentence message by trying different combinations of numbers to identify the key. They were fortunate enough to have found the correct key after trying only a quarter of the possible key combinations. However, they would have to go through the same process to decode any other message and it could take up to sixteen months to try all the possible number combinations.

Question. Does the Secure Public Networks Act set the limit at 56 bit DES forever?

Answer. No. The SPNA sets the 56 bit DES limit for non-key recovery products exported under a license exception (after it is reviewed once and approved, exports of the product do not require a separate license for each sale) but provides for the President to increase that level. It also creates a panel of government and industry experts which will review the foreign availability of encryption products and make recommendations to the President on what level of non-key recovery products should be allowed for export under a license exception. There is no bit length on the export of key recovery products. Non-key recovery products above the 56 bit DES level could still qualify for individual license and the SPNA provides for expedited review for the export of stronger products to banks, financial institutions, foreign subsidiaries of U.S. companies and other classes of users.

Question. What are other countries doing with regards to encryption?

Answer. We believe it is important to recognize that the United States is not the only nation concern about how a neutral technology like encryption can be misused in the furtherance of crime. Other nations such as Russia, Israel, and France today control the use of encryption within their borders as well as maintaining export restrictions. Therefore, when claims are made that strong encryption is available overseas, the Latin saying "caveat emptor"—let the buyer beware—should be foremost in the mind of the consumer. What is advertised as strong encryption may not be. Since other nations have the same concerns, it is not just a possibility but a likelihood that foreign governments hold keys to encryption software and harware produced overseas. Already Russia, Israel, and France have imposed import restrictions on encryption products and others have stated their intention to implement similar restrictions if the United States permits the mass export of strong encryption products.

Question. How can we be sure this policy won't harm U.S. computer companies selling products overseas?

Answer. Others have argued that foreign markets will not accept key recovery encryption. In fact, American companies are already marketing and selling their key recovery products overseas. The European Union is running eight pilot programs in five countries to test a trusted third party system—their version of a key management infrastructure. Companies such as Microsoft and Trusted Information Systems are participating in these pilot programs. Further, since law enforcement officials both here and abroad have expressed their need for key recovery products and key management infrastructures, the market for key recovery products will likely grow even larger as other nations move into the digital age.

REP. LOFGREN/SAN JOSÉ RESPONSE

(1) Charge: bill would force citizens to put descrambling keys in the hands of third parties.

Response: Sec. 101 recognizes that it is lawful for private parties to use any type of encryption in the USA.

Sec. 102 prohibits federal and state mandates for third party escrow of keys in communications between private persons.

The bill does create market based incentives for the deployment of encryption based on key recovery. It is the goal of the bill to encourage the private sector to develop, offer and profit from the provision of key recovery services.

(2) Charge: bill would force the government to use key recovery software.

Response: The federal government is the largest purchaser of software. It is making a rational market choice to purchase the type of products that do not undermine our law enforcement or national security needs. This creates a market for key recovery technology and is a vote of confidence in its reliability.

(3) Charge: bill would require private citizens to use key recovery when they buy anything on line.

Response: Secs. 101 and 102 assure that private parties can use whatever form of encryption they chose. It is our hope that the market will move to key recovery technology.

(4) Charge: There are practical difficulties setting up a centralize key recovery system.

Response: Yes that is true, but the SPNA does not set up a centralized system. It uses market incentives to establish a decentralized system of "key recovery" not "key escrow".

(5) Charge: Governments tend to "abuse liberties" and bill would "allow virtually anyone at any level of law enforcement to have access to private information on the flimsiest pretext.

Response: Sec. 106 (1) requires that law enforcement must have lawful authority over the encoded information before it can get access to the decoding keys.

Sec. 106 (3) establishes a uniform subpoena to minimize risk of confusion among private sector key recovery agents.

Sec. 106 (4) requires audits of subpoenas to assure that lawful authority is not exceeded and requires the Attorney General to take "disciplinary investigatory and prosecutorial actions against those discovered to exceed lawful authority.

Sec. 105 makes it a crime to exceed lawful authority to obtain or use decoding keys.

Sec. 107 authorizes civil suits against the federal government if a federal agent who exceeds lawful authority.

(6) Charge: There is no middle ground on this issue. Either you allow people to keep their keys or you do not.

Response: This is a false choice. Personal security and public safety can be balanced. People have not stopped using the telephone because law enforcement with a properly executed warrant can tap a wire. The SPNA provides strong privacy protections and also assures that, under limited, constitutionally approved procedures, federal, state, and local law enforcement officials can do their jobs protecting our citizens.

Senator KERREY. Mr. Chairman and Members of the committee, first off, again, I appreciate the opportunity to testify. I will try to go quickly through this testimony and then get into any questions that you might have of me.

I will begin by saying that the current law is unacceptable. The status quo is unacceptable. The law needs to be changed, for a range of reasons, and I appreciated very much Senator Grassley's comments earlier because the law as we have drafted it—and I have spoken with many members already in the Senate and a few in the House, as well, in positions of responsibility and/or just individuals who have direct concern with this matter.

Senator Grassley has raised some concern about domestic encryption. The law that we put together doesn't just deal with the exportation of encryption, and I think you will see as you look at the modification that Senator John Kerry put on it in the Commerce Committee that it substantially advances the ball on the exportation of encryption.

Title I deals with domestic uses of encryption, for the very reasons that Senator Grassley was raising. Title II deals with Government procurement. Regardless of whether or not we are able to come to agreement on exportation of encryption, the U.S. Government buys a lot of product and we have got to make a decision, are we going to have a key recovery system. How is it that we are going to accommodate the concerns for security of law enforcement, the concerns about security from national security people, but also from people at the IRS or people in other Government agencies? So there is Government procurement. The third title deals with exportation of encryption, and the fourth title deals with a voluntary system of development for key management, as well as escrow agents.

Again, as I say, the current law is unacceptable, and the reason it is unacceptable is that in the commercial sector people are concerned about the absence of security. On the Government operations side, we are concerned about the absence of security. It is difficult to operate, again, whether it is USDA or IRS or other agencies that are trying to do business on the Net.

Last, there is a concern about privacy coming from individuals in the private sector, and most noteworthy, the concern about privacy is not that the Government is going to come snooping in and try to find out what they are doing, but what other private sector people are going to do. I have got some examples that I would list. The examples could go on at considerable length. Senator Grassley just listed one out of Denver. There are many other examples.

The FBI recently reported that a hacker collected 100,000 credit card numbers from an Internet provider. A Texas woman received a letter full of threatening sexual comments from an inmate of a Texas prison who gained information on her personal life from a computer data base. A car dealership in New Jersey used their company's access to credit information to open false accounts in their customers' names and then charged thousands of dollars of merchandise to those accounts. A child rapist in a Boston hospital used a former employee's password to access information on the young hospital patients and then made obscene phone calls to girls as young as eight.

The list can grow, Mr. Chairman. One only has to look at the newspaper over a couple of days to accumulate additional examples about citizens whose privacy is being violated as a consequence of people who are skilled in using the network and using that skill to invade an individual's privacy.

There is a growing consensus that the Congress must act and that it must act soon to enhance security on America's computer networks. There are a number of examples of individuals being compromised online that I have given, and again I cannot emphasize enough the capacity to make that list even longer. I can't emphasize enough either that when you hear many of the arguments in the debate about encryption, you would think that the Government is out snooping on private citizens, but it is the private citizen concern for somebody who is skilled in the private sector that is producing most of the privacy problems.

The Internet is a vibrant, exciting, and important mode of communication and commerce. Unfortunately, many Americans regard using a credit card on the Internet or transmitting personal data via a computer network as risky business. According to Business Week, a small fraction of Americans make online purchases. A recent survey found that the biggest deterrent to computer users making purchases online was lack of confidence in Internet security.

Concerns about privacy and security are well-placed, Mr. Chairman. A popular net browser was found to provide Web site operators direct access to users' hard drives and personal information is gathered and then bought and sold on the Internet. For the Internet to be a successful environment for commerce, for Government service, and for personal communications, the security on the public networks must be improved.

There is little doubt that encryption technology is an essential to enhanced security on the public networks. The problem is that certain types of encryption technologies, if fully integrated into communication networks, would cripple the ability of our law enforcement and national security agencies from protecting Americans from criminal and terrorist attack, and I cannot be sure, as well, as an individual whether that encryption is going to solve my privacy problems.

Fortunately, there is a technology that is being developed in the marketplace that guarantees maximum security, meets the demonstrated market need, and does not destroy law enforcement's ability to protect Americans. That technology is key recovery encryption. The advantage is that the private sector wants and needs this technology. A workable system of key recovery is also desperately needed by business to assure that valuable data is not lost with the departure of any employee holding the keys to encrypted company information.

Mr. Chairman, the Secure Public Networks Act that was passed out of the Commerce Committee and amended, I think, in a fashion that substantially improves it, is a good-faith effort to balance the competing equities and find a workable plan to enhance security online. As this committee investigates the needs of law enforcement and business, I urge you to consider using the approach taken by this legislation.

The Secure Public Networks Act relies on market forces and incentives rather than heavy-handed mandates to enhance security on public networks, and punishes those who would violate privacy or misuse encryption technology. And I emphasize this punishment is the first time we have had such punishment. There is no current punishment for misuse of wiretaps. There is in this legislation not only a review process that is unique, but, in addition, there are criminal punishments for people who misuse this authority.

Our legislation creates strong privacy protections for network users, preserves the right of private citizens to use encryption, creates market-based incentives for the development and deployment of encryption systems which use key recovery technology, limits Government access to decoding keys, and penalizes those who would abuse their authority to violate privacy.

The bill finds a sensible compromise to the 5-year debate that has been raging over encryption exports by providing for an immediate liberalization of the rules for the export of encryption products without a license and a process of continuous review every 3 months by a Government-private sector board of encryption export policies to assure that only a national security finding by the President himself can block the free export of encryption products that are generally or will be imminently available in foreign markets.

The bill also provides for speedy consideration of individual licenses which can permit the sale of encryption products to foreign customers, even if the product is stronger than what can be exported without a license. The SPNA makes it easier to export encryption software than current law.

The legislation is also tough on those who would use encryption technology to commit crime or abuse their authority or position of trust to violate privacy and property rights. The bill includes an entirely voluntary system of Federal registration for key recovery agents and certificate authorities. These providers of services of trust would be required to meet minimum standards which would give users confidence that their security is being protected when they use a registered agent or authority. Registration and the use of registered agents and authorities are entirely voluntary.

Mr. Chairman, it is not unusual—it is quite common, in fact—for the Federal Government to create a standard in order for the marketplace to develop. In order for the marketplace to develop, in my judgment, Mr. Chairman, we do need standards in this area. By embracing a market-driven approach to the development of key recovery infrastructure, business, law enforcement, and national security needs can be carefully balanced, while strong encryption is made available to protect the security of users.

There is a need and a market demand for key recovery technology. Rather than using regulatory mandates, the Secure Public Networks Act uses the buying power of the Federal Government and market-based incentives to encourage the deployment of a network infrastructure which provides users total confidence in the security of their communications without compromising the limited, lawful and legitimate needs of law enforcement and national security. This legislation strikes the balance between commerce and national security which is missing from bills which deal just with encryption exports.

I would like to take a moment to address concerns that some have expressed about certain provisions of this legislation. Regarding Government access to key recovery information, our bill provides no additional authority to law enforcement to access encoded information. Before law enforcement can gain access to decoding keys, they need lawful authority over coded information. Any law enforcement official who exceeds their lawful authority will be discovered and prosecuted.

As to the linkage between the use of key recovery and federally registered certificate authorities, no one is required to participate in the Federal system. Those who don't want the benefits of SPNA are free to opt out of the system. The legislation is fully consistent with the President's Electronic Commerce White Paper, and I am confident that it can be the basis of meaningful, productive compromise between the Congress, the industry, and administration.

Mr. Chairman, I want to emphasize again I believe there is a very powerful and urgent need to create security in America's public networks, and I applaud you, Mr. Chairman, and other members of this committee—the ranking member, Senator Leahy—for your leadership and for bringing the matter to the center of the public debate.

Finally, Mr. Chairman, again, I am prepared to answer any questions that you have, and I appreciate the opportunity to testify and I appreciate your indulgence for my introduction of questions and answers that have been raised earlier.

The CHAIRMAN. Well, we are happy to have you here and we appreciate your testimony. I think Senator Leahy has some questions.

Senator LEAHY. I do, Mr. Chairman, just briefly.

Senator Kerrey, I know you have worked hard on S. 909, and certainly in your capacity as the vice chairman of the Senate Intelligence Committee you have probably looked at this whole issue of encryption as much or more than anybody here.

If you take S. 909 as it was voted out of the Commerce Committee, is that supported by the Administration?

Senator KERREY. I do not know. The President, as I understand it, is reviewing it at the moment. I do not know if it has the support of the Administration. My belief is the process, Senator, for me was—first of all, you are quite right. There is a concern that I have got that came from my work on the Senate Select Committee on Intelligence, but my concern is also connected to work that I have done with the Internal Revenue Service, work that I have done in public education, trying to bring relevant curricula into both the homes and the classrooms. So it is a broader concern based upon a variety of experiences.

My belief was, with great respect to you, that your legislation was not likely to be enacted, not likely to move. I think it can be incorporated substantially into a broader piece of legislation. I went around and talked with many people, including the Administration——

Senator LEAHY. Well, the reason I asked——

Senator KERREY [continuing]. And briefed the Administration and briefed many other Members of Congress. My belief is the Administration is likely to support it, but I can't give you that guarantee at the moment.

Senator LEAHY. Director Freeh's testimony today indicates that the bill is not adequate, but I will let him to speak to it himself in that regard.

I would like to know, are there companies or private sector groups that support S. 909 or have endorsed this bill?

Senator KERREY. That, I don't know either, Senator. Again, I think the starting point for us must be to say that we have got to change this law. Anybody that wants to bring language and say, here is where I want to change it, I think they should be allowed to come and say, here is some specific language that I want to bring.

I know that law enforcement, for example, has raised some concerns saying that the key recovery system should be mandatory. They raised some concern about the additional sanctions that are in the legislation for people who violated the domestic use of encryption, as well as some people in the private sector, I know, have raised some concerns.

Regardless of where the concerns come from, I think that we, the people who write laws—our message needs to be uniform, and that is we intend to deliver the President a piece of legislation he can sign. In order to do that, whatever your objection is, it needs to be specific enough that we can accommodate it, and it needs to be accurate. You need to address the legislation, whatever the vehicle is—address the piece of legislation with a specific recommended language change.

Senator LEAHY. Well, I will suggest one of my concerns is the scope of the authority given to the Secretary of Commerce in S. 909. As I read it, the Secretary would be able to issue regulations controlling the practices, responsibilities and requirements for both certificate authorities and key recovery agents. In fact, if somebody violated those regulations, they could face up to 5 years in jail and $100,000 in civil penalties.

I mean, I don't see anything in here that would stop the Secretary of Commerce, after consulting with the FBI and the NSA, from issuing a regulation that requires key recovery agents to use only clipper chip, even though that was roundly turned down before.

Senator KERREY. I disagree with you, Senator. I mean, section 402, in title V, describes the registration of certificate authorities, the registration as well of key recovery agents. We have given the Secretary of Commerce the guideline. The idea is to develop a market. The idea is——

Senator LEAHY. You have given him the authority, but he could, under those regulations, after consultation, do some of the very same things that the Congress not only did not embrace in earlier times, but made very clear across the political spectrum, both parties, that they shunned.

Senator KERREY. Well, that is always the case, Senator. When we passed a piece of legislation that deregulated telecommunications, a lot of us are not happy with the way that is being implemented. So it is always the case, whether it is a health issue or a commerce issue, that we have to exercise oversight, and if we don't like the way it is being implemented, we come back and we change the law.

Senator LEAHY. Well, yes, but I mean look at that. I mean, we passed a telecommunications bill which was going to lower cable rates and it was going to do some of these other things, and cable rates have shot up.

Senator KERREY. Let me use another example. We passed——

Senator LEAHY. There has been no oversight from anybody. What I am suggesting——

Senator KERREY. We passed a welfare bill, Senator, and the President signed it, and supporters and opponents are looking for ways to improve it. We don't presume that as a consequence of enacting legislation that that is the end of the game. We know that it is going to be implemented.

Senator LEAHY. What I am suggesting we do is we write it right in the first place instead of turning something over that is written so broadly that it would allow an administration appointee to put into place something that has already been roundly rejected. And knowing the galactic pace ofttimes of the Congress, especially with anything that has any complexity whatsoever, you and I will probably be matching age records by the time anything would happen on it.

My concern is that having floundered around without either a legislative or administrative solution that we now write a strong legislative solution, knowing that that might be easier to change if it doesn't work than to turn it over for an administrative solution, especially with an administration that has not shown an ability to keep up with the demands on encryption, and this administration has not, nor did the administration before it.

Senator KERREY. Well, I mean the law that came out of the Commerce Committee provides something that currently we don't have, which is a public and a private sector board, immediate liberalization to 56 DES, and a 3-month review. If this board says we ought to go to 128, only the President for national security reasons can override that. Every 3 months, it provides a review that we currently don't have, Senator.

If there are specific concerns about section 403 or section 404 or section 405 that need to be changed, I mean let us look at it. Let us change it if you want to put language in there that says you cannot use clipper chip.

Senator LEAHY. We will.

Senator KERREY. I am just saying, in general, we wouldn't pass anything up here—we would never pass legislation up here if we

44-452 - 97 - 2

said, well, we can't pass anything because we are concerned about how the executive branch is going to implement it.

Senator LEAHY. But that is not the issue. What I am saying here is we have something that has numerous new criminal penalties. Obviously, we will look at it. I mean, with all the criminal penalties and others in there, this committee will——

Senator KERREY. Which criminal penalties, Senator, don't you like?

Senator LEAHY. I think that the committee should be looking at all the criminal penalties that are in here. These are things that, naturally, the Judiciary Committee will want to look at. I mean, I am not saying——

Senator KERREY. The reason I raised the criminal penalty issue, Senator, is there are criminal penalties in here that law enforcement doesn't like because it protects people's privacy and it gives them new power that they don't currently have. So I mean the reason I raised that right then is that I have been hearing from a lot of people on the private sector side that presume that the criminal penalties were falling only on the citizen. That is what the San Jose Mercury editorial presumed, and that is not true. The law imposes new criminal penalties to protect privacy.

Senator LEAHY. I am not here to defend the San Jose Mercury, especially after one of their earlier series. But what I am suggesting is that—and part of this has been because the history of this administration and the previous administration has been so far behind the curve on encryption matters that we ought to be very clear, whether it is in your committee, your proposal, mine and Senator Burns', or mine and Senator Hatch's, or anybody else's, that we write as clear a piece of legislation as possible. I think it can be done.

I do not agree that we could never pass legislation if we assume the Administration will not carry it out. But I do know after 23 years here that administrations react far better with legislation if we provide very clear guidelines to it, just as the courts do, too. I am suggesting that we write it, and I suggest that we can write it and have it in place by this Fall, a strong piece of legislation that allows the United States to be the leader in the world in this area of encryption, instead of going in such a haphazard fashion that the Europeans and the Asians will take over all this market and we will not have the kind of controls that I think all of us would believe that we do need for both law enforcement and national security purposes.

The CHAIRMAN. I would like to get to the FBI Director and Mr. Crowell, but if there are any other questions?

Senator FEINSTEIN. Mr. Chairman, I have one.

The CHAIRMAN. Senator Kyl, and then I will come to Senator Feinstein.

Senator KYL. Mr. Chairman, I won't ask Senator Kerrey a question in view of the time and the fact that we do need to hear from the other witnesses. I simply want to suggest something that perhaps will balance what the distinguished ranking member has said.

I fully support the efforts of Senator Kerrey and Senator McCain and others who have attempted to find a balance in respect of these issues that can gain legislative support and support from the President. My own view is that the legislation does not go far enough, and I have spoken to Senator Kerrey about this. I am especially concerned about the liberalization of the export controls.

The reason that I say this is to simply make the point that there is not just one point of view. There is not just an industry point of view, and I am concerned that some day this very committee is going to be holding an oversight hearing and it will be reviewing a terrorist incident in which American lives were taken. Fingers will be pointed and questions will be asked about how this could have happened. Distinguished law enforcement people will say to us, do you remember when we testified before you and told you that you had the chance to do something now?

Director Freeh testified before us on June 4 and made the point that we still had time to do something about this problem. The time is a wasting, and that is why I support Senator Kerrey's effort, though I don't totally agree with it, to try to get legislation that can be passed this year. I don't want to be sitting up here a couple of years from now and have law enforcement officials say to us, Senators, you had the opportunity to protect American lives and you didn't do it and that is why this problem occurred, not because of any fault of law enforcement. I don't want to be in that position, Mr. Chairman, and that is why I support the effort of Senator Kerrey and others.

The CHAIRMAN. Thank you, Senator Kyl.

Senator Feinstein.

Senator FEINSTEIN. Thank you very much, Mr. Chairman. I would echo Senator Kyl's concerns, and also Senator Grassley's. I tend to be supportive of this legislation, and I would like to thank you for your longstanding effort in this regard, both you and Senator McCain, Senator Kerrey.

Having said this, I am a relative newcomer to what is a very complicated issue. I also represent a big computer-producing State, so I recognize I am on difficult ground. But, would you address yourself to the exact situation that Senator Grassley raised and how your legislation would impact this situation?

Senator KERREY. Well, first of all, Senator, what this legislation attempts to do is solve a broader problem, not just the exportation of encryption. So you find in the legislation that the exportation of encryption is actually——

Senator FEINSTEIN. I am not talking about the exportation of encryption.

Senator KERREY. I understand that. I was going to get to your question, but I was going to use your question to illustrate the breadth of this law.

Title I deals with the export use of encryption for the first time. Many people who are talking about new criminal penalties are talking about new criminal penalties that are in title I. Today, I am not restricted at all in using any encryption I want to domestically, and as far as I am concerned, that is fine, except where encryption was being used with criminal intent.

So, what we have is in section 104 of this first title—in section 104 of the first title it says, "Whoever knowingly encrypts data or communications in furtherance of the commission of a criminal offense for which the person may be prosecuted," and then goes on to list the penalties, as well as describing the unlawful use of domestic encryption, "to obtain or use key recovery without lawful authority, exceeding lawful authority in decrypting data, breaking encryption codes, intercepting on a public communications network, impersonating another person," as well as three or four additional things.

The things that Senator Grassley was talking about, as well as other domestic concerns about the use of encryption to accomplish an unlawful objective, are addressed in this title I.

Senator FEINSTEIN. I am not understanding. Would the case in Colorado that the Senator mentioned—how would this law enable, with a voluntary key recovery system, the police to have broken the code?

Senator KERREY. The answer is it may not. The answer is it may not. It does set in law for the first time penalties for using encryption. You could actually arrest and bring a charge of using encryption to commit an unlawful act. But because—this is Senator Kyl's point—because it is a voluntary system, because it is not a mandatory system, there will be individuals out there who will say I am just not going to use key recovery. So it doesn't provide a universal guarantee that the cases that Senator Grassley is talking about will allow law enforcement people to either be able to get a stream of communication or to get into stored data.

Senator FEINSTEIN. So there is nothing mandatory on the youngster that encrypted that data to have required that he had a key recovery system?

Senator KERREY. That is correct.

Senator FEINSTEIN. Therefore, law enforcement could be in exactly the same position with your legislation that they were without it?

Senator KERREY. They would not be in the same position because they could bring a charge for unlawfully using encryption in order to perpetrate a crime. In the specific case that Senator Grassley has raised, they may not be able to bring a sufficient amount of evidence to bring that case. I would let Director Freeh answer that.

The answer directly to your question is because it is a voluntary system, it is not fool-proof. There are individuals out there who could still use encryption and not use key recovery, and law enforcement would be prevented either from getting the stream of communication while it is being done or getting access to the stored data.

Senator FEINSTEIN. Now, without revealing the classified briefing that you participated in and that we had recently, what is puzzling to me is that Colorado law enforcement doesn't have any recourse to be able to break into this encrypted system to solve a crime. I had thought that there was recourse presently available to them for that. Director Freeh is nodding no. Do you agree that that is the answer?

Senator KERREY. I agree that that is the answer. Again, we do attempt to put changes in the law in title I that would provide an opportunity for law enforcement to go after somebody who is using encryption to carry out a crime. But because it is a voluntary system, because it is not mandatory, because it is a voluntary system, the situation that Senator Grassley described earlier—if that individual wasn't voluntarily using a key recovery system both for the communication and for the stored data, and they used something 56 or above, it would be very difficult for law enforcement to crack it.

Senator FEINSTEIN. Now, have you read the June 17 memorandum from the Center for Democracy and Technology which specifically states how your legislation would expand law enforcement surveillance authority and curtail constitutional rights specifically relating to the fourth and fifth amendments? Have you had a chance to review that?

Senator KERREY. No.

Senator FEINSTEIN. Essentially, what this memorandum contends is that your legislation would authorize the Government to obtain private keys and other decryption information without a court order and without notice to the individual whose privacy would be affected. Could you react to that?

Senator KERREY. Senator, let me disclose to you that I am not a lawyer. What I do is I write laws and, you know, sometimes lawyers come in and say, you have got it wrong. So if somebody can reference the specific section—in this case, I think they are talking about section 106, but whatever section they are talking about, if they have a specific section and they say, we think this needs to be changed, I am willing to listen to any proposed changes.

But what we attempted to do was maintain the status quo as far as court orders going for wiretaps. So when law enforcement tries to get a wiretap, they have to get a court order. We are trying to maintain the same in this, except for two additional provisions that I suspect were not in this June 17 memo. Since they are trying to make a case that the law is bad, they are not likely to include in their comments anything about this law that would actually increase the protection for the individual.

There are two additional provisions in this law that are very important. One is the Attorney General's review, and I don't know what Director Freeh's view of that is, but my guess is there will be some in law enforcement who will object both to the review and to the criminal penalties that are there imposed on people who use this key recovery system and use this court order authority in an illegal fashion.

So I mean the attempt is to maintain the status quo, with additional review and additional powers actually against law enforcement people that use this authority improperly.

Senator FEINSTEIN. It is section 106 that we are——

The CHAIRMAN. Senator, I would like to move on. We have to go to the next witnesses.

Senator FEINSTEIN. Well, may I just ask this, Mr. Chairman? Perhaps if we could get the memorandum to the Senator and his staff, if you could respond in writing to this, it would be very helpful to me.

Senator KERREY. I would love to.

Senator FEINSTEIN. Thank you very much.

The CHAIRMAN. Senator Ashcroft.

Senator ASHCROFT. Thank you, Mr. Chairman.

Senator Kerrey, I am interested in the export controls provisions of your bill or those in other bills. What kinds of export controls do you envisage, and at what level are exports controlled in your bill?

Senator KERREY. We go immediately to 56-bit, and we have a provision in there as well, again, that Senator John Kerry put on as an amendment in the Commerce Committee that creates a new public-private sector board that reviews this standard every 3 months and makes a judgment, and only if the President overrules that judgment for national security reasons would that judgment not prevail. So under the law, as amended by the Commerce Committee, that provision is in the legislation. There is also an expedited procedure that Commerce can provide people that make special cases for the need to do export.

Senator ASHCROFT. Are you aware of the group of young people who cracked the 56-bit code as was reported in the Wall Street Journal on July 19? I guess that was the day after you submitted your measure. It seems to me that we are in a universe that is dynamic here, and that every time someone thinks we have got a secure thing that we can put in the law, the developments in the computer industry, the power and speed of cracking the codes, make a laughingstock out of what we have just done.

Senator KERREY. Well, this one—I didn't laugh when I read it. In this case, I believe—I don't remember the numbers that they used, but they had an impressive number of computers operating in parallel to be able to crack it. What this does is make the case that for law enforcement and national security concerns, unless you have got a key recovery system, it is going to be very difficult for them to protect this country. I mean, that is what I saw in this.

Second, I would say, Senator, that it also makes the case that the likely attack point is not going to come from a government. I mean, increasingly, as we look at threats to the United States, it is not the Nation state, not some other nation state that is a threat to us.

Senator ASHCROFT. I guess the point that I would be moving toward—and it doesn't seem to be the point that you are addressing, but that is OK—is that I believe there are going to be robust encryption necessities, first, because codes are crackable. And, second, I think the marketplace is going to respond to those necessities. I mean, it is already responding to the necessities.

The Siemens-Nixdorf Company in Germany advertises on the Internet now and it says, buy our new Trusted Web Information System. Siemens-Nixdorf is part of the German Siemens Group. Their new product called Trusted Web, which incorporates 128-bit public key, private key, whichever approach you want. This advertisement announces a joint venture between these folks—and it says this, "Trusted Web is an independent European product, and hence is not subject to the export restriction imposed on the U.S. Government in relation to encryption software."

So what you have is in the marketplace advertisements for substantially robust encryption, twice as strong as what you would allow in your bill, being offered to both people inside and outside the United States. It seems to me that, with that, I wonder what the bill really achieves by limiting the exports of American business to half the encryption quality that is necessary. I say necessary because with 56-bit being breakable, and having been demonstrably breakable even with technology which we are now past, I think this is a real serious problem.

Senator KERREY. I agree with you, Senator. First of all, Commerce has just recently negotiated with some companies allowing them—financial institutions, in particular—to use——

Senator ASHCROFT. I am concerned about that. I think our financial institutions definitely need that. But they are not done. We have car companies, for example, that don't want to complete their designs in the United States now. They have placed some of their people overseas so that they can compute with their overseas plants with higher rates of encryption than we have now. I don't think we should be forcing U.S. manufacturers to place part of their operations in overseas markets.

Senator KERREY. I completely agree with you. In fact, the legislation allows for both an expedited process and a review process that would greatly accelerate the use of exportation of encryption.

Second, I would say using the Germans as an example is, I think, a weak argument. No. 1, you can look at other things that the Germans do and we would not want to emulate it. We would not want, for example, to say, well, Germany is selling to Iran. You know, they have got an embassy in Iran. Let us start doing business with Iran. I mean, let us use the German approach to exportation in other areas. We would absolutely reject that out of hand.

Second, the German approach to domestic communication is much more invasive than anybody in the United States would either suggest or approve of. So very often what we hear—and the reason I raise this, Senator, is very often what we hear in this whole debate is, gee, the foreigners are already doing all the stuff and they are taking away our market share and they are damaging our capacity to compete.

No. 1, Commerce is working with private sector companies, for the reason that you have identified. And, No. 2, this bill does attempt to accommodate that, but I don't think it would be wise for us to use some other nation, particularly one that has demonstrated a willingness to deal with almost anybody.

Senator ASHCROFT. If the Senator doesn't mind, I would just like to say that that is not my point. Germany doesn't become important because it is Germany. It just becomes important to define what is available in the marketplace, and regardless of how you feel about Germany and whether you have disrespect for what they have done in other arenas, the point is that the marketplace is offering 128-bit encryption, not only in Germany but in other settings. As a matter of fact, our marketplace uses 128-bit encryption for its domestic use.

Senator KERREY. That is correct.

Senator ASHCROFT. We have a very strange anachronism here. The only thing you can't do with 128-bit encryption in the United States is send it out of the country. And it seems to me that with our marketplace using 128-bit, with producers manufacturing it around the world, we ought to be very careful about saying that we can consume it, we can use it, we can use it for robust encryption, but we can't produce it.

Senator KERREY. I accept your premise. In fact, that is one of the purposes of this legislation. But let us presume we can't deal with export. Let us say that the conflict between national security and domestic concerns is too great and this Congress can't deal with it. I say drop that title. Let us drop it. Let us say to the business sector we will drop that title; we won't even deal with it.

I still have a domestic concern. I still have a concern about Government procurement. I still have a need to make decisions in other areas, and I think that the language is an attempt that will find some arguing that we have liberalized too much in the exportation.

Senator ASHCROFT. Let me ask——

The CHAIRMAN. Senator, I want to get to the FBI Director.

Senator ASHCROFT. Mr. Chairman, has my time expired?

The CHAIRMAN. Yes, but I will be happy to go one more question, if we can.

Senator ASHCROFT. Thank you, Mr. Chairman.

Under the first section of the bill, it is made a criminal offense to use encrypted information in the commission of a crime. If an individual who keeps his tax returns on his computer encrypts the information and is subsequently found to have violated the law, is he guilty of a second crime because he sought to protect the integrity of his tax information on his computer by encryption?

Senator KERREY. I would say no. If you, with your much longer and deeper and more impressive experience with law and law enforcement, say it does, I am willing to accommodate changes. I mean, the object is not to do what you have just described. I would say the answer should be no.

The attempt is to deal with domestic issues such as the one that was raised by Senator Grassley earlier, and the attempt is to deal with people who are using encryption for the effort to carry out a criminal act. I mean, that is the reason that that is being——

Senator ASHCROFT. Having resisted the chairman to this point, I now yield and thank the Senator and thank the chairman.

The CHAIRMAN. Well, I thank my colleague.

Senator ASHCROFT. Mr. Chairman, I would just ask that my statement be made part of the record.

The CHAIRMAN. Without objection, it will be included.

[The prepared statement of Senator Ashcroft follows:]

PREPARED STATEMENT OF SENATOR JOHN ASHCROFT

Mr. Chairman, thank you for the opportunity to provide a few comments at the beginning of this debate in the judiciary committee. For two years the Commerce Committee has debated this issue and just two weeks ago the full committee voted out a bill that even the sponsors characterize as "not perfect." Anything we do in this area will have a significant impact on the future of the encryption and software industries here and around the world. These are two high-tech industries where the U.S. is currently the unequaled leader. So, whatever we do needs to be as "perfect" as we can make it.

Many argue that if the U.S. continues to enforce the existing export policy on encryption, which permits 40 bit exports and with special permission for up to 56 bit, then law enforcement will be able to apprehend terrorists, stop illegal gamblers and arrest child pornographers. However, this argument assumes that these criminals cannot and do not acquire robust encryption from other countries. This is false many times over. Robust encryption is available. Germany, Japan, and the United Kingdom all have companies that have developed, promote, and sell 128 bit encryption. Even the supporters of the Administration's approach, as expressed in the legislation recently voted out of the Commerce Committee, admit that criminals who want robust encryption can get it for use in their current dealings. This issue is a red herring.

I have here the homepage of Siemens-Nixdorf which is no fly by night operation, but a subsidiary of Siemens, an international conglomerate. They not only tout the 128 bit sophistication of their encryption to sell their product, but the fact that they can sell it to their customers without having to tell the government how it works, the way that American companies would have to do.

Claims have also been made that high levels of encryption would allow criminals to flourish and therefore must be limited. Mr. Chairman, we do not outlaw photography because some deviants misuse the technology to take pornographic pictures of children, or outlaw the telephone because some criminals call one another in the furtherance of their crimes. I find this argument the most troubling not only for the future of technology, but the future of this country as well, because at its core it says that Americans should expect lower standards of privacy in their electronic communications using computers.

I simply ask, why? Why should it be easier to "wiretap" email than it is to wiretap a phone-line? What is the compelling reason to reduce the right to privacy and protections against unreasonable search and seizure guaranteed by the Bill of Rights? Why should we pull down the Fourth Amendment to open the door for big brother in this particular field as opposed to others?

Mr. Chairman, it appears to me that at the most fundamental level, this debate is about the relationship of our citizens to our government. We all must take steps to ensure that the rights of our citizens are not violated, that the guarantees passed down to us by the Founding Fathers is not casually discarded. Our citizens should be able to communicate privately, without the government listening in—that is one of our most basic rights and principles, paid for dearly at Lexington and Concord and on every battlefield where an American soldier has died.

As we work to provide law enforcement with some necessary amount of access, let us do it only in a manner consistent with our Constitution, as we have been able to do in the past in regards to telephone lines and computer hard drives.

The Founding Fathers carefully crafted the Constitution to protect our most basic liberties in this country. Those protections have kept Big Brother from intruding into our private lives for over 200 years. Some would advocate the removal of these protections, and leave citizens exposed to the invasion of privacy, for the sake of security. The Founding Fathers understood all too well the need for protection from random government searches of personal property. I doubt they would ever suggest that every citizen provide the government a key to their homes, their bank accounts, or their diaries so federal agents could intrude or-invade at will.

Wrongfully using the cry of national security in this debate does not benefit anyone. A threat to national security of another sort occurs if we force U.S. companies to fall behind technologically by restricting them from competing in an already established, operating, and competitive global market. National security is also compromised when we force U.S. companies to transact business outside of the U.S. using obsolete encryption that is vulnerable to joy-seeking hackers and organized criminals and is therefore unsafe and unprotected communication. Businesses, doctors, consumers, patients, and others have legitimate reasons for wanting to protect the privacy of the information they transmit electronically.

Companies must be able to protect their transmissions from unwanted hacking, not only by those with malicious intent but those who are out for a lark as well. Companies will protect their information as best they can for both domestic and international transmission regardless of what we do. The market for stronger encryption exists and if we force U.S. companies out of the competition, companies in other countries will meet the demand for this product.

It is curious that after the two year debate in the Commerce Committee in which the Administration argued passionately in the hearings and in private meetings with the FBI and NSA against allowing 128-bit encryption out into the international market, that the Administration itself announces, on June 25, that they will now allow the export of 128-bit encryption for bank transactions involving software. This is an implicit admission of the vulnerability of the 56-bit strength encryption which we have been assured for two years was adequate to meet the legitimate needs of business. The legislative compromise offered in the Commerce Committee would only have exported 128-bit with key recovery for trusted parties. The Administration now advocates the export of 128-bit length encryption for banks without any key recovery device, which is a more liberal export position than the one they opposed in the Commerce Committee.

My point, Mr. Chairman is that this debate must change. We cannot continue to focus on the key length since these standards become obsolete on a daily basis. We need to focus on allowing trustworthy parties to use robust encryption, in their transactions and in the development of software and hardware.

No nationwide key recovery system, or a new licensing requirement for certificate authorities, should be brought to the floor without thorough examination, analysis and understanding. We must understand the impact of these provisions, economically as well as technologically, before a bill is brought to the Senate Floor.

With robust encryption readily available globally, by simply downloading it from the World Wide Web, will we really accomplish by restricting U.S. exports to an obsolete standard, whether 40, 56 or any other particular bit length? Is the best approach to have big brother hold the keys to everyone's encrypted messages? Would we advocate giving the keys to all our homes to the federal government on the chance that one day they may want to search the premises and it would be easier to get in with the key?

Mr. Chairman, we must proceed carefully with these decisions. Simply spouting rhetoric on an issue involving complex technology and competing national values will not solve the problem or allow us to move forward with a coherent, sensible, national policy.

The CHAIRMAN. I want to thank you, Senator Kerrey. You have certainly carried the ball for your bill, and we appreciate having you here and having the bill to begin with so that we have an even greater basis for discussion of these matters. So we appreciate all the efforts you have put forward and thank you.

Senator KERREY. It hasn't been a pleasure, but it has been an honor.

Senator LEAHY. And a delight.

The CHAIRMAN. Well, we are going to remember that comment, I will tell you. [Laughter.]

At this particular point, I would like to turn to two individuals who have worked tirelessly to bring about a meaningful resolution to the encryption debate—FBI Director Louis Freeh, and William Crowell, Deputy Director of the National Security Agency. We are very pleased to welcome both of you here. We appreciate the work that you do and we look forward to taking your testimony at this time.

We will start with you, Director Freeh.

PANEL CONSISTING OF LOUIS J. FREEH, DIRECTOR, FEDERAL BUREAU OF INVESTIGATION, WASHINGTON, DC; AND WILLIAM P. CROWELL, DEPUTY DIRECTOR, NATIONAL SECURITY AGENCY, WASHINGTON, DC

STATEMENTS OF LOUIS J. FREEH

Mr. FREEH. Thank you, Mr. Chairman, Senators. It is a privilege, as always, to appear before this committee, and let me compliment you, Mr. Chairman, the other Senators, Senator Kerrey, who just left, for really exercising some leadership and momentum in this area. It is a very complex area. It is not a law enforcement/anti-law enforcement issue. It is a complex one, but it is one which demands and has now received the attention of the Senate and the House, and we are very pleased to be part of that discussion.

A couple of years ago when the public safety issue loomed with respect to losing our court-authorized access to conversations of criminals and spies and terrorists, the digital telephony issue, this committee, and the chairman and vice chairman in particular, took personal control and leadership over that issue. After a very difficult and protracted period of negotiations where industry, law enforcement, all the other related interests came to the table, you fashioned a piece of legislation, the Law Enforcement Assistance Act of 1994, which, not only in 1997, but in years to come, law enforcement agencies, whether they be State, local, or Federal, will look back to that statute and really credit this committee and Senate with preserving, without altering the protections of privacy and without infringing on commerce, the continuation of our ability to access by court order the conversations of people who would do great harm to our people and our national security.

This is really a continuing part of that debate. If we have access, per court order, to the conversation of someone who has committed a crime or is about to commit a heinous crime, whether it be an act of terrorism or a kidnapping, and the Federal, State, and local officers who are listening to that court-authorized conversations or looking for the data which is stored somewhere can't understand it, the access really is not meaningful.

If we have all the legal authorities and the technical accessibility to that information, but we can't understand it in real time, it doesn't do us and the people that we have to protect and the country very much good. The gentleman sitting next to me, who I also thank and compliment for his leadership in this area, has done studies and looked at studies which tell us very clearly that to decrypt real-time a message bit—and that is a couple of words and phrases—with a 56-level-bit encryption using a $30 million Cray computer would take a little bit over a year. That is fine if you are doing historical research.

If you are looking for a kidnapping victim or we want to find the information which is in Yousef's encrypted file because he is planning to blow up 11 airliners in the Western Pacific, I can't wait a year and several days to get that information. So it is a very critical law enforcement and public safety issue. It is very much a continuation of the problem which was successfully tackled and solved here with respect to digital telephony, and I raise that because I want to try to overcome the notion that this is a new technology problem for law enforcement. It is really a continuation in many ways of what we solved in 1994.

I am of the view—and I represent here not only the FBI, but as reflected in some of the remarks by the members here, the interests of all of our State and local enforcement agencies around the country. There are resolutions which the committee has seen issued by the International Association of Chiefs of Police, representing 17,000 police departments around the country; the National Association of District Attorneys; the National Sheriffs Association.

There is unanimity with respect to law enforcement that although encryption is a very important commercial and economic issue for the United States, and it certainly is, it is equally a very important public safety and national security issue. That is the balance in the policy which has heretofore not been achieved and what we strongly urge is reflected in any legislation that is derived from this discussion.

Our view is that unless a balanced approach to encryption is adopted that includes a viable key recovery infrastructure, our ability, the ability of law enforcement, to investigate and sometimes prevent the most serious crimes and terrorism will be severely impaired and that our national security will be jeopardized. Although there has been continuing and shifting debate even within the Administration about the way to achieve the balance in that policy, the law enforcement interests which I have just recited have not changed or modified over the entire period.

We have dazzling telecommunications abilities. The technologies that are being developed and being deployed and those to come are tremendous. No one in law enforcement disputes that clearly, in today's world, and more so in the future, the ability to encrypt both transitted communications as well as stored data is vital for business, for national security. We are very, very strong advocates of the most robust encryption. We have the same interest that everyone else in this room has in protecting information, whether it be intellectual property or privacy. We are only asking that some balance be maintained and that the right which was given to us by the Framers in 1791 to access evidence of crimes be preserved in a changing technology.

There is another aspect to the encryption that, if left unaddressed, will also have, in our view, severe public safety and national security ramifications. One of the few remaining vulnerabilities in some of the most complex and dangerous crimes is the ability to understand real-time the communications of spies and criminals or terrorists and the access to stored data and evidence. It is really one of the few and diminishing windows that we have in the most difficult cases that we work on.

To give you a little bit of a perspective of electronic surveillance and court-authorized access to transitted communications, in 1996, if you add all of the court orders for electronic surveillance, Federal, State and local, it comes to 1,159, not the thousands or hundreds of thousands that sometimes are indirectly suggested.

The Federal Government only performed 13 more of those court orders than the State and locals. In fact, for 1996, for the first time the majority of all of those 1,149 court orders were done by the Federal Government. But the State and locals—your district attorneys, your sheriffs, your police departments—they do almost an identical amount and they rely very heavily on their ability to access and understand real-time these conversations.

Under a key recovery approach—you have heard much about that—the key recovery agent could certainly be a private company, a bank. It is not advocated that it be a Government agency or a Government-controlled agency. We are content to have any trusted third party that meets the minimum standards of security and reliability to hold in trust keys and to only access those keys under judicial procedures. You can make those judicial procedures as high or low as you think appropriate, and it is important in many ways that that procedure be exclusively controlled by some form of judicial procedure.

When law enforcement needs to decrypt criminal-related communications or computer files, they too, under conditions strictly prescribed by law, would, by this process, obtain for specific objectives and with whatever probable cause standards are required those keys for the purposes necessary to carry out their public safety obligations.

I also would suggest to you that this is an area where I think that a Government policy and action by the Congress is necessary.

I do not believe that we can leave this issue solely to market forces and economic forces to be completely implemented and looked at prospectively with all the public safety concerns that are brought to the table.

If you recall, back in the digital telephony debate there were many very good arguments about letting industry and the marketplace deal with this issue. It is a public safety issue which in many respects is one of the first obligations of Government, and I think that in this particular area there needs to be a Government policy. There needs to be some input beyond what the market forces would simply allow, which is why I think the establishment of a key recovery infrastructure is necessary and needs to be implemented.

Senator I will, because of the time, submit my prepared remarks for the record, and let me just highlight a few other points in an effort to save some time here.

With respect to some of the legislation which is being introduced, we applaud the efforts of Senators Kerrey and McCain with respect to 909. It does take significant strides in the direction of protecting public safety by encouraging the use of key recovery encryption through market-based incentives and other inducements.

Unfortunately, all the legislative proposals still allow for the widespread availability and use of any type of encryption product within the United States without adequate assurances that the impact on public safety and effective law enforcement will be addressed. The enactment of any of these bills without including legislative accommodations that adequately address the public safety needs of law enforcement in the United States will, in our view, have a negative impact on public safety.

The argument heard many times that the encryption genie is out of the bottle and that there is nothing we can do is, in my view, not a very good one. The same argument, by the way, was made with respect to digital telephony, and it was clear that the situation could be addressed, has been addressed, even though there was some embedded infrastructure that still needs to be taken care of.

Nobody ever contends that a key recovery system is going to prevent all criminals in all places at all times from committing crimes. But our view is that if we have a policy that responsibly encourages the building and promulgates a key recovery system, we are going to keep more windows open for public safety opportunities than in a world where we have no policy with respect to encryption and the most robust form of encryption is allowed unimpeded here and everywhere else.

Congress has on many occasions accepted the notion that electronic surveillance is important and necessary under strict judicial control and guidelines. We think that certainly there is nothing in the proposed bill by Senators McCain and Kerrey which increases law enforcement authority, which does any damage to the Constitution or the Bill of Rights. It simply allows law enforcement to keep pace with a technology which was certainly not in the contemplation of the Framers of the Constitution.

I could cite many cases where electronic surveillance and court-authorized ability to understand real-time has saved thousands of lives. I think that we cannot quickly or casually take the position that there is nothing we can do about encryption and, although there are valid public safety reasons, it is too expensive and too complicated to address. I think that we have an obligation and a life-and-death necessity to make sure that we have the access to information that is necessary to investigate and protect people.

Over the last couple of years, the number of cases in the FBI where we have encountered encryption which has impeded investigations has increased fairly significantly. The number of instances where stored data has been in the form of encrypted programs and hard drives is proliferating. I cannot tell you now, nor would I tell you that encryption is in any significant way impeding our law enforcement and public safety mission or our ability to protect national security.

But I am not so sure, as Senator Kyl points out, that myself or my successors years from now will come back and tell you the same thing. I think the nature of this technology is that it is increasing very, very quickly, and that what we need to do is establish a policy that protects this access before that window comes down.

Major drug traffickers in cases around the country are now utilized very encrypted communications to conceal their efforts from law enforcement. Seventy-one percent of all the court-authorized surveillances by State, local, and Federal agencies are in narcotics-related cases, and some of these large organizations and cartels are using that technology to our distinct disadvantage.

Let me just say in closing that in support of our position for a balanced encryption policy, we rely on the fourth amendment to the Constitution, adopted in 1791. That amendment, very wisely written by the Framers, of course, protects with great constitutional safeguards the right for people to be protected and private in their papers and homes. But it also allows in that same amendment the application and the ordering by judges of search warrants and court orders to get access to the communications and evidence that criminals commit.

An unlimited, robust encryption infrastructure without any key recovery for law enforcement, in my view, changes very dramatically the balance of that fourth amendment, in that for the first time in the history of the republic the law enforcement authorities will not be able to execute court orders which will direct us and order us to obtain evidence of criminal activity. That is a very important point, I think, in this debate, that if a technology such as encryption is not carefully dealt with, my view is that you will not be avoiding the expansion of powers for law enforcement; you will be very severely changing the balance of the fourth amendment to the distinct disadvantage of the people that we protect.

So, again, I applaud you for your interest and your leadership here, and I think it is critical, really a matter of life and death in the years to come, that we have some law enforcement access and window to this great technology so we can live safer.

Thank you.

The CHAIRMAN. Well, thank you, Director Freeh.

[The prepared statement of Mr. Freeh follows:]

Prepared Statement of Louis J. Freeh

Mr. Chairman and members of the committee, I appreciate the opportunity to discuss the issue of encryption and I applaud your willingness to deal with this vital public safety issue.

The looming spectre of the widespread use of robust, virtually uncrackable encryption is one of the most difficult problems confronting law enforcement as the next century approaches. At stake are some of our most valuable and reliable investigative techniques, and the public safety of our citizens. We believe that unless a balanced approach to encryption is adopted that includes a viable key management infrastructure, the ability of law enforcement to investigate and sometimes prevent the most serious crimes and terrorism will be severely impaired. Our national security will also be jeopardized.

For law enforcement, framing the issue is simple. In this time of dazzling telecommunications and computer technology where information can have extraordinary value, the ready availability of robust encryption is essential. No one in law enforcement disputes that. Clearly, in today's world and more so in the future, the ability to encrypt both contemporaneous communications and stored data is a vital component of information security.

As is so often in the case, however, there is another aspect to the encryption issue that if left unaddressed will have severe public safety and national security ramifications. Law enforcement is in unanimous agreement that the widespread use of robust non-key recovery encryption ultimately will devastate our ability to fight crime and prevent terrorism. Uncrackable encryption will allow drug lords, spies, terrorists and even violent gangs to communicate about their crimes and their conspiracies with impunity. We will lose one of the few remaining vulnerabilites of the worst criminals and terrorists upon which law enforcement depends to successfully investigate and often prevent the worst crimes.

For this reason, the law enforcement community is unanimous in calling for a balanced solution to this problem. It is called "key recovery" encryption and, in our view, any legislative approach that does not achieve such a balanced approach seriously jeopardizes the long-term viability and usefulness of court-authorized access to transmitted as well as stored evidence and information. Electronic surveillance and search and seizure are techniques upon which law enforcement depends to ensure public safety and maintain national security.

Under one type of key recovery approach, a decryption "key" for a given encryption product is deposited with a trustworthy key recovery agent for safe keeping. The key recovery agent could be a private company, a bank, or other commercial or government entity that meets established trustworthiness criteria. Should encryption users need access to their encrypted information, they could obtain the decryption key from the key recovery agent. Additionally, when law enforcement needs to decrypt criminal-related communications or computer files lawfully seized under established legal authorities, they too, under conditions prescribed by law and with the presentation of proper legal process, could obtain the decryption key from the key recovery agent. This is the only viable way to permit the timely decryption of lawfully seized communications or computer files that are in furtherance of criminal activity. The key recovery information would be provided to the law enforcement agency under very strict controls and would be used only for its intended public safety purpose. Under this approach, the law-abiding would gain the benefits of strong, robust encryption with emergency access capabilities and public safety and national security would be maintained—as manufacturers produce and sell encryption products that provide key recovery.

This solution meets industry's information security and communications privacy needs for strong encryption while addressing law enforcement's public safety needs for timely decryption when such products are used to conceal crimes or impending acts of terrorism or espionage.

Some have argued that government policy makers should step aside and let market forces solely determine the direction of key recovery encryption, letting market forces determine the type of technologies that will be used and under what circumstances. They argue that most corporations that see the need for encryption will also recognize the need for, and even insist on, key recovery encryption products to secure their electronically stored information and to protect their corporate interests should an encryption key be lost, stolen or used by a rogue employee for extortion purposes.

We agree that rational thinking corporations will act in a prudent manner and will insist on using key recovery encryption for electronically stored information. However, law enforcement has a unique public safety requirement in the area of perishable communications which are in transit (telephone calls, email, etc.). It is law enforcement, not corporations, that has a need for timely decryption of communications in transit. There is extraordinary risk in trusting public safety and national security to market forces that rightfully are protecting important but unrelated interests. Law enforcement's needs will not be adequately addressed by this type of an approach.

It is for this reason that government policy makers and Congress should play a direct role in shaping our national encryption policy and adopt a balanced approach that addresses both the commercial and the public safety needs. The adverse impact to public safety and national security associated with any type of "wait and see" or voluntary market force approach would be far too great of a price for the American public to pay.

Several bills have recently been introduced which address encryption. Language in some of the proposed bills makes it unlawful to use encryption in the furtherance of criminal activity and set out procedures for law enforcement access to stored keys in those instances where key recovery encryption was voluntarily used. One of these bills, S. 909, takes significant strides in the direction of protecting public safety by encouraging the use of key recovery encryption through market-based incentives and other inducements.

Unfortunately, these legislative proposals still do not contain adequate assurances that the impact on public safety and effective law enforcement of the widespread availability of encryption will be addressed. We look forward to working with you to develop legislative accommodations that adequately address the public safety needs of law enforcement and a balanced encryption policy.

Further, some argue the encryption "genie is out of the bottle," and that attempts to influence the future use of encryption are futile. I do not believe that to be the case. Key recovery encryption products can, with government and industry support, become a standard for use in the global information infrastructure.

No one contends that a key recovery-based encryption policy will prevent all criminals, spies and terrorists from using non-key recovery encryption. But if we, as a nation, act responsibly and build systems and products that support and rely upon key recovery, all facets of the public's interest can be served.

And as this committee knows, export controls on encryption products exist primarily to protect national security and foreign policy interests. However, law enforcement is more concerned about the significant and growing threat to public safety and effective law enforcement that would be caused by the proliferation and use within the United States of a communications infrastructure that supports strong encryption products but cannot support timely law enforcement decryption. Without question, such an infrastructure will be used by dangerous criminals and terrorists to conceal their illegal plans and activities from law enforcement, thus inhibiting our ability to enforce the laws and prevent terrorism.

Congress has on many occasions accepted the premise that the use of electronic surveillance is a tool of utmost importance in terrorism cases and in many criminal investigations, especially those involving serious and violent crime, terrorism, espionage, organized crime, drug-trafficking, corruption and fraud. There have been numerous cases where law enforcement, through the use of electronic surveillance, has not only solved and successfully prosecuted serious crimes and dangerous criminals, but has also been able to prevent serious and life-threatening criminal acts. For example, terrorists in New York were plotting to bomb the United Nations building, the Lincoln and Holland tunnels, and 26 Federal Plaza as well as conduct assassinations of political figures. Court-authorized electronic surveillance enabled the FBI to disrupt the plot as explosives were being mixed. Ultimately, the evidence obtained was used to convict the conspirators. In another example, electronic surveillance was used to prevent and then convict two men who intended to kidnap, molest and then kill a male child.

Most encryption products manufactured today do not provide for timely law enforcement decryption. Widespread use of non-key recovery encryption or communications infrastructure that supports non-key recovery encryption use clearly will undermine law enforcement's ability to effectively carry out its public safety mission and to combat ultra-dangerous criminals and terrorists.

This is not a problem that will begin sometime in the future. Law enforcement is already encountering the harmful effects of encryption in many important investigations today. For example:

- Convicted spy Aldrich Ames was told by the Russian Intelligence Service to encrypt computer file information that was to be passed to them.
- An international terrorist was plotting to blow up 11 U.S.-owned commercial airliners in the far east. His laptop computer which was seized during his arrest in manilla contained encrypted files concerning this terrorist plot.

• A subject in a child pornography case used encryption in transmitting obscene and pornographic images of children over the Internet.

• A major international drug trafficking subject recently used a telephone encryption device to frustrate court-approved electronic surveillance.

Requests for cryptographic support pertaining to electronic surveillance interceptions from FBI field offices and other law enforcement agencies have steadily risen over the past several years. For example, from 1995 to 1996, there was a two-fold increase (from 5 to 12) in the number of instances where the FBI's court-authorized electronic efforts were frustrated by the use of encryption that did not allow for law enforcement access.

Over the last three (3) years, the FBI has also seen the number of computer related cases utilizing encryption and/or password protection increase from 20 or two (2) percent of the cases involving electronically stored information to 140 or seven (7) percent. These included the use of 56 bit data encryption standard (DES) and 128 bit "pretty good privacy" (PGP) encryption.

Just as when this committee so boldly addressed digital telephony, the Government and the Nation are again at an historic crossroad on this issue. The International Association of Chiefs of Police, the National Sheriff's Association and the National District Attorneys Association have all enacted Resolutions supporting a balanced encryption policy and opposing any legislation that undercuts or falls short such a balanced policy. If public policy makers act wisely, the safety of all Americans will be enhanced for decades to come. But if narrow interests prevail, then law enforcement will be unable to provide the level of protection that people in a democracy properly expect and deserve.

CONCLUSION

We are not asking that the magnificent advances in encryption technology be abandoned. We are the strongest proponents of robust, reliable encryption manufactured and sold by American companies all over the world. Our position is simple and, we believe, vital. Encryption is certainly a commercial interest of great importance to this great nation. But it's not merely a commercial or business issue. To those of us charged with the protection of public safety and national security, encryption technology and its application in the information age—here at the dawn of the 21st century and thereafter—will become a matter of life and death in many instances which will directly impact on our safety and freedoms. Good and sound public policy decisions about encryption must be made now by the Congress and not be left to private enterprise. Legislation which carefully balances public safety and private enterprise must be established with respect to encryption.

Would we allow a car to be driven with features which would evade and outrun police cars? Would we build houses or buildings which firefighters could not enter to save people?

Most importantly, we are not advocating that the privacy rights or personal security of any person or enterprise be compromised or threatened. You can't yell "fire" in a crowded theater. You can't with impunity commit libel or slander. You can't use common law honored privileges to commit crimes.

In support of our position for a rational encryption policy which balances public safety with the right to secure communications, we rely on the fourth amendment to the Constitution. There the Framers established a delicate balance between "the right of the people to be secure in their persons, houses, papers, and effects (today we might add personal computers, modems, data streams, discs, etc.) Against unreasonable searches and seizures." Those precious rights, however, were balanced against the legitimate right and necessity of the police, acting through strict legal process, to gain access by lawful search and seizure to the conversations and stored evidence of criminals, spies and terrorists.

The precepts and balance of the fourth amendment has not changed or altered. What has changed from the late eighteenth to the late twentieth century is technology and telecommunications well beyond the contemplation of the Framers.

The unchecked proliferation of non key recovery encryption will drastically change the balance of the fourth amendment in a way which would shock its original proponents. Police soon may be unable through legal process and with sufficient probable cause to conduct a reasonable and lawful search or seizure, because they cannot gain access to evidence being channeled or stored by criminals, terrorists and spies. Significantly, their lack of future access may be in part due to policy decisions about encryption made or not made by the United States. This would be a terrible upset of the balance so wisely set forth in the fourth amendment on December 15, 1791. I urge you to maintain that balance and allow your police departments, district attorneys, sheriffs and Federal law enforcement authorities to continue to use their most effective techniques to fight crime and terrorism—techniques well understood and authorized by the Framers and Congress for over two hundred years.

I look forward to working with you on this matter and at this time would be pleased to answer any questions.

The CHAIRMAN. Let me just say for the record that Senator Specter has been here, but he had to go back to the Governmental Affairs Committee where they are examining the campaign finance problems. So I will put his statement in the record.

[The prepared statement of Senator Specter was not available at presstime.]

The CHAIRMAN. Director Crowell, we will turn to you now and we look forward to taking your testimony, and then we will have some questions for both of you. I think we will have 5-minute rounds and go from there.

Director Crowell.

STATEMENT OF WILLIAM P. CROWELL

Mr. CROWELL. Mr. Chairman, thank you for inviting me to testify on the technical aspects of the Administration's key recovery policy.

To be successful, the technical underpinnings of the Nation's encryption policy must be sound. My written testimony goes into detail about many of the technical issues, but for now I would like to discuss in fairly straightforward, non-technical language some of those issues. However, I will also address some of the frequently voiced misconceptions about the Administration's position on key recovery and on building trusted key management infrastructures.

First, as the chairman stated earlier, we believe that users will need key recovery. If you are locked out of your house, what do you do? You break a window or a door, you call a locksmith, or you go get an extra key that you left with a neighbor or a trusted friend. If you didn't have these reasonable fallback options for getting into your locked house, you would probably start by using very weak locks or no locks at all, since you couldn't afford to abandon your house and all of its contents if you couldn't get in again.

Individuals and businesses with a need to protect sensitive and valuable information will be faced with similar choices. They could use no encryption at all, which would weaken their privacy. They could use very weak encryption to protect the information, which would not be satisfying. They could abandon the information if and when they are locked out, which would not be economically sound. Or they could use strong encryption and plan ahead for the inevitable day that they lose their key. They could use key recovery-based encryption.

Senator Ashcroft earlier commented on the breaking of 56-bit DES. What, in fact, happened was that 78,000 computers on the Internet were used for a period of 96 days to break one message that was encrypted in a DES algorithm. I don't think that if you were using encryption, even DES, you could afford to go to 78,000 of your closest friends in order to be able to recover the one important piece of information that you needed to recover.

The CHAIRMAN. We were kind of pleased that it was a Utah kid who broke the—[Laughter.]

One of the many.

Mr. CROWELL. One of the many, and he happened to be assigned the lucky key. That is the essential piece of information.

Senator LEAHY. We are going to write him into the legislation.

The CHAIRMAN. Yes, we may call it after him.

Mr. CROWELL. At the individual level, this is what key recovery is all about, ensuring that all the benefits of encryption are not overshadowed by its drawbacks.

Now, let us look at public safety. Law enforcement will need key recovery as well. Director Freeh has already clearly expressed the need for a balanced approach in legislation addressing key recovery. That approach would allow for the use of strong encryption by individuals and businesses, while still addressing law enforcement's need for timely—I stress timely—decryption of enciphered communications used to conceal crimes.

Law enforcement needs to maintain its legal authorities to access evidence in the information age. Court-ordered wiretaps and physical searches or seizures currently enable law enforcement to listen to or to read the information of the suspected criminal. The U.S. Supreme Court has repeatedly reaffirmed that such court orders are permitted under the Constitution to protect public safety, and Congress has also passed laws to that effect.

Encryption without key recovery begins removing the power that society has given the courts and can result in court orders without teeth, and law enforcement will be without a valuable tool in the era of encrypted communications and in the information age. Some may say that there is another tool that can preserve law enforcement's authorities. They suggest that more computing power would enable law enforcement to determine the criminal's needs, but compute power is not the answer.

In the case that I just cited, it took 78,000 computers 96 days for one message. That was with 56 bits. With 64 bits, that would have been about 6,000 years, and with 128 bits it wouldn't be twice as much; it would be 8.6 trillion times the age of the universe. So we shouldn't base the policy that we develop on the number of bits of cryptography without understanding the consequences of doing that.

So far, I have discussed the technical reasons for key recovery. For a moment, I would like to address the relationship between key recovery and key management infrastructures. Those arguing against key recovery often incorrectly blur the distinction between the two.

Key management infrastructures enable people to communicate securely using encryption. They provide the trust that binds cryptography to real applications. They provide essential support services to encryption users by helping with the generation, authentication, distribution, and very importantly the revocation of encryption keys that are no longer valid. Until trusted key management infrastructures are developed, the promise of encryption and electronic commerce will remain largely unfulfilled.

The Administration, contrary to what some will say today, does not advocate a single, large, complex key management infrastructure. Instead, it advocates incentives for the market to develop its own approaches to a decentralized system of key management infrastructures. Key recovery is a value-added service offered as a part of key management infrastructures. It is like an encryption insurance policy. If you lose your keys, you can easily recover from the loss.

Yes, it is possible to build key management infrastructures without key recovery, but I think the potential consequences of widely used encryption without key recovery are enormous. We have already discussed the law enforcement implications, but also consider the consequences when your last will and testament, if those become lawful in a computer, is unreadable because no one knows where to get the keys, or doctors are unable to refer to your health records during an emergency because there is no backup key, or a disgruntled employee encrypts your business accounting records and holds the key hostage.

Is key recovery too expensive an insurance policy? I don't think so. Contrary to what you may be hearing, key recovery is achievable. Recently, the Center for Democracy and Technology published a paper that said the commercial and academic world simply does not have the tools to properly analyze or design the complex systems that arise from key recovery. This is only one of many incorrect statements made about recovery.

Let us look at the facts. Key recovery is complex, but achievable. There are over 60 companies who have either already built key recovery products or that are in the process of supporting the building of key recovery products, and they are members of an alliance that is doing exactly what the naysayers say can't be done. Many of these companies are in the States that you represent, and if you don't mind, Mr. Chairman, I would like to submit a copy of a description of the Key Recovery Alliance and a list of the members who are in that alliance.

The CHAIRMAN. Without objection, we will make that part of the record.

Mr. CROWELL. Thank you, Mr. Chairman.

[The information referred to follows:]

IBM INDEX SecureWay

HOME NEWS PRODUCTS & SOLUTIONS CONSULTING & SERVICES LEARNING CENTER

Global deployment of strong encryption nears as key recovery alliance welcomes 22 new members

Industry group accelerates growth of secure electronic business

Find out who the new alliance members are

TORONTO, May 6, 1997... Twenty-two major additional manufacturers, high-tech companies and security innovators such as Boeing, Mitsubishi Electric America, Intel and Silicon Graphics have joined the Key Recovery Alliance to accelerate the growth of security-rich global electronic business. Formed in 1996, the Key Recovery Alliance is a group of 61 international companies that are facilitating the worldwide use of strong encryption.

Encryption is critical to the security of sensitive information that is either stored electronically or sent over public networks like the Internet. Key recovery is a new method that allows for authorized access to encrypted information. "Keys" are encryption tools that lock and unlock data. Key recovery could be an effective tool to meet commercial, private and institutional needs.

The Key Recovery Alliance meets quarterly. During the third meeting of the alliance held April 24 to 25 in Toronto, members discussed the progress of the various working committees that meet regularly.

The committees and their missions are:

- Technology Requirements Committee -- works to achieve interoperability of key recovery technologies while supporting a wide range of exisiting industry solutions;
- Policy Committee -- reports on cryptographic regulations worldwide;
- Deployment Committee -- identifies requirements for worldwide deployment of key recovery and identifies means to expedite that deployment;
- Business Scenarios Committee -- identifies global business requirements for key recovery;
- Outreach Committee -- disseminates clear, concise, understandable information about key recovery.

The alliance represents a broad cross-section of information technology providers and customers from around the world that have joined together to address the business needs created by the emergence of network computing and electronic business.

Key recovery alliance members

Last updated: 5/6/97

New alliance members

Baltimore Technologies
Paddy Holahan
353-1605-4399
paddy@baltimore.ie

Boeing
Kjell Carlsen
206-865-3500
kjell.carlsen@pss.boeing.com

Cryptomathic
Dr. P. Landrock
45-8620-2000

Frontier Technologies Corp.
Dr. Prakash Ambegaonkar
414-241-4555
drp@frontiertech.com

Fujitsu Ltd.
Haruki Tabuchi
tabuchi@saint.nm.fujitsu.co.jp

GemPlus
Corrine Bonifas
33-4-42-36-5147
corrine.bonifas@ccmail.edt.fr

Hitachi
Shinichi Fukushima
81-45-826-8532
fukushsi@soft.hitachi.co.jp

Intel
Tom Potts
503-264-6277
tom_potts@ccm.jf.intel.com

IRE
Garry S. Meyer
410-931-4833
gmeyer@ire.com

Mitsubishi Electric America
Eisaku Takeda
81-4674-1280
etakeda@iss.isl.melco.co.jp

nCipher Corp.
Carol Atack
44-1-22-3723600
carol@ncipher.com

NEC
Teiji Okumura
81-423-33-1282
okumura@bs1.fc.nec.co.jp

Open Horizon, Inc.
Jahan Moreh
310-476-3767
jmoreh@openhorizon.com

Portland Software
Dagmar Glier
503-220-2300
dagmar@portsoft.com

RedCreek Communications
Cary Hayward
510-745-3952
caryh@redcreek.com

RPK
Jack Oswald
408-479-7874
joswald@msn.com

Silicon Graphics, Inc.
Gayle LeDoux
415-933-2968
ledoux@corp.sgi.com

Spyrus
Russ Housley
408-576-5624
housley@spyrus.com

Sterling Commerce
Mary VanZandt
972-868-5764
mary_vanzandt@stercomm.com

Tandem
Chris Russell
408-285-2390
russell_chris@tandem.com

Technical Communications Corp.
George Simmons
508-287-5100 ext. 266
gsimmons@tccsecure.com

Toshiba
Toshiaki Saisho
81-44-549-2244
saisho@isl.rdc.toshiba.co.jp

Existing alliance members

America Online	Apple Computer *	Atalla *
Certicom	Compaq Computer Corp.	CygnaCom Solutions, Inc.
Cylink Corp.	Data Securities International, Inc.	Digital Equipment *
Digital Signature Trust Company	Entrust Technologies	First Data Corp.
Gradient Technologies, Inc.	Groupe Bull *	Hewlett-Packard *
IBM *	ICL	McAfee
Mitsubishi Corporation of Japan	Motorola	Mytec Technologies, Inc.
NCR Corp *	Network Systems Group of Storage Tek	Novell, Inc.
PSA	Price Waterhouse	Racal Data Group
Rainbow Technologies	RSA * of Storage Tek	SafeNet Trusted Services, Corp.
Secure Computing Corp.	SourceFile	Sterling Commerce
Sun Microsystems, Inc. *	Trusted Information Systems, Inc. *	Unisys
UPS *	Utimaco Mergent	VPNet Technologies
Sligos	Silicon Graphics	SourceFile
Spyrus	Sterling Commerce	Sun Microsystems *
Tandem	Technical Communications Corp	Telequip
Trusted Information Systems *	Unisys	UPS *
Utimaco Mergent	VPNet Technologies	

* Charter members of the key recovery alliance

Mr. CROWELL. Options for key recovery will allow a choice for individuals and private business. Companies may set up their own key recovery centers, their own key management infrastructures, establish their own certificate authorities, self-escrow their keys, or they may opt to use a trusted third party, just as individuals may choose to do as well. Key recovery may also be accomplished by splitting key information among several entities or by storing information needed to recreate a key. Despite what may be said today, the Administration does not want to see digital signature keys stored at all. That would be an unsafe practice.

Just a quick mention of foreign views, since that came up earlier in Senator Kerrey's testimony. Ambassador Aaron has been serving as our envoy for encryption and he has been carrying on discussions with foreign governments about their policies in the encryption area. The one thing that is common among all of them is that they all want some form of key recovery. It is also true that they have not been able to agree about how to do that.

He is continuing those talks and he hopes that that will lead to increasing agreement among the nations about how to do this in an international sense. But we do not advocate creating a single, monolithic, international key management infrastructure or key recovery system, as will be suggested today.

The Administration does not wish to prescribe how key recovery should work. The best interests of society will be served by innovative key recovery solutions developed by private industry. The Administration is seeking to create a climate which encourages such technological creativity. Despite the claims made by some people, the Administration does not want to hold the keys of private citizens and business. This is a fundamental feature of the Administration's policy and one that is often misrepresented by those who are opposed to the policy.

So, Mr. Chairman, in summary, the Government's key management infrastructure initiative and its key recovery policymakes technical sense and it is good policy for individuals, businesses, and law enforcement. The policy is constructed to support the use of strong encryption with the voluntary use of key management infrastructures and key recovery, and the United States is now well ahead the rest of the world in this debate and in understanding the intricacies and complexities of encryption policy. The development of key management infrastructures and the use of key recovery make good technical sense and I urge you to support it.

Thank you very much.

The CHAIRMAN. Well, thank you so much.

[The prepared statement of Mr. Crowell follows:]

PREPARED STATEMENT OF WILLIAM P. CROWELL

INTRODUCTION

I appreciate the opportunity to comment on key recovery and key management infrastructures, and to discuss with you NSA's involvement with the development of the Administration's encryption policy. Since NSA has both an information security and a foreign signals intelligence mission, encryption touches us directly.

NSA's role in support of the Administration's initiative has been that of a technical advisor. For decades, NSA has been the nation's center of cryptographic expertise. We have played an important role in using cryptography to produce the safeguards that control our nuclear arsenal, enable our military commanders and policy makers to communicate securely anywhere in the world, provide our intelligence customers with vital information to support U.S. interests, and protect classified and sensitive-but-unclassified information. I believe it is important for the nation's encryption policy makers to base their decisions on the best possible information, and I would like to help clarify several issues for the record.

THE USE OF ENCRYPTION CAN BE A SIGNIFICANT BENEFIT TO AMERICA

The country is now engaged in a national discussion on encryption centered on how to accommodate the private interests of individuals and businesses with the public interests of law enforcement and national security. How we resolve this will affect how well the nation succeeds in the information age.

Some would argue that if we overemphasize the public interests, we risk a world with too much government access and too few secrets. Others argue that if we overemphasize the interests of the private sector, we risk a world with perhaps too many secrets—for example, a world in which terrorists, organized crime, and hackers acquire the capability to operate with impunity. Both of these extremes are unpalatable and are therefore not part of the Administration's policy. We need to strike a balance that provides adequate protection for both individuals and businesses, and for society as a whole.

The White House recently defined a policy initiative that is designed to accelerate growth in the use of encryption. Some believe the administration's initiative is about key recovery and export controls, but in the broadest sense the initiative deals with the preparations we must make as a nation to use information technology to its full potential. It is an attempt to create an international framework in which the use of strong encryption will grow. I cannot overemphasize either the importance or the difficulty of moving this initiative from concept to reality.

Encryption usage has the potential to enable citizens to use technology that will make their lives more convenient, enhance the economic competitiveness of U.S. industry, combat frivolous and criminal access to private and valuable information, and deny adversaries from gaining access to U.S. information wherever it may be in the world. That's the good news. The bad news is that the encryption in most commercial products today has very little chance of being used to its full potential until support infrastructures are established that enables the encryption to be used widely and with integrity. Furthermore, if encryption is used by criminals and other adversaries (e.g., terrorists) to help hide their activities, the public safety of U.S. citizens, and citizens of other countries, may be placed in jeopardy. This is a problem whether support infrastructures exists, or not.

The U.S. must address these challenges. Instead, we seem mired in an unfocused debate about bit lengths, brute force attacks, and product "availability" that often takes place in press releases, newspaper editorials, and Internet Newsgroups. We all need to focus-in on what will enable encryption to be used to its potential. The way to do this is to mutually acknowledge the interests, roles, and responsibilities that industry and governments have in this issue.

OVERVIEW OF KEY MANAGEMENT INFRASTRUCTURE AND PUBLIC KEY ENCRYPTION

Crypto products use algorithms and keys to encrypt and decrypt information. The algorithm combines the key with the information that a person wants protected or authenticated. The keys must be unique, random number streams generated by a trusted authority and delivered by a trusted means to the users. The system of people and processes that provide these services is called a key management infrastructure (KMI), and it enables keys to be generated properly, securely transported, authenticated, and stored.

For years, secure KMIs consisted of people hand-delivering keys to each pair of potential communicators. Such secure KMIs became impractical when a large number of people needed to potentially communicate. Furthermore, security was often degraded when keys were compromised during the delivery stage. Even computer delivery of keys did not solve these problems. In general, the use of encryption was not widespread because of these KMI complexities and limitations.

A type of encryption technology called public key technology was invented to address the KMI scalability problem and reduce the possibility of key compromise during delivery. Public key encryption does not eliminate the need for KMIs, it only changes what products and services we expect from the infrastructures.

A public key infrastructure (PKI), a type of KMI, does not require shared, confidential keys to be pre-placed in order for people to communicate. Instead, it uses two related keys—a public key and a private key—and allows the public encryption key to be made known and stored in publicly-accessible places. There is no magic involved, only the use of complex mathematics and other techniques to effectively hide the part of the key that must be kept secret.

A PKI's services are for:

1. Verifying user identities
2. Generating user public and private key pairs
3. Linking user identities with their keys
4. Accessing the database of user identities and keys
5. Verifying the integrity of user identities and keys
6. Deleting invalid user identities and keys
7. Dealing with compromised or lost keys

All of the above services are necessary to enable public key-based encryption products to be used widely, securely, and with integrity. The certification of the public key value for each individual using public key encryption is the absolute foundation of trustworthy public key encryption. Without this certification service, users of computer networks have no way of verifying who they are talking to or who has signed documents or commercial transactions in digital transactions.

INFRASTRUCTURES ARE NEEDED TO SUPPORT THE WIDESPREAD USE OF ENCRYPTION

Today, businesses hope to use encryption to expand into the 'new world' of electronic commerce (EC), but the lack of robust KMIs leaves EC pioneers shortchanged. For this reason, KMIs are the keystone of the Administration encryption policy reform proposal. Encryption has little chance of being used to its fullest potential, here or overseas, until there is an international key management framework in place. Unfortunately, there has been too much emphasis on algorithms and key lengths in the encryption debate. There is much more to the issue of trust than a good encryption algorithm. The algorithm gets you perhaps 5 percent of the way there. Without a trustworthy infrastructure to support it, an encryption algorithm's value is comparable to that of a bank vault door on a cardboard box. Many commercial information products and services are facing a tide of resistance because of their lack of security or trust.

When I say trust, I mean that you must be willing to bet your company's future not only on the strength of your algorithm, but on the integrity of those who:

• Issue the encryption certificates that vouch for your identity and the identity of those you deal with;

• Build the directories that allow others to know how to communicate securely with you; and,

• Assist you if you believe your encryption key or certificate has been compromised or lost.

Rhetoric aside, there is very little disagreement in the software or hardware industry that KMIs are needed to increase the use of encryption. The system integrity fostered by such infrastructures will allow us to have the same confidence in electronic commerce that we now have in signatures on paper contracts or in handshakes with business partners, and is needed to achieve our vision of global electronic commerce with secure interoperability.

Trustworthy encryption support infrastructures do not exist widely today, other than in the KMIs used by the Defense Department and other specialized areas where it is essential to the viability of systems. The Administration's recommended KMI-focused approach intends to help fill that void by helping U.S. KMIs to grow, addressing the nation's public safety interests, and helping to open doors for U.S. encryption overseas.

THE KMIs WILL NEED TO SUPPORT KEY RECOVERY

As the EC pioneers build KMIs to support large numbers of encryption users, they will need to provide the capability to regain access to their encrypted data when encryption keys are lost, corrupted, destroyed, or otherwise unavailable. This feature, commonly referred to as "key recovery", is a means to ensure greater safety and trust, and there are compelling business reasons for it. Key recovery ensures, for example, that:

• Employees can recover encrypted Email or files in the event that the disk that holds their encryption key crashes;

• Corporations are not held hostage to a disgruntled employee who sabotages company files by encrypting valuable company intellectual property; and,

• Companies can pass accounting audits, even if archived data had been encrypted with an expired encryption key.

The KMI is a logical place to support key recovery. While key recovery may not yet be widely recognized as a user requirement, analogies to key recovery are common in the workplace. Today, computer system administrators help users recover their forgotten passwords. Similarly, most offices securely maintain spare door and desk keys for emergency use.

Certainly users should have the ability to choose their own responsible agents to generate and store their keys, but the government's public safety responsibilities will require that law enforcement, with proper authorization, be able to gain access to such keys. Without key recovery, law enforcement agencies will be unable to decrypt encrypted criminal files and communications since modern commercial encryption can prevent computerized "brute force attacks" against the criminal communications. The Administration proposes to use privately-operated KME data recovery features to support authorized law enforcement investigations, rather than creating a separate infrastructure that solely supports those investigations.

A GLOBAL SOLUTION DEPENDS ON INDUSTRY/GOVERNMENT COLLABORATION

The Administration's encryption policy satisfies a cross-section of society's needs. The policy enables industry and government to work together to develop and build the infrastructures for managing encryption keys. Industry can bring their market knowledge and infrastructure technology and services to the collaborative effort, while the U.S. government can contribute decades of KMI expertise, and extensive in-place working relationships with foreign governments.

The Administration has engaged various industry and international groups to further define the infrastructure concept. All agree that the emergence of KMIs is necessary. Some in industry, however, continue to seek immediate relaxation of existing export controls on encryption. The Administration is mindful that any such relaxation must be consistent with the objective of encouraging the development of robust, full-featured, key management infrastructures that support key recovery.

MYTHS AND DISTRACTIONS IN THE ENCRYPTION DEBATE

I would like to help clarify some of the frequently-repeated factual errors regarding encryption so we all can stand on firm ground during the formation of the nation's encryption policies.

The encryption debate has often been mischaracterized as a struggle between the high-tech industry, which wants unlimited freedom to sell encryption products worldwide, and the government which is perceived as wanting to prevent the spread of encryption. Such myths, and other threads of the encryption debate, are unsound. They do not address the issues at hand, they can cause unnecessary conflicts among the parties to the debate, and they ultimately delay the resolution of the hard problems. These myths and distractions include brute force attacks, comparisons to earlier key escrow initiatives, and encryption availability and use.

It is Short-Sighted To Base Long-Term Encryption Policy On Bit Lengths And Brute Force Attacks

You may have heard news accounts of a University of California Berkeley student who recently decrypted a message that was encrypted with a 40-bit key using 250 workstations as part of a contest from RSA Inc. This so-called "challenge" is often cited as evidence that the government needs only to conduct "brute force" attacks on messages when they are doing a criminal investigation. In reality, law enforcement does not have the luxury to rely on headline-making brute force attacks on encrypted criminal communications. I think you will find it useful to see for yourselves how increased key sizes can make encryption virtually unbreakable. Ironically, the RSA challenge proves this point.

• If that Berkeley student was faced with an RSA-supplied task of brute forcing a single PGP-based (128-bit key) encrypted message with 250 workstations, it would take him an estimated 9 trillion times the age of the universe to decrypt a single message. Of course, if the Berkeley student didn't already know the contents of part of the message—RSA provided some of the unencrypted message content to assist those who accepted the challenge—it would take even longer.

• For that matter, even if every one of the 29,634 students enrolled at UC Berkeley in 1997 each had 250 workstations at their disposal—7,408,500 computers (cost: ~$15B)—it would still take an estimated 100 billion times the age of the universe, that is over 1 sextillion years (1 followed by 21 zeros), to break a single message.

• If all the personal computers in the world—~260 million computers—were put to work on a single PGP-encrypted message, it would still take an estimated 12 million times the age of the universe, on average, to break a single message (assuming that each of those workstations had processing power similar to each of the Berkeley student's workstations).

Clearly, encryption technology can be made intractable against sheer compute power, and longterm policies cannot be based on bit lengths. Brute force attacks cannot be the primary solution for law enforcement decryption needs. This line of argument is a distraction from the real issues at hand, and I encourage you to help put this debate behind us.

Estimated Time Needed to Recover a Single Key Using the 250 Workstations Used By the Berkeley Student Who Solved RSA's 40-Bit Challenge*

Number of bits	Average time	Time if key is found ⅓ of the way through the full exhaust **
40	5.5 hours	3.6 hours.
56	41 years	27 years.
64	11 thousand years	7 thousand years.
80	690 million years	455 million years.
128	13 trillion times the age of the universe	9 trillion times the age of the universe.

Notes:
- *RSA gave away part of the decrypted text to those trying to solve the challenge.
- ** Berkeley student recovered RSA Challenge 40-bit key ~33 percent into exhaust attack.
- Average point at which a key is recovered during an exhaust attack = 50 percent.
- Berkeley student performed 100 billion operations per hour using 250 workstations.
- Age of the universe = ~15 billion years.

The Administration's Approach To Encryption Policy Reform Is Very Different From Earlier Key Escrow Initiatives

Some have argued that the Administration's recent policy initiative is the same as previous key escrow initiatives. Their argument is disingenuous and incorrect. The KMI initiative is about creating an environment in which commercial encryption can flourish. Just as significant, the Administration's proposal differs significantly from previous key escrow initiatives because:

- It eliminates the focus on bit lengths;
- The government doesn't hold the keys;
- A separate key escrow infrastructure is not required;
- Keys can be held overseas;
- It doesn't prescribe algorithms or limit them to hardware; and,
- Users' data recovery needs can be met.

With these impediments addressed, industry and government can work to develop encryption products that will win acceptance in foreign markets and establish infrastructure services to support those products.

Several major companies recognize these profound changes and have formed business ventures to thrive within the new climate. In October 1996 IBM formed the Key Recovery Alliance and that alliance has already grown to over 50 domestic and international companies. Alliance members include Apple, Mitsubishi, Boeing, DEC, Hewlett Packard, Motorola, Novell, SUN, America Online, Unisys, and RSA.

Despite Being Available, Encryption is Not Being Widely Used

Most measurements of encryption are inadequate (incomplete or inconclusive) since they do not show how many people are using encryption. Encryption can be measured in a number of ways. Depending on how it is measured, one could misconstrue the data to conclude that "the encryption genie is out of the bottle" or that the bottle is tightly plugged. The fact of the matter is that encryption is widely available (e.g., embedded in tens of millions of commercial software products) but, based on our impressions from market surveys, etc., is not widely used.

Those who argue that government encryption policies are outdated because "the encryption genie is out of the bottle" (i.e., there are many products advertised to contain encryption and some of them are available from the Internet) must consider two important perspectives.

First, encryption is not now being, and will not be, used to its fullest potential (with confidence by 100s of millions of people) until there is an infrastructure in place to support it.

Encryption is not a genie that will magically solve the security problem. Nor is the Administration trying to 'keep the plug in the bottle'. The Administration wants to help promote a full range of trusted security services providing privacy, authentication, and data integrity while simultaneously fulfilling public safety and national security responsibilities for our government, and governments worldwide.

Second, serious users of security products don't use free security products from the Internet. The president of a prominent Internet security corporation was recently asked in a magazine article on this issue: "Since encryption technology is available as freeware off the Internet, why would anyone pay a company for it?" He responded by saying: "Freeware is worth exactly what you pay for it. I'd rather not implement security systems using software for which the source code is available to any 12-year-old who thinks being a hacker is fun." In other words, when determining what encryption you use to protect valuable business secrets, you should consider who you're getting it from, how it got to you, and whether you'll receive support when you need it.

U.S. ENCRYPTION POLICIES ARE ADDRESSING CONCERNS THAT THE REST OF THE WORLD IS ALSO FACING

The U.S. is not the only nation which has concerns that encryption use by criminals can threaten public safety. All countries that are major producers of cryptography control its export. Some of those countries have voiced their displeasure with the U.S. decision to export 56-bit encryption.

Though the U.S. does not have domestic restrictions, some countries do through import controls of encryption and its domestic use. Recently, France, Israel, and Russia imposed import and domestic use restrictions, and several Asian, South American, and African countries have informally done so for many years.

At this point, it would be over-generalizing to say that the world has agreed to an approach on key recovery, but it is accurate to say that all governments want authorized access to encrypted information. The U.S. is not the only nation that recognizes the dual-edged nature of the encryption tool.

WRAP UP

The Administration is basing its policies on the foundation that the need for robust commercial encryption will grow and it has proposed policy reforms to ensure that American companies and the public, can flourish in the future encryption market. The Administration's approach is not past its time, it is just in time. The fundamental issue in play is how industry will build key management infrastructures to support mass market products with encryption. If infrastructures are built that support key recovery, then the export control debate can be concluded. Otherwise, governments worldwide are likely to resist the use of those products because of public safety concerns.

Though the Administration's proposed policies will have a significant impact on NSA, I believe they are a reasonable response to a complex, interdependent set of issues. I hope that the Administration can continue to work with Congress and industry to reach a resolution of these issues. Thank you for the opportunity to address this important matter.

The CHAIRMAN. We will have one 5-minute round and keep the record open for written questions that any Senator on the committee can submit.

Director Freeh, please give us your thoughts from a law enforcement perspective of S. 909, the McCain-Kerrey bill. Do you believe that bill meets your needs, and if it doesn't, where does it fall short?

Mr. FREEH. Senator, I think it goes very far in meeting the law enforcement needs. It is the best single, balanced approach to the issue that I have seen and I commend everyone who has worked on that very much. I would go a little bit further with respect to the part of the legislation that deals with the domestic use of encryption.

With respect to section 402, the section as written now makes the storage of key recovery by certificate authority issuers, those who issue public keys, a voluntary event. It certainly encourages the use of that, but it makes it voluntary. From a law enforcement point of view, and again speaking not just for the FBI, but for all the State and local associations I mentioned, we would suggest that one way to better implement and, with more encouragement, establish a key infrastructure system would be for the certificate authorities to be licensed, and that the licensing requirement require that they place the key in some trusted third party.

Now, that doesn't mean that people have to use certificate authorities. They could decide not to use them, which still makes it a voluntary use of encryption. But if they do use a certificate authority issuing a public key, we would encourage that the licensing require the storage of a public key with a trusted third party. I think that would go very far in meeting our major concern, which is the domestic use of encryption.

The CHAIRMAN. I am sure that you recall our efforts in the last Congress to pass the Economic Espionage Act. Now, that bill was passed in part to provide a strong deterrent from theft of proprietary information and trade secrets, and it has been argued that the widespread proliferation of encryption provides an even more meaningful and direct deterrent from such espionage.

Do you agree with that proposition and, if so, how do you believe the Administration's current position of tightly controlling the proliferation of encryption can be reconciled with our desire to thwart economic espionage?

Mr. FREEH. I certainly agree that the economic espionage statute is a very, very strong instrument and will become more so in the future in terms of protecting trade secrets, intellectual property, and that robust encryption is a very critical part of the policies and the objectives behind that statute.

I don't think the objective of providing and preserving for a 200-year history the ability of law enforcement to access and understand the criminal intentions or crimes or objectives of people either attempting economic espionage or any other crime is inconsistent with that. We are not saying that—the key recovery systems with a trusted third party, not a Government trusted third party, do not impede the successful use by companies to protect their trade secrets. I don't think the two are inconsistent at all.

The CHAIRMAN. Now, it is my understanding that there are no current domestic controls on the use of encryption. What does the FBI do now if you are confronted with encrypted information?

Mr. FREEH. Many times, there is nothing we can do. We have, as I mentioned earlier, and had for many, many months after seizure——

The CHAIRMAN. So if sophisticated terrorists and/or organized criminals and/or drug lords are able to use encrypted information, there is not much you can do under current law?

Mr. FREEH. No. We do not have the technical ability to what they call brute-force-access the information on any real-time basis. If it is a very low level of encryption, we can do that. If it is a very high level of encryption, we cannot do that, nor can many of the other agencies involved in our work.

The CHAIRMAN. Well, let me turn to Senator Leahy. We appreciate the testimony of both of you. It has been very enlightening. Senator Leahy.

Senator LEAHY. Thank you, Mr. Chairman. The director had mentioned the digital telephony legislation, and I remember that one very well. It was basically a piece of legislation sponsored by me in the Senate and by Congressman Edwards in the House. We spent a great deal of time leading up to its passage. We actually passed it by unanimous consent, but that was after months of work with everybody.

I would hope we might have a similar process on this area of encryption. We have not had the same kind of process that we had with the digital telephony bill. We saw how well it worked doing it there, and I think that if we did the same thing here—and I pass this on not for the two witnesses, but maybe beyond them to the Administration. If we could have a similar process, I think we could have a similar result. Without it, I don't think it is going to be possible because I don't think you are going to get the kind of unanimity necessary on such a complex issue.

Now, I have always felt that certain encryption users are going to want to use a key recovery system. You are not going to take the chance that you have got a great deal of information in your computer and somebody gets run over by a truck and you don't have any way of getting it. But what about key recovery for a phone conversation or a fax transmission?

I mean, once the communication has been delivered, you store the decoding key or decryption information. Isn't this kind of a useless expense? I mean, why would a user of encryption want to use key recovery encryption for communications such as a telephone conversation or a facsimile transmission?

Director Freeh.

Mr. FREEH. Senator, it is a good point. I think the encryption users—and there are many different categories of users—certainly would have different interests and different formats. In business or in commerce, the decryption of the in-transit communication may not be important unless there is a lawsuit the next week and somebody has to try to retrieve what exactly was the electronic commerce dimensions of the message that was sent.

I can tell you that from law enforcement's point of view, not only with respect to stored data, but critically with respect to in-transit data, we have a daily and vital interest in understanding that real-time. All of our electronic court-authorized wiretaps depend on that understanding.

Senator LEAHY. I understand that, and I mean also if you have recorded something, you may want to be able to get the key to go back and decrypt what you have recorded, which might be useless otherwise. But the commercial user in most instances would not want to carry on the added burden, would they?

I mean, you fax something. Here is our proposed data for tomorrow's board meeting on what our profit and loss is for the year. Now, they may send that on an encrypted fax because they don't want to affect the stock market, or whatever reason, before the board meeting tomorrow or 2 days later or something like that. I mean, if they have received the fax, they are not going to have any reason to keep the key.

Now, you might want a key to be in there if you were tapping that line for a particular reason, but do you think that there is going to be a market or a consumer interest in a key recovery encryption for communications over telephone and fax?

Mr. FREEH. I agree that there certainly would be a dissimilar interest between that example and law enforcement, which is exactly my point that you can't let the market forces deal with this public safety issue because their interests are quite distinct from ours.

Senator LEAHY. But, you see, that raises my next issue. I understand the idea of going after the crime lord and a number of other people, the money launderers, and so on. But do we put an imposition on all of the people who might use this to keep that system and keep those records for all these normal communications on the odd chance that out of the 10 million of that day, there may be one that you want to go after? In fact, I would assume the only way you are going to get industry to do that is to mandate it, and I am asking whether it seems like a very good thing to mandate.

Mr. FREEH. Well, I agree with you that you are putting a burden on the users of encryption, but, you know, you are putting a burden on everybody who uses the telephone when you mandate, as you did in 1994, that software switches be written with access.

Senator LEAHY. It is a somewhat different thing, though. I mean, I pick up the phone and I call my brother in upstate New York. I don't have to keep a record of that. Now, if either one of us is under investigation—and I am going under the assumption we are not, and if he is watching this, he will probably call me up and ask me what it is all about. But assuming that neither one of is, there is no record of that. Now, if we are, you are going to have the ability under the digital telephony law to go in somewhere and tap this conversation. But I don't have to keep a record.

What we are saying is we are going another step further. We are saying now, if you are going to be using encryption, you have got to keep a record of it, even though I might, for whatever reason, be using that encryption just to call my brother to say, hey, are you going to be at the family reunion next month?

Mr. FREEH. Well, I guess my answer to that would be that there is nothing in the proposed statutes, any of them, which would require anybody to use key recovery encryption or systems. What we are saying, though, is that we would like to build an infrastructure which encourages that to the greatest extent, which is why we ask the common carriers to spend millions of dollars to write software to give us access to their switches.

Most of the people who use those switches are never going to be burdened in terms of the authority, but, you know, we are looking for that one or two cases——

Senator LEAHY. But for this, they would be.

Mr. FREEH. Not if they are not required to use the key recovery encryption. I don't see how they would be burdened. In private conversations, you and your brother——

Senator LEAHY. Then how are you going to get it? How are you going to get it if you are going to be tapping?

Mr. FREEH. No. You would need to tap it to get the access to the communication and if they are using a non-key-recovery product, we can't get access to it, and there is nothing that requires them to use that product.

The CHAIRMAN. Your time is up.

Senator LEAHY. Yes, my time is up. Could I just ask for the record—Deputy Director Crowell said that he has a list of Key Recovery Alliance members that seem to support this, at least the way I understood his testimony. I would be interested in who those are because I know Trusted Information Systems is one member of that Key Recovery Alliance and they seem to take just the opposite view.

Mr. CROWELL. Trusted Information Systems is a member of the alliance and has testified before Congress in favor of key recovery. I have heard their testimony on the House side. Among the others are several foreign companies, like Mitsubishi Corporation of Japan.

Senator LEAHY. But are they supporting the Administration's view?

Mr. CROWELL. No. They support the notion of key recovery.

Senator LEAHY. OK; I had the impression that——

Mr. CROWELL. I was not trying to say that they supported the Administration plan.

Senator LEAHY. That is my misunderstanding. I just wanted to make sure that was clear. Thank you.

The CHAIRMAN. Thank you, Senator.

Senator Kyl.

Senator KYL. Thank you, Mr. Chairman.

Director Freeh, in your prepared testimony on page 11, you cite four specific examples where law enforcement is already encountering harmful effects of encryption. I wonder if you could briefly describe those for us first. Second, if you could go back over a question which I think is confusing many, and that is the issue of whether or not, with a voluntary system like the McCain-Kerrey bill provides, law enforcement is going to have the ability in all cases to tap into a system and prevent the abuses that you have described are beginning to occur. If not, what use would it be to law enforcement to have a voluntary system in place.

In other words, what difference does it make for you? Are you at least somewhat better off with it, and if you could give us some kind of context to answer the question that seems to be confusing many here? Could you first of all describe some of those situations?

Mr. FREEH. Yes, Senator, certainly. One of them I referred to briefly—there was a conspiracy subsequently proven in a prosecution in the Southern District of New York where a group of individuals were going to blow up 11 U.S.-owned commercial airliners in the Western Pacific within a 48-hour period. We got access through the Filipino police authorities to the laptop computer that was used by the lead co-conspirator to plan these attacks. One of the files in that laptop computer was encrypted, and encrypted to the point that for months and months thereafter nobody in law enforcement or any other service was able to understand or decrypt that. That is just one case in that category.

We know people like Ames were told by their Soviet handlers to use encrypted computer software. The Innocent Images cases, which was a child pornography initiative the FBI has done for several years, has indicated and evidenced several instances where people are using encrypted programs and software to transmit obscene and pornographic images of children. Many drug trafficking cases, and some which are ongoing as we speak, have now encountered telephone encryption devices to the extent that the court-authorized—the judge's order to get and understand those conversations is a nullity because they can't understand them real-time.

Senator KYL. So in certain cases, if somebody wants to plan a crime or wants to communicate with somebody else with respect to a crime and they have a system that is encrypted without any key recovery, probably through brute force you are not going to be able to crack it and law enforcement is out of luck and the citizenry may suffer as a result. Is that a fair summary?

Mr. FREEH. That is exactly right.

Senator KYL. Now, what you are proposing is that at least the ability of law enforcement to get at this be enhanced. So what good does it do if you have a voluntary key recovery system?

Mr. FREEH. A voluntary system which will encourage corporations—Mr. Crowell referred to 60 companies, including many American companies, who have adopted the notion of key recovery products and are building key recovery products. The more infrastructure, the more banks, the more motor vehicle agencies, the more supermarkets that use key recovery products, the more opportunities or points of access or windows law enforcement will have to access those communications.

One example I would give you is, you know, John Gotti never incriminated himself on the telephone. For years, court orders directed to his telephone communications turned up no evidence of a crime because he was aware of the fact that he was being listened to. So he took measures to avoid electronic surveillance. In fact, what he used to do is he used to talk in an attic on Mulberry Street which was swept, he thought, every day and felt very confident. What would happen then is his underlings would come out of the meeting and they would get on the telephone and call everybody to execute his orders.

So the example is we want an infrastructure that gives us points of access and some opportunities to get real-time understanding of the information. We are not going to prevent the John Gottis or the Aldrich Ameses or the Cali cartel from using encrypted communications, but if we just lay down, which is what we will do if we don't have a policy, and say anybody can use any encryption wherever they want, no rules, no restrictions, then we will severely limit over time and ultimately eliminate any access points that we can get to.

Senator KYL. Quickly while the light is still yellow, in fact, wouldn't you have to turn to more intrusive methods of surveillance to the extent that they are permitted by the Constitution?

Mr. FREEH. Yes, we would have to resort to more intrusive methods.

Senator KYL. Like what?

Mr. FREEH. Well, instead of, you know, a court order that listens to conversations and makes it easier to minimize innocent conversations, we would need to have microphones in places where we have never had them. We would have to go in and maybe on an hourly or daily basis look at hard drives and disks, which right now we don't need to do. I don't think we could do that job, by the way.

Senator KYL. Not as a matter of limitation by the Constitution, but simply being too difficult?

Mr. FREEH. Too difficult, too dangerous, and too compromising.

Senator KYL. Thank you very much, and I would like to submit some questions to you, pursuant to the chairman's suggestion, with respect to your suggestions on the legislation. Do you have any concerns about the law enforcement punishment and any possible chilling effect that that would have on law enforcement doing its duty on the McCain-Kerrey bill?

Mr. FREEH. I actually don't Senator. I will read it again, but we read it over when it was mentioned and I do not.

Senator KYL. Thank you very much, and thank you very much, Mr. Crowell, for your testimony, too.

Thank you, Mr. Chairman.

The CHAIRMAN. Thank you, Senator.

Senator Feinstein.

Senator FEINSTEIN. I think, Mr. Freeh, you have made a clear and compelling case for key recovery. I think, if understood by the American people, they would be supportive, in the dominant majority, of key recovery. The question I have, as Senator Kyl was asking, is does a voluntary system really do it?

I remember a while ago getting briefed from Ambassador Aaron on his efforts in the European Community to get concurrence for a key recovery system, and to the best of my knowledge this has not yet happened. Mr. Crowell read the name of one major Japanese company that would subscribe to a system of key recovery. I would like to ask what you gentlemen can tell us about securing a global, private sector, positive response to key recovery.

Mr. FREEH. Senator, let me begin that and I will let Bill answer the other half of it. You know, a lot of the countries have taken a much more aggressive approach to encryption. In France, in Israel, in Russia, they have mandated key recovery systems and actually have looked at their export controls in response to our modification of import controls. The United Kingdom and Germany are looking very seriously right now at controlling and requiring key recovery, so this is a very dynamic situation. I know in speaking to my——

Senator FEINSTEIN. And the Japanese?

Mr. FREEH. Do you have an update on that? I am not sure.

Mr. CROWELL. There are discussions ongoing with the Japanese.

Senator FEINSTEIN. For a mandated system?

Mr. CROWELL. No, for a voluntary system in their case. That is the approach that they examined in Japan.

Mr. FREEH. The second part of your question—in my discussions with my law enforcement counterparts in many, many different countries, most recently with the new Home Secretary in Great Britain who is very concerned about the encryption issue, I believe there will be effective means to have bilateral and even multination agreements with respect to sharing and accessing and protecting keys, but we need an infrastructure.

They are, quite frankly, looking to the United States for the leadership in the legislation. Whatever the Congress does or does not do in this area will be very persuasive—I don't know of Bill agrees with me—on many, many countries that are waiting to see what the United States does with respect to this issue.

Senator FEINSTEIN. Well, let me just urge you, then, not to backtrack. I understand the forces at play here, but I think it is very important for the future security of the world that we come to grips with a system of key recovery that gives law enforcement what it needs without impinging on individual rights, and I believe it can be done. I don't see a reason why it can't be done.

What concerns me is that I get so many conflicting signals on key recovery that I really don't know what to think. I, for one, will be very much guided by what you gentlemen believe is in the best interests of public safety and national security in any piece of legislation. So, I would just like to urge you to be as dominant in this area as possible and not to get downtrodden, so to speak, by companies who have their own individuals interests at stake rather than the public's or the Nation's security interests.

Mr. FREEH. Thank you, Senator.

Senator FEINSTEIN. Thank you.

The CHAIRMAN. Thank you, Senator.

Senator Ashcroft.

Senator ASHCROFT. Thank you, Mr. Chairman.

Director Crowell, you indicated that people would need key recovery in the private sector. Are key recovery systems being developed to respond to that need now by the marketplace?

Mr. CROWELL. Yes, Senator, there are some being developed.

Senator ASHCROFT. Both domestic and abroad?

Mr. CROWELL. Both domestic and abroad.

Senator ASHCROFT. Is there any reason why someone who needs it can't have it now?

Mr. CROWELL. The products are not widely available yet for personal use, but there is no reason why people couldn't have their own system of key recovery.

Senator ASHCROFT. So the need for key recovery in the private sector is not a need for us to pass legislation. As a matter of fact, there is key recovery available in the private sector currently——

Mr. CROWELL. No.

Senator ASHCROFT [continuing]. And it is something to which the market is responding and you can buy from Siemens overseas or from companies here.

Mr. CROWELL. No. I disagree with you, Senator. There is a need for legislation that has to do with how that key recovery system, when it is established, relates to things like law enforcement. Do they have the authority to address that key recovery agent and recover the keys?

Senator ASHCROFT. Well, that is not the need for the private citizen. That is the need for law enforcement.

Mr. CROWELL. Well, I just didn't want to answer the question too narrowly.

Senator ASHCROFT. I didn't think you wanted to answer the question. [Laughter.]

Recently, the Federal Government, the Administration, authorized 128-bit encryption for financial institutions. Why did it do that?

Mr. CROWELL. It was done because there has been a long history, almost 18 years now, of allowing banks and financial institutions to have strong encryption.

Senator ASHCROFT. Well, was that needless? You have provided us charts saying that 128-bit encryption would require 13 trillion times the age of the universe to break.

Mr. CROWELL. If I may just continue my answer, sir, there is a longstanding history of allowing them to do it, and there also is a longstanding history of the banks providing for documentation and other records necessary for law enforcement needs. So there was a belief that it was in keeping with the Administration's policy.

Senator ASHCROFT. It occurs to me that one of the points you sought to make was that we really don't need robust encryption. It takes so long to decipher these things. There is no need for it. But, apparently, the Administration feels that there is a need for it because they not only went above the 56-bit level, they more than doubled the 56. This goes up geometrically, it is my understanding. They went all the way to 128-bit, and I may be using the wrong terminology because I am not conversant here.

But it seems to me that to say that you don't need this, on the one hand, and to provide it without keys, without anything to the financial institutions of this country, on the other hand—there is a little tension there and I don't understand the resolution of that tension.

Mr. CROWELL. Senator, my testimony specifically said that the Administration encourages the use of strong encryption.

Senator ASHCROFT. I understand that and that is good. I believe we ought to encourage the use of strong encryption and I think we ought to make it possible.

Now, Director Freeh, do you recommend that we have a mandated encryption system?

Mr. FREEH. No, I don't, Senator.

Senator ASHCROFT. So any business that didn't choose to have—pardon me. A key deposit system is what I am talking about. Anybody that chose not to participate in depositing a key wouldn't have to under the kind of proposal——

Mr. FREEH. No, would not have to, it is my understanding.

Senator ASHCROFT. So that any criminal or terrorist that chose to have very robust encryption would be allowed to do that and would be allowed to communicate with other terrorists for those purposes without depositing a key for recovery either by law enforcement or anyone else?

Mr. FREEH. That is right.

Senator ASHCROFT. They would accept certain risks if they didn't have a key—for example, that somebody who knew the key could disappear or that the key would be destroyed, so that they couldn't recover their data. But that would be a thing that they could—and so your presumption is basically that lawbreakers and terrorists will, in some measure, willingly use key recovery systems that are voluntary?

Mr. FREEH. Well, I would go beyond that, maybe unwittingly use those. But those would be the opportunities that we would be able to take advantage of. There is an assumption here that nobody in the categories of spies, terrorists or criminals are going to, you know, do anything to help me do my job.

Senator ASHCROFT. Well, you keep using examples, like in order to protect us from serious terrorist attack by complex organizations, and you talk about cartels. It seems to me that they would be pretty adept at minimizing their risk of detection and it is very unlikely that they would voluntarily participate in a system that was not mandated.

Mr. FREEH. Well, I agree and disagree. I don't think they are going to participate in any system that helps law enforcement and leads to their detection. As someone many years in law enforcement, that is a given in our work. On the other hand, you know, there are many more opportunities with a key recovery infrastructure that they are going to——

Senator ASHCROFT. Slip up.

Mr. FREEH. They are going to slip up.

Senator ASHCROFT. And they might do some of their business in a key recovery system and others of their businesses in encrypted system that offered no——

Mr. FREEH. That is right. You know, there are different degrees of criminals. I had a wiretap when I was a young FBI agent where we had two organized crime people on a telephone and they were really worried about electronic surveillance, so they whispered to each other. [Laughter.]

You know, we are not always dealing with rocket scientists. But if very robust encryption is available in Radio Shack, we are going to have it at a much more comprehensive level. We are just looking to keep some windows in the network available for us.

Senator ASHCROFT. Well, yes. It is available closer than Radio Shack now. I mean, at least Pretty Good Privacy, Mr. Zimmerman's product, is on the Internet.

Mr. FREEH. Yes. You can download some of that stuff, sure.

Senator ASHCROFT. You indicated that there are some countries where they have mandated encryption systems with key recovery and deposit. Have they been able to enforce that? Have they been able to implement it? It is one thing to tell the population of a country—I could understand that the Soviet Union might say we don't want anybody to have any secrets here, so we are going to mandate a key recovery system, and they have done so.

Mr. FREEH. Yes.

Senator ASHCROFT. And so have a whole list of other countries with far fewer commitments to civil liberties than we have. It is not an impressive list to me for that reason, but have they been able to implement it?

Mr. FREEH. I don't know what the success is in France or Israel, for instance. Maybe you know, Bill.

Mr. CROWELL. I believe in France it is fairly successful, since they essentially have the telecommunications company that provides modem access cooperating with them. So if they have a modem that they cannot understand, they essentially take it off the air.

Senator ASHCROFT. I thank the chairman for the time.

The CHAIRMAN. Thank you, Senator.

I want to personally thank both of you for your testimony here today.

Senator LEAHY. Somebody mentioned PGP. I sent a letter out to the internet and this is what my signature looks like under that encryption. My wife says it is the only time it has been legible. [Laughter.]

The CHAIRMAN. I was thinking the same thing.

Senator LEAHY. I do want to note, Mr. Chairman, we asked the FBI at the last oversight hearing a number of questions in this area and we have yet to get responses. I know things have been pretty busy, and I am not going to repeat the questions here, but I do need them.

I would also make one last comment, if I could, that when we had the clipper chip hearing, a Justice Department witness used the example of a criminal using a bank to move illicit money out of this country and the clipper chip was needed to allow the Government to monitor these illegal transactions. Now, the Commerce Department's new encryption rule would allow exactly that, using encryption of any key length stronger than 56-bit DES for direct home banking software for customers worldwide.

So after saying that it was a terrible thing, now they say if you have got a Colombian drug lord in Cali doing money laundering through New York, they can do it. So the Administration has not been a model of consistency on this whole issue. I would throw that out for whatever it is worth.

The CHAIRMAN. You would limit it to this issue? [Laughter.]

Senator LEAHY. I don't mean to be picking on just this Administration. On this particular issue, no administration has been a model of consistency. [Laughter.]

The CHAIRMAN. Well, we are grateful to have both of you here. We do want to solve these problems. Sometimes, they seem insoluble to us up here.

Senator LEAHY. I would not have their job for anything facing encryption, though. I think it should not be left for anybody up here to assume that encryption does anything but make the job of the FBI and the NSA infinitely more difficult. It does.

The CHAIRMAN. Well, I personally miss Bill Casey, who didn't need any encryption. [Laughter.]

Well, thank you both for being here. We appreciate your testimony.

Mr. CROWELL. Thank you very much, Senator.

Mr. FREEH. Thank you.

The CHAIRMAN. We are grateful to our law enforcement people and to our national security people for the efforts that they put forth in these matters and we want to thank them.

We are pleased to have four industry and academic leaders in the encryption policy debate in our third panel today. First, we will hear from an old friend of mine, Ken Dam, of the University of Chicago Law School, who chaired the National Research Council's committee to study national Cryptography. A comprehensive report was released in May 1996 and is known as the CRISIS, or Cryptography's Role in Securing the Information Society, report.

Our second witness is from Utah, Mike MacKay, vice president of Corporate Architecture for Novell, Inc. Mike, we are happy to have you here and look forward to hearing your testimony.

Our third witness is Peter Neumann, principal scientist at the Computer Science Laboratory of SRI International, and author of "Computer-Related Risks." And our final witness today is Raymond Ozzie, founder and chairman of Iris Associates, a wholly owned subsidiary of Lotus Development Corporation. So we are happy to have you here as well.

We will begin with you, Ken. Now, I am going to have to limit you to just a few minutes each, 5 minutes each. Can you summarize in that? We will put all statements in the record as though fully delivered, but we are all running out of time here.

Mr. Dam.

PANEL CONSISTING OF KENNETH W. DAM, CHAIR, COMMITTEE TO STUDY NATIONAL CRYPTOGRAPHY POLICY, NATIONAL RESEARCH COUNCIL, CHICAGO, IL; MICHAEL MACKAY, VICE PRESIDENT, CORPORATE ARCHITECTURE, NOVELL, INC., OREM, UT, ON BEHALF OF THE BUSINESS SOFTWARE ALLIANCE AND THE SOFTWARE PUBLISHERS ASSOCIATION; RAYMOND OZZIE, CHAIRMAN, IRIS ASSOCIATES, WESTFORD, MA, ON BEHALF OF THE BUSINESS SOFTWARE ALLIANCE; AND PETER G. NEUMANN, PRINCIPAL SCIENTIST, COMPUTER SCIENCE LABORATORY, SRI INTERNATIONAL, MENLO PARK, CA

STATEMENT OF KENNETH W. DAM

Mr. DAM. Thank you, Senator, Senator Leahy. I am glad you mentioned the report, so I won't have to. What I will do is I will summarize the report. Several other people testifying here were members of the committee. They will talk about other things, and I will be willing to answer questions about particular points from my own point of view. But right now, I am speaking essentially for the committee.

We were asked to examine the balance among various national security, law enforcement, business, and privacy interests, and we were composed of individuals with expertise in many of the relevant fields. The fact that we were able, as individuals with diverse interests and stakes, to come to a strong consensus demonstrates that agreement on policy in this area is indeed possible.

Furthermore, the cleared members of the committee unanimously concluded that the debate over national cryptography policy could be carried out in a reasonable manner on an unclassified basis. So I think those are two important lessons there.

Now, all parties agree that encryption is one of the very most important tools for protecting all forms of electronic information, albeit it is only one tool. The policy dilemma stems from the fact that while it is an important tool to protect the Nation's businesses and the privacy of individuals, it can also be used, as we have heard this morning, for a variety of illicit and illegal activities.

In our deliberations, we came to the conclusion that this picture of law enforcement and national security competing against privacy and business needs for confidentiality was an incomplete picture. After all, protecting a company's proprietary information against industrial spies is very much a part of law enforcement. Protecting critical national information systems and networks against unauthorized intruders is a key responsibility of national security. Thus—and this is a very important point and I think it was borne out by the testimony here earlier this morning—the use of cryptography can actually help law enforcement and national security, as well, of course, as hindering them.

Let me just go over a few of our findings and recommendations. First of all, we emphasize the role of market forces in policy. We argue that a national policy on cryptography that runs counter to user needs and against market forces is unlikely to be successful over the long term, and I think that the Administration is slowly coming around to this same view. So we would emphasize that whatever is going to be done has to harness and take advantage of market forces rather than working against them.

Now, with regard to key recovery, which is what you are really focusing on today, we concluded that key recovery is a promising technology. But—and this is something we haven't really talked about this morning—it is relatively unproven and it entails its own risks. It is promising for the reasons that have been indicated, but many unresolved issues remain.

For example, the extent to which key recovery agents can actually protect keys is unknown. Key recovery agents involve people and when people are involved, human vulnerabilities and weaknesses may lead to compromises of the system. Wholesale compromise of keys could lead to catastrophic losses for business and individuals. I refer to this as the "open says me" problem.

Second, the introduction of key recovery features into encryption products may introduce technical vulnerabilities that could be exploited by an adversary, and no one knows how likely such an eventuality is or who all of the adversaries might be.

Then there are questions about liability. While a business may enter into a contractual arrangement with a key recovery agent that specifies liabilities—but, of course, that would be up to the private firm or individual to do—a customer or supplier of that business who is damaged by the compromise if the key may not have the ability to recover unless recovery is permitted, and the bill we have been looking at leans in the other direction.

Now, while resolving some of these issues may ultimately require legislation, key recovery is so new today that it is speculation rather than an experience which would underlie any legislation in this area. Rather than aggressively promoting key recovery encryption as a proven technology, we concluded that the Government should explore key recovery for its own internal uses to gain working experience with this technology and to demonstrate its utility in a convincing way to the commercial sector.

Even if and when commercial utility is demonstrated, we believe that adoption of key recovery systems or standards by the commercial sector should be voluntary and based on business needs, not Government pressure. So we are definitely opposed to the idea of making it mandatory. We don't think enough is known about how to implement this on a large scale. We believe that since it could be circumvented technically, it is not at all clear that it will be a real solution to the most serious problems that law enforcement authorities feel that they will face. There is a real risk that it will be used by everybody but the criminals we are trying to reach.

Third, to adopt a particular solution at this time would likely have a significant negative impact, and I do believe there is a recognition of that point in saying that there are 60 companies out there with solutions and we are going to let them use their solutions so long as they are subject to certain regulation. So I think that is a step forward.

Fourth, we felt that there is not enough known yet about how the market will respond to key recovery, nor how it will prefer the concept to be implemented, if at all, to really mandate it as this time. So we felt that a policy of deliberate exploration rather than aggressive promotion would be the best that we would be prepared to recommend.

There is a lot more in my prepared testimony. I think at this point not only has my time elapsed, but it would be better to hear from some of my colleagues here who will be able to address some of the questions that need to be faced. I would emphasize to this committee how important I think it is that they grab hold of this legislative train and take a very close look at many of the proposals within the legislation, the McCain-Kerrey bill, particularly with regard to subpoena power, and so forth, but also with regard to how fast all this is to be implemented because if we implement it before we have solutions to these technical issues, we may actually be creating new vulnerabilities for our American business and for individuals.

Thank you.

The CHAIRMAN. Thank you, Mr. Dam.

[The prepared statement of Mr. Dam follows:]

PREPARED STATEMENT OF KENNETH W. DAM

Good morning, Mr. Chairman and Members of the Committee: As you probably know, I chaired a committee of the National Research Council which last year released a report entitled Cryptography's Role in Securing the Information Society. Asked to examine the balance among various national security, law enforcement, business, and privacy interests, we were composed of individuals with expertise in many relevant fields: computers, communications, and cryptography; law enforcement, intelligence, civil liberties, national security, diplomacy, and international trade; and it included individuals from the private sector; both vendors and users. The fact that these individuals, with diverse interests and stakes, were able to come to a strong consensus demonstrates that agreement on policy in this area is indeed possible. Furthermore, 13 of the 16 members of the committee received security clearances to examine the classified material alleged to be relevant to the debate. These cleared members unanimously concluded that the debate over national cryptography policy can be carried out in a reasonable manner on an unclassified basis.

All parties to the debate over encryption policy agree that it is important to protect personal financial transactions, medical records, and corporate secrets—such as bidding information and proprietary research—from criminals and corporate spies. All parties also agree that encryption is one very important tool for protecting all forms of electronic information.

But the policy dilemma arises from the fact that while encryption is a vital tool for protecting the legitimate information interests of the nation's businesses and the privacy of its citizens, it can also be used in a wide range of illegal or harmful activities—by terrorists, by hostile military forces, by drug cartels, and so on.

However, in May 1996, our committee concluded that this picture of law enforcement and national security competing against privacy and business needs for confidentiality was incomplete. After all, protecting a company's proprietary information against industrial spies is very much a part of law enforcement. Protecting critical national information systems and networks against unauthorized intruders is a key responsibility of national security. Thus, as the committee pointed out, the use of cryptography can help law enforcement and national security as well as hinder them. We also found that export controls to discourage the export of strong encryption had a negative impact on information security products available to the domestic market, even though the domestic market was and is ostensibly unregulated.

THE ADMINISTRATION'S POLICY APPROACH

The Administration's approach to the policy dilemma was—and is—to rely on a technology known then as key escrow and now as key recovery. This policy includes:

- liberalizing export controls conditioned on developer agreement to build and market key recovery products in the future.
- connecting key recovery to the use of a public key infrastructure that would otherwise be used for authentication and confidentiality purposes.
- development of a yet-to-be-formulated Federal Information Processing Standard for key recovery.

RELEVANT NRC FINDINGS AND RECOMMENDATIONS

Our report addressed many of the issues raised in today's debate over key recovery, and I want to relate to you some of our committee's relevant findings and recommendations. For example, we found that policies that support key recovery have been motivated primarily by law enforcement needs, rather than by those of national security, and that key recovery has much less utility for national security than for law enforcement.

The role of the market

We emphasized the role of market forces in policy. In particular, we argued that national policy on cryptography that runs counter to user needs and against market forces is unlikely to be successful over the long term. Market-friendly policy would emphasize the freedom of domestic users to determine cryptographic functionality, protection, and implementations according to their security needs as they see fit, including the use or non-use of key recovery. For example, businesses have articulated a need in many cases for recovering the keys to encrypted files, but not such a need for monitoring the content of their encrypted communications. Furthermore, the development of products with encryption should be driven largely by market forces rather than by government-imposed requirements or standards.

On key recovery

As noted earlier, key recovery is functionally the same as escrowed encryption, though the details are different in some cases. We concluded that while key recovery encryption is a promising technology, it is relatively unproven and entails its own potential risks. It is promising because if it is properly implemented and widely deployed, it could allow law enforcement and national security authorities to obtain legally authorized access to relevant encrypted data in specific instances. Similarly, it would enable businesses and individuals to recover encrypted stored data to which access has been inadvertently lost.

On the other hand, many unresolved issues remain. For example:

- The extent to which key recovery agents can protect keys is unknown. Key recovery agents involve people, and when people are involved, human vulnerabilities and weaknesses may lead to compromises of the system. Wholesale compromise of keys could lead to catastrophic losses for businesses.
- The introduction of key recovery features into encryption products may introduce technical vulnerabilities that could be exploited by an adversary, and no one knows how likely such an eventuality is.
- Liability issues are unresolved. While a business may enter into a contractual arrangement with a key recovery agent that specifies liabilities, a customer or supplier of that business who is damaged by the compromise of a key may not have similar recourse. Furthermore, there is a tension between reducing liability through statute to promote key recovery and reassuring users that their interests will be protected in the event of large losses.

While resolving some of these issues may ultimately require legislation, key recovery is so new today that it is speculation rather than experience that would underlie any proposed legislation in this area.

Rather than aggressively promoting key recovery as a proven technology, we concluded that the government should explore key recovery for its own internal uses to gain working experience with this technology and to demonstrate its utility in a convincing way to the commercial sector. Even if and when commercial utility is demonstrated, we believe that adoption of key recovery systems or standards by the commercial sector should be voluntary and based on business needs, not government pressure.

We took this stand for several reasons.

- First, not enough is yet known about how best to implement key recovery on a large scale. The operational complexities of a large-scale infrastructure are significant, and approaches proposed today for dealing with those complexities are not based on real experience. A more prudent approach to setting policy would be to develop a base of experience that would guide policy decisions on how key recovery might work on a large scale in practice.

• Second, because of the ease with which key recovery can be circumvented technically, it is not at all clear that key recovery will be a real solution to the most serious problems that law enforcement authorities feel they will face. Administration officials freely acknowledge that their various initiatives promoting key recovery are not intended to address all criminal uses of encryption, but in fact those most likely to have information to conceal will be motivated to circumvent key recovery encryption products.

• Third, information services and technologies are undergoing rapid evolution and change today, and nearly all technology transitions are characterized by vendors creating new devices and services. Imposing a particular solution to the encryption dilemma at this time is likely to have a significant negative impact on the natural market development of applications made possible by new information services and technologies. While the nation may choose to bear these costs in the future, it is particularly unwise to bear them in anticipation of a large-scale need that may not arise and in light of the nation's collective ignorance about how key recovery would work on a large scale.

• Fourth and most importantly, not enough is yet known about how the market will respond to key recovery, nor how it will prefer the concept to be implemented, if at all. Given the importance of market forces to the long-term success of national cryptography policy, a more prudent approach to policy would be to learn more about how in fact the market will respond before advocating a specific solution driven by the needs of government. This is especially true when the reaction of export markets to key recovery is unknown and keysharing or information-sharing arrangements between governments have not yet been established.

A process of deliberate exploration rather than aggressive promotion would allow the development of a body of experience demonstrating that key recovery encryption does not pose undue risks to users. In a market-driven system, this body of experience will begin to accrue in small steps. As this body of experience grows, government will have the ability to make wise decisions about the appropriate rules and regulations that should govern key recovery agents. These include issues such as standards, liability, contract terms, and so on.

Since our report was released in 1996, a number of vendors have indeed released products or made product announcements about-encryption products that support key recovery. As the key recovery products of these and other vendors are adopted and used in the private sector and by government, experience with this technology will grow. In several years, this accumulated experience could well induce our committee to revisit its conclusions. After all, we explicitly cast our report in transitional terms, rather than address the issues once and for all.

Finally, we recognized that considerations of public safety and national security made it undesirable to maintain an entirely laissez-faire approach to national cryptography policy. Consequently, we crafted several recommendations to describe what we thought were appropriate affirmative steps, and I can describe these if you wish.

As a footnote, our committee tackled a very controversial problem and came to consensus on it. Had we operated in conformance to the requirements of the Federal Advisory Committee Act, such a consensus would have been impossible to reach.

That concludes my prepared testimony, and I am pleased to address any questions you may have.

The CHAIRMAN. Let us turn to you, Mr. MacKay.

STATEMENT OF MICHAEL MACKAY

Mr. MACKAY. Thank you. Good morning, Mr. Chairman. My name is Michael MacKay. I am the vice president of Corporate Architecture at Novell, Inc. Novell is one of the world's largest network software companies, with an installed base of roughly 55 million users, which represents a significant portion of the growing worldwide Internet. Novell was founded and is headquartered in the State of Utah. We also have major operations in the State of California, in San Jose, and throughout the world.

This morning, I am speaking on behalf of Novell, as well as the Business Software Alliance and the Software Publishers Association. I would also like to say that while I am specifically not speaking on behalf of the Key Recovery Alliance, in fact, Novell is a member of the Key Recovery Alliance. I was personally instrumental in engaging Novell's participation with that organization, and so am quite familiar with that.

I would like to thank you, Mr. Chairman, for holding these hearings and for the careful consideration you are giving to encryption. This is not an easy issue. I would also like to thank you for being at the forefront of the effort to promote and protect one of America's most valuable assets, its intellectual property. As you know, these issues are extremely important both to the American software industry and to the U.S. economy. I would also like to thank Senator Leahy for all this work in this area as well.

Novell and the commercial computing industry are busy building worldwide networks that will serve as the engine for electronic commerce and communications in the next century. This engine promises to provide a major boost to economic growth and a dynamic source of new companies and jobs. As these networks mature, security is and will become an evermore critical foundation of them. Unfortunately, in industry, our ability to provide security that our customers in business and the commercial sector are demanding is being severely compromised by the Administration's current export controls on encryption.

I will focus on one aspect of the Administration's encryption policy, its mandatory key recovery scheme. My message is simple. The Administration's mandatory key recovery scheme is too complex, too costly, and too vulnerable, and we don't believe it will work. Allow me to explain why in seven points.

No. 1, we believe a huge bureaucracy will be necessary in order to manage it. The Administration's plan assumes a system involving dozens of governments, thousands of companies, tens of thousands of law enforcement offices, and millions, growing to hundreds of millions of users. This system will manage tens or hundreds of millions of public-private key pairs and potentially upwards of billions of recoverable session keys across thousands of different products. The bureaucracy needed to manage it, we believe, could rival that of the Social Security Administration or the IRS.

No. 2, the technology does not yet exist to create and smoothly operate a mandatory key recovery scheme that is reliable and which is comprehensive to the magnitude and complexity which has been proposed. In its zeal to see the system established, we believe the Administration has overlooked some tremendous and considerable technical barriers, and it is unclear that a system can be built, much less in the next few years. As Novell's own CEO, Dr. Eric Schmidt has said, "Perhaps the technology to create such a system will be available in my lifetime, but it is not available today."

No. 3, the cost is likely to be prohibitive. Even under the most favorable circumstances, the cost of managing billions of keys around the world is likely to be very high. Unfortunately, there are no cost estimates that have been provided, nor any mention of any careful cost/benefit analysis or who is, in fact, even going to pay or how this will be paid for as it is rolled out.

No. 4, none of the necessary international treaties are in place. Despite years of insisting that bilateral and multilateral treaties necessary for a worldwide key recovery system can be negotiated and are around the corner, we still don't have a single one.

No. 5, criminals and terrorists won't use it. In fact, they will probably do their best to circumvent, as the point has been made earlier today. The stated purpose of the Administration's mandatory key recovery scheme is to strengthen law enforcement and national security, goals with which we all agree. It is unlikely, however, that criminals and terrorist groups will use a system that requires them to provide their keys to third parties who can give them back to Government officials on demand for real-time use.

No. 6, Government programs should not preempt market forces. The private sector is pursuing key recovery programs motivated by commercial business requirements that allow for voluntary deposited encrypted keys with third parties or for self-escrow. The private sector is creating these programs because our customers, business, are demanding it for their stored data. We do not believe, however, that there is a market demand for covert, real-time access to communications, which the Administration has insisted be part of this mandatory system.

No. 7, it may actually result in greater vulnerability for users. Given the scale and scope of the Administration's proposal and the type of system that it implies, comparatively minor design flaws could compromise the overall utility and operational integrity of the system. Lurking in any key recovery system and any security system are design and implementation flaws or operational weaknesses that could inadvertently give unauthorized access to sensitive information.

For these reasons, we do not support the Administration's key recovery scheme and we believe that there are serious problems with Senate bill S. 909 as well. Instead, we recommend that the Administration work with the private sector to build on market-driven initiatives that are technically practical, affordable, and accomplish many of the same ends.

In closing, I would like to urge you, Mr. Chairman, to continue to play an active role in this issue, as any legislation dealing with encryption and key recovery will pass through this committee. We do support the ECPA and Pro-CODE legislation—we believe that this is excellent model legislation—and look forward to working closely with you and the committee to resolve these issues.

Thank you.

The CHAIRMAN. Well, thank you very much. I can assure you that members of this committee are going to play an important role and we are taking this very seriously, and we appreciate the testimony all of you are bringing here today.

[The prepared statement of Mr. MacKay follows:]

PREPARED STATEMENT OF MICHAEL MACKAY

My message is simple: The Administration's key recovery scheme is too complex, too costly and too vulnerable. It will not work.

1. A huge bureaucracy will be necessary to manage it. The Administration's plan would involve dozens of governments, thousands of companies and tens of thousands of law enforcement offices managing billions of keys. The bureaucracy could rival the IRS.

2. The technology does not yet exist to create and smoothly operate a reliable system of this magnitude and complexity. To quote Novell's chairman and CEO, Dr. Eric Schmidt, "Perhaps the technology to create such a system will be available in my lifetime; it is not available today."

3. The cost is likely to be prohibitive. Even in the most favorable circumstances, the cost of managing billions of keys across an international bureaucracy would be high.

4. None of the necessary international treaties is in place. Despite years of insisting that the treaties are just around the corner, the Administration has not signed a single one.

5. Criminals and terrorists will avoid using it. They will not use a system that requires them to deposit their keys with third-parties who can give them to law enforcement officials.

6. Government programs cannot preempt market forces. The private sector is developing key recovery products, but there is no market demand for the Administration's scheme.

7. It may actually result in greater vulnerability for users. A system of this complexity would inevitably have flaws that may undermine the security of law abiding citizens.

For these reasons, we cannot support the Administration's key recovery scheme. Instead, we recommend that government work with the private sector to build on market-driven initiatives that are technically feasible, affordable and accomplish many of the same ends. We support S. 376 (the Encryption Communications Privacy Act), S. 377 (the Promotion of Commerce OnLine in the Digital Era) and H.R. 695 (the Security and Freedom through Encryption Act). We believe, however, that S. 909 (The Secure Public Networks Act), which the Senate Commerce Committee passed out of mark-up last week, entails a key recovery scheme that will not work and is a step backwards.

INTRODUCTION

Good Morning. My name is Mike MacKay, and I am Vice President of the Corporate Architecture Group at Novell, Inc. Founded in 1983, Novell is the world's leading provider of network software. Novell has an installed base of 55 million users, which is about the size of the worldwide Internet. Our flagship products include IntranetWare, Groupwise, Novell Directory Services (NDS), Managewise and BorderManager. The company offers a wide range of network solutions for distributed network, Internet/Intranet and small-business markets, as well as the network computing industry's most comprehensive education and technical support programs.

I appreciate the opportunity to appear today before this Committee on behalf of Novell, the Business Software Alliance (BSA) and the Software Publishers Association (SPA).

The BSA promotes the continued growth of the software industry through its international public policy, education, and enforcement programs in 65 countries throughout North America, Europe, Asia, and Latin America. BSA worldwide members include the leading publishers of software for personal computers including Adobe, Apple Computer, Autodesk, Bentley Systems, Lotus Development, Microsoft, Novell, The Santa Cruz Operation, and Symantec. BSA's Policy Council consists of these software publishers and other leading computer technology companies including Computer Associates, Compaq and Sybase.

The SPA represents more than 85 percent of the U.S. packaged software market. Its 1,200 members are both large and small software publishers and developers in the business, consumer, education, Internet and client/server markets worldwide. SPA and its members are dedicated to serving the needs of the software publishing community by addressing relevant issues and providing solutions to specific industry concerns.

But I am really here today to speak on behalf of the tens of millions of users of American software products—users who are also trying to create a world of digital commerce.

American individuals and companies are rapidly becoming networked together through private local area networks (LANs), wide area networks (WANs) and public networks such as the Internet. Combined, these private and public networks are the economic engine driving electronic commerce, transactions and communications. This engine is being choked by the lack of availability of strong encryption products.

Users are demanding the ability to use encryption to protect their electronic information and to interact securely worldwide. They do not want to put sensitive personal information and confidential business information on-line without this protection. Fortunately, American companies do have exciting and innovative products that can meet this demand and compete internationally. But unless the current unilateral U.S. export restrictions are changed to allow the use of strong encryption, American individuals and businesses will not be active participants in this new networked world of commerce—let alone continue to be the leaders in its development.

During the past few years, we have witnessed a lengthy debate on U.S. encryption policy. Industry has argued forcefully that the U.S. government must implement a contemporary and practical policy for export controls on encryption to maintain U.S. competitiveness, keep American jobs, protect the public interest and facilitate electronic commerce. We have also explained at great length that the genie is out of the bottle since strong encryption is already readily available oversees.

For these reasons, we strongly urge all of you on this Committee to support legislation such as S. 376, the Encryption Communications Privacy Act (ECPA), and S. 377, the Promotion of Commerce On-Line in the Digital Era (Pro-CODE) Act since they place industry on a level international playing field, provide consumers with choice, and strengthen our national security.

I would like to thank all of the members of the Senate Judiciary Committee, and especially Senator Hatch, for holding this hearing on encryption, and Senator Leahy for introducing legislation, as well as Senator Ashcroft for cosponsoring Pro-CODE. I also want to thank Congressman Goodlatte for introducing H.R. 695, the Security and Freedom through Encryption (SAFE) Act, which was recently adopted by the full House Judiciary Committee without amendment.

While these bills differ in some respects, they all modernize export laws regarding software and hardware with encryption capabilities. In doing so, they permit American software companies to compete on a level international playing field and to provide computer users with their choice of adequate protection for their confidential information.

Unfortunately, last week the Senate Commerce Committee reported out S. 909, the Secure Public Networks Act, which promotes the Administration's mandated third party key recovery access and is a significant step backwards for American consumers. In fact, far from being a compromise, S. 909 is actually worse than the status quo. S. 909 sets up an extremely convoluted domestic key recovery system that is even more detailed than the one originally proposed by the Administration and requires the President to try to make it a worldwide system. This complex a key recovery scheme will inevitably sacrifice business and consumers' security and drastically increase their costs unnecessarily.

Indeed, the primary focus of my comments today is key recovery. While this issue has attracted much attention, it has been treated in only superficial terms. Despite all of the talk about a worldwide key recovery system, no one has answered even the most basic questions about how it would operate. Who will manage it? Is it technically feasible? How much will it cost? Will other governments support it? How vulnerable is it? I will examine these questions in my testimony.

THE PROBLEMS WITH THE ADMINISTRATION'S KEY RECOVERY SCHEME

My message is simple—The Administration's key recovery scheme is too complex, too costly, and too vulnerable. It will not work. Let me explain why.

First, a huge bureaucracy will be necessary to manage the Administration's key recovery scheme. The Administration's proposal assumes that we can effectively accommodate the needs of dozens of governments, thousands of companies, tens of thousands of law enforcement offices, and millions of users. It also assumes that we can handle tens of millions of public-private key pairs and billions of recoverable session keys across thousands of different products. This is a very tall order.

To put this challenge in perspective, Novell currently has 55 million users worldwide, each of which could reasonably be expected to generate 10–100 keys a day. If we assume that all of Novell's consumers use 30 keys on average per day and work 250 days a year, over 400 billion keys would have to be managed and stored just for Novell's customers alone over a one year period. As the number of people using computers and the Internet grows, the number of keys that must be managed will explode. By the end of the decade, a key recovery system capable of accommodating all of the potential users around the world would have to be capable of handling hundreds of billions of keys. The bureaucracy to manage this key recovery system is likely to rival that of the Social Security Administration, the Internal Revenue Service, or the U.S. Postal Service.

Second, the technology does not yet exist to create and smoothly operate a reliable system of this magnitude and complexity. Advocates of a worldwide key recovery system conveniently overlook the tremendous technical barriers posed. It is unclear that such a system can be built at all, much less in the next few years. As Novell's CEO, Dr. Eric Schmidt stated, "Perhaps the technology necessary to create such a system will be available in my lifetime; it is not available today."

Third, the cost of the Administration's key recovery scheme is likely to be prohibitive. No one has attempted to estimate the cost of the proposed key recovery system. This is not surprising since any cost estimates would have to be based on a management system that is without precedent, technology that does not yet exist, international treaties that have yet to be negotiated and legal responsibilities that have not been formulated. Under even the most favorable circumstances, however, the cost of managing hundreds of billions of keys around the world with guaranteed real-time response across different computer systems will be enormous.

Software and hardware vendors will be the first to pay the price since they will have to modify their existing and planned encryption technology to accommodate the Administration's requirements. They also will likely have to contribute funds to help develop the key recovery system. But U.S. vendors cannot afford to foot the entire bill, especially if their foreign competitors do not have to meet the same requirements and can sell a vastly cheaper product. This puts the U.S. software industry at a distinct competitive disadvantage.

Key recovery agents also will have to expend money trying to determine their rights and obligations under the Administration's certification rules. These agents will enter into the key recovery business only when they are provided some type of government immunity from prosecution for keys that are disclosed in a non-negligent manner; otherwise, the agent's liability could be too great.

Consumers will also have to pay a price since much of the cost of building, managing and maintaining such a system will be passed on to them. But if the infrastructure carries too high a price tag, consumers simply will not use it. Instead, they will engage in risky, unprotected electronic transactions, or try to avoid them altogether.

Ultimately, then, it is likely that the U.S. taxpayer will have to bear much of the cost of creating this infrastructure and supporting the key recovery agents. We should have a careful accounting of the expense involved and a public debate of the cost-benefit analysis before we saddle American taxpayers with this burden.

Fourth, none of the international treaties necessary for the Administration's key recovery scheme is in place. Bilateral and/or multilateral agreements must be negotiated and foreign governments' rights and responsibilities must be defined before the Administration's key recovery system can be created. Despite years of insisting that these treaties were just around the corner, the Administration has yet to conclude a single bilateral, much less multilateral, agreement with another government on key recovery. Nor has the Administration outlined any rights or responsibilities for foreign governments requesting access to U.S. decryption keys held by key recovery agents. It is not even clear whether these keys are subject to civil discovery in addition to criminal discovery.

Vendors and consumers need to know their legal rights before they will invest in and use key recovery technology. Bilateral key recovery agreements could allow foreign courts to abrogate a U.S. citizen's constitutional rights under the First, Fourth and Fifth Amendments by granting the authority to request keys to decrypt an intercepted message or stored data without a U.S. warrant. Some activities that are legal in the United States might be illegal under another country's laws. Moreover, the foreign country might suspect criminal activity and obtain keys necessary to convict a U.S. citizen in a foreign court, even in absentia. In addition, foreign governments or government employees may use reciprocal key recovery arrangements for purposes of industrial espionage. Americans are highly unlikely to trust these governments to protect the confidentiality of sensitive information, just as foreign firms will be wary of the U.S. government.

Fifth, criminals and terrorist groups will avoid using the Administration's key recovery scheme. The stated purpose of the Administration's key recovery scheme is to strengthen law enforcement and national security. But it is unlikely that criminals and terrorist groups will use a key recovery system that requires them to provide their keys to third-parties who can, in turn, give them to government officials. It is not clear that a global key recovery scheme can be designed so that it is impossible to circumvent, let alone with sufficient guarantee to make it impossible for criminals to avoid using it. Criminals have already shown that they can easily evade lawful wiretap and key escrow warrants and subpoenas by using a stolen or cloned cellular phone to connect to the Internet. There is no indication that they will not do the same when it comes to the Administration's key recovery scheme.

There is already strong evidence that unilateral U.S. export controls have not been effective in restricting the availability of encryption abroad. It is easy to obtain strong, non-key recovery encryption over the Internet. Moreover, foreign firms have seized the opportunity created by U.S. export controls on encryption to move into this market. A 1996 Department of Commerce study confirmed the widespread availability of foreign manufactured encryption programs and products. An on-going industry study, reveals that as of January 1996, there were 570 foreign programs and products available from 28 countries, 229 of which employ Data Encryption Standard (DES). There are also 823 American programs and products—378 with DES—readily transferable abroad with a modem and public telephone line (See Crypto Survey: Worldwide Survey of Cryptographic Products, Trusted Information Systems, Inc., January 11, 1996.)

Two specific examples are worth mentioning. First, the Apache Group, based in the U.K., announced last April that its Apache Unix Internet Server software with very strong encryption had a 29 percent market share, today it has a 43 percent market share. BSA has also learned that approximately six foreign companies in Germany, Belgium, Switzerland, the U.K., Ireland, and Australia have recognized the void for stronger encryption products. These companies have responded to local customer demand for stronger encryption by developing add-on products that allow anyone with a Web browser to download software off the Internet and thereby upgrade their "export-crippled" U.S. products from 40-bits to 128-bits. In developing these add-on products they neither require nor depend on any technical assistance from U.S. companies. To the contrary, they utilize standard programming techniques and free, public-domain versions of encryption algorithms and Internet security protocols to develop products that completely avoid U.S. export controls.

The General Accounting Office also confirmed in 1995 that sophisticated encryption software was widely available to foreign users on foreign Internet sites. For example, Pretty Good Privacy (PGP) provides 128-bit encryption that can be used instead of or in addition to key recovery systems and is available for free on the Internet. Individuals can easily transmit U.S. developed programs overseas using a modem and the public telephone network without fear of detection. Clearly, the Administration's export controls are in no way preventing foreigners, let alone those with criminal intent, from obtaining access to encryption products.

The blue ribbon National Research Council (NRC) Committee panel echoed many of these views and called for U.S. policies that foster the broad use of encryption technologies in its May 1996 CRISIS Report ("Cryptography's Role in Securing the Information Society"). The Committee concluded that as demand for products with encryption capabilities grows worldwide, foreign competition could emerge at levels significant enough to damage the present U.S. world leadership in information technologies products. The Committee felt it was important to ensure the continued economic growth and leadership of key U.S. industries and businesses in an increasingly global economy, including American computer, software and communications companies. Correspondingly, the Committee called for immediate and easy exportability of products meeting general commercial requirements—currently the 56-bit DES level encryption—with periodic updates. The Committee also recommended a policy of "deliberate exploration" for key escrow and key recovery, rather than one of "aggressive promotion."

Sixth, the Administration's key recovery scheme assumes that government mandated programs can preempt market forces. The private sector is already pursuing key recovery technology to enable emergency access to stored data files, including stored e-mail. Some companies have voluntarily requested that third parties hold the keys for their stored data. Others have opted for split-key regimes that allow a series of third parties to hold their keys. Novell is working with several other companies in the Key Recovery Alliance (KRA), which is a pro-active, private sector effort to develop market-based solutions for key recovery.

By demanding mandatory key recovery with government approved third party key recovery agents, the Administration is trying to preempt these private sector key recovery efforts. The Administration appears to have a "field of dreams" strategy that assumes if they mandate a key recovery infrastructure, consumers will use it. Instead, the government is likely to discover that if it tries to override market forces and demonstrated, requirement-based consumer demand, few will use it.

The Administration's new regulations are too tenuous to drive the creation of mass market encryption products. The key management infrastructure envisioned by the Administration is not in place, and it is unclear how it would work for millions of individuals who are not in large corporations or government. Consequently, companies are reluctant to develop products for it.

The Administration's efforts to build a world-wide key recovery system will meet with much greater success if it capitalizes on market forces rather than tries to preempt them. Given time and the proper incentives, the private sector will come forward with products that can accommodate a variety of key recovery encryption options. As these key recovery and data recovery encryption products are widely used, they will provide the government with much more information for law enforcement purposes. The government should not attempt to create a global key recovery infrastructure, but to work with industry to design and test any proposed key recovery solutions, especially since industry will fund the pilot programs and provide the investment necessary to build it.

Seventh, the Administration's proposed key recovery scheme may actually make consumers more vulnerable. Cryptography experts report that "secure cryptographic systems are deceptively hard to design and build properly * * * Very small changes frequently introduce fatal security flaws * * * [A]dding key recovery makes it much more difficult to assure that such systems work as intended. It is possible, even likely, that lurking in any key recovery system are one or more design, implementation, or operational weaknesses that allow recovery of data by unauthorized parties." (See The Risks of Key Recovery, Key Escrow, and Trusted Third Party Encryption, A Report By An Ad Hoc Group of Cryptographers and Computer Scientists, May 1997.)

One of the inherent problems of providing third parties with backdoor access to the plaintext of an encrypted message without the knowledge of the original party is that it provides a quick and easy path for successful hackers. Moreover, it is uncertain whether Government employees, let alone private firms, can be trusted with a large concentration of keys to secrets potentially worth trillions of dollars. As in any other security system, the human element—especially those working for the company providing the security—provides the greatest opportunity for defeating the security system. Recent news stories are full of reports about those in responsible positions who have betrayed their trust for a variety of reasons ranging from differing ideological convictions to bribes. Some espionage cases demonstrate that even those who have received exhaustive background checks and who take frequent polygraph tests may not be trusted. Thus, Americans are unlikely to turn over the ability to access all of their keys to third-parties who must provide under certain circumstances access to this information to governments around the world.

WE STRONGLY SUPPORT LEGISLATION THAT PROVIDES NEEDED EXPORT CONTROL RELIEF

The ECPA, Pro-CODE and SAFE bills recognize that it makes little sense for the U.S. government to require individual export licenses for the export of software that is generally available by virtue of being mass marketed commercially, distributed via the Internet, or found in the public domain. Nor should computer hardware be controlled simply because it incorporates such software. In short, if it is already available to millions of people and readily transferable electronically, then it makes little sense to continue trying to control such exports.

Importantly, these bills do permit the Secretary of Commerce to prevent exports to countries of terrorist concern or other embargoed countries pursuant to the Trading With the Enemy Act or the International Emergency Economic Powers Act.

We think the time for export control relief is now! It should not be held hostage to the Administration's desires and plans for a pervasive, government directed, infeasible, expensive key recovery scheme.

CONCLUSION

The Administration's key recovery scheme will not work. It entails a massive worldwide bureaucracy. It is based on technology that does not yet exist. It is in all likelihood prohibitively expensive. It hopes for treaties that have never been signed. It assumes that criminals who do not want to use it will have no other choice. It tries to preempt market demand. And it may actually increase the vulnerability of law abiding citizens who do use it. Taken together, these conditions spell failure. The Administration would be much better off trying to build on legitimate market-based key recovery systems.

As part of the Administration's encryption policy, its proposed key recovery system is undermining the competitiveness of U.S. firms, siphoning away American jobs and undermining public safety. U.S. export controls prevent American software and hardware companies from supplying their customers with strong encryption to meet their legitimate needs for information security and thereby directly threaten the continued success of our industry. Moreover, because U.S. vendors invest more heavily in developing products for worldwide markets, export controls also delay the introduction of sophisticated security products in the U.S. market, leaving American computer users' electronic information vulnerable to hackers and other intruders. U.S. export controls also threaten to dislodge continued American leadership in developing the Global Information Infrastructure.

One last and very important point. The interests of computer users, hardware and software companies and privacy groups are not opposed to those of law enforcement and national security. As the NRC Committee found, encryption prevents crime by protecting the trade secrets and proprietary information of businesses and correspondingly reducing economic espionage. Encryption also promotes the national security of the United States by protecting "nationally critical information systems and networks against unauthorized penetration." Thus, the NRC Committee found that on balance the advantages of more widespread use of encryption outweighed the disadvantages and that the U.S. Government has "an important stake in assuring that its important and sensitive * * * information * * * is protected from foreign government or other parties whose interests are hostile to those of the United States."

The time for action is now. In order to keep U.S. vendors on a level international playing field, American jobs at home and American computer users adequately protected, the U.S. government must nurture market-driven key recovery systems and update export controls to reflect technological and international realities.

Thank you.

The CHAIRMAN. We will go to you, Mr. Ozzie, and then we will wind up with Mr. Neumann.

I am going to ask Senator Kyl to watch over the committee for a few minutes because I have got to go into another meeting and resolve some Judiciary Committee problems. But I am paying strict attention to what you are saying, so please know that we are not ignoring it.

We will go to you, Mr. Ozzie, then to Mr. Neumann.

Senator LEAHY. I should note for the record, Mr. Chairman, a note that I passed the chairman—I think that we have created and are creating a very important record, and I commended the chairman for having this hearing. I realize everybody has had to stay here a long time, but there is a possibility of actually getting some legislation this year and I think the record of this hearing is going to be one of the most important parts of that.

STATEMENT OF RAYMOND OZZIE

Mr. OZZIE. Thank you. Good morning, members of the committee. My name is Ray Ozzie. I am chairman of Iris Associates, which is a wholly-owned subsidiary of Lotus Development and IBM Corporation, which is a founding member of the Key Recovery Alliance.

Although I am testifying today as a representative of the Business Software Alliance, I was also a member of the National Research Council committee that produced the CRISIS report, which I wholeheartedly endorse as the most balanced analysis of cryptography policy issues to date. Again, I would like to thank the chairman and Senator Leahy for your efforts in tackling this tough issue.

Over the past 12 years, I have worked to create a product called Lotus Notes, which is a secure messaging and information management system for businesses. I hope to give you a unique perspective today because in Notes we have commercially deployed encryption, certificate management, and key recovery technologies far more broadly than any other product to date, with about 13 million users worldwide.

I have two points that I would like to make to you briefly today that I feel are frequently either overlooked or not stated properly. The first point that I would really like to make is that strong, secure encryption doesn't just aid criminals, it prevents crime. That is why our customers are buying it. Surely, we are all aware that criminals will use it to conceal their own activities and commit crimes, but virtually every major business in this country and in the world today, and governments worldwide, now run on and now depend upon these secure computer networks to operate every single day.

These organizations are simply under attack. They are under attack from within, they are under attack from the outside, and they are looking to cryptography in products from vendors such as myself to help them reduce their exposure to break-ins, to disclosure of trade secrets, insider trading, corporate espionage, covert transactions. The demand is coming from them. We are not just putting it in, you know, for fun. They are asking us very strongly, and the demand is increasingly dramatically month after month because of the growth of the networks. It is not just the Internet. It is because of the growth of their own internal networks and because companies are being victimized. So encryption is the most effective tool that we have at our disposal to help them prevent themselves from being victimized. We see it as a way to fight crime, as opposed to, you know, other ways of viewing it.

My second point today is that given my experience in building systems, because that is what I do—I build the kinds of systems that we are talking about here—large-scale key management and recovery systems are inherently imperfect and, if they are mandated, will likely result in an increase in crime, as opposed to a decrease, as they are intended.

In developing our product, Notes, we designed the most secure system possible that we could develop. We try to make it easy for our customers to manage keys and certificates for their employee populations, which tend to be in the hundreds of thousands of individuals. But while we have done our best to build a secure system and our customers have made huge investments in trying to manage these systems properly, security breaches still occur with some regularity, and it is because it all comes down to people and human fallibilities.

People choose bad or obvious passwords. People write them down or tell other people. People are mischievous or they are tempted, or sometimes they are dishonest. We need people to manage these systems, and the systems that are being managed are spread out throughout the globe. We have to trust people across the globe to manage these distributed systems.

Given my experience, if we mandate the creation of key management and recovery systems for hundreds of millions of people and businesses, I can guarantee you, given my experience, that the systems will be imperfect and there will be compromise, and we will have created significant new opportunity for abuse and crime that don't exist today and don't have to exist if corporations are given key recovery tools that they can manage themselves.

In conclusion, I would like to state that I am very happy that, finally, the impact of technology on society has been brought to this level. Encryption is surely one aspect of high technology and there have been many benefits of high technology to society, but there have been abuses and there will continue to be abuses, and these are issues that belong at this level.

The good news, however, is that, overall, high-technology trends favor a peaceful and orderly society. If you look at the raw amount of interpersonal communications that is happening with just telephones and fax machines and pagers and all of these different devices that we are producing, the raw growth of unencrypted communications gives law enforcement dramatically more ability to investigate and prevent crime than they have in the past.

The use of wireless communications continues to skyrocket, giving law enforcement more opportunity to track the physical location of criminals while they are communicating wirelessly. The use of video surveillance has skyrocketed and the cost has gone down, giving law enforcement more opportunity to watch and report criminals' public activities. And the Internet itself as an open information marketplace brings child pornographers and the radical fringe more out into the open, making them easier to spot and know where to target investigations. Surely, terrorists and child pornographers will use these technologies toward their own end. They are truly dual-use technologies, but we also need them to protect our own networks. Good, strong encryption is one of the most effective tools that we have to prevent crime on our networks today and our companies need it today.

So thank you for the time.

[The prepared statement of Mr. Ozzie follows:]

PREPARED STATEMENT OF RAYMOND OZZIE

I am Chairman of Iris Associates, a wholly-owned subsidiary of Lotus Development and IBM Corporation. I also served on the Committee of the National Research Council's Committee to Study National Cryptography Policy that prepared the CRISIS (Cryptography's Role in Securing the Information Society) Report.

BSA supports S. 376, S. 377, and H.R. 695 because they all provide badly needed, immediate export control relief. Today, however, I would like to share with you my perspective on key recovery systems from the standpoint as the creator of Lotus Notes. Over twelve million people use Notes every day to communicate with one another and to collaborate using PCs and over networks such as the Internet. Notes represents the world's largest commercial deployment to date of a cryptographically secured general purpose messaging and information system. It is also the world's largest deployment to date of a commercial key management infrastructure, which makes my company's experiences quite relevant in today's key management and key recovery debate.

My company's experiences bear out the conclusions of the National Research Council's CRISIS Report, especially with regard to easy exportability of strong encryption and the need to go slowly on key recovery systems. Unfortunately, S. 909, the Secure Public Networks Act, recently adopted by the Senate Commerce Committee, does not align with the conclusions of the CRISIS Report. I believe that the debate on S. 909 was flawed as it did not take into account two critical points:

(1) Strong, secure encryption does not just aid criminals, it prevents crime. It is obvious that encryption can be used by criminals. However, virtually every major business and government worldwide now depends upon computer networks that communicate with other computer networks. Information security is critical to the integrity, stability and health of both corporations and governments and their computer networks. There is no substitute for good, widespread, strong cryptography when attempting to prevent crime through these networks. For these reasons, corporations are now demanding 56-bit DES as a minimum, and much longer key-length, stronger encryption for financial applications as well as many other applications such as enterprise-wide messaging systems.

(2) Large scale key management and recovery systems are inherently imperfect and, if mandated, will cause an increase in crime. In our customer experiences, no single technology or technique has yet withstood the test of time in keeping information secure. Relying upon a single technology or technique for anything creates a single point of failure, which entails too many risks for consumers—whether they are governments, businesses or individuals—to endure. Our customers, especially our larger customers, have learned through trial and error that in order to manage the keys of hundreds of thousands of people, they must use a variety of techniques to keep their system's security in check.

These companies have found the need to compartmentalize not only information, but also the management of keys, so that if critical keys are compromised in one area, the entire organization's security is not compromised. They have found the need to keep diversity in their security systems, so that if a single technology fails or is used improperly, the effect on the entire organization is limited. Most significantly, they have learned that the weakest aspect of large-scale system security is the human element. Security compromises (and thus crime) through misjudgment, carelessness, mischievousness, temptation, and outright dishonesty, is the rule—not the exception—in any large-scale systems deployment.

Good morning, Mr. Chairman, and members of the Committee. My name is Raymond Ozzie, and I am Chairman of Iris Associates, a wholly-owned subsidiary of Lotus Development and IBM Corporation. I also recently had the honor of serving as a member of the National Research Council's Committee to Study National Cryptography Policy that prepared the CRISIS (Cryptography's Role in Securing the Information Society) Report. However, today I am testifying as a representative of the Business Software Alliance (BSA), of which Lotus is a member.

The Business Software Alliance promotes the continued growth of the software industry through its international public policy, education, and enforcement programs in 65 countries throughout North America, Europe, Asia, and Latin America. BSA's worldwide members include the leading publishers of software for personal computers including Adobe, Apple Computer, Autodesk, Bentley Systems, Lotus Development, Microsoft, Novell, The Santa Cruz Operation, and Symantec. BSA's Policy Council consists of these software publishers and other leading computer technology companies including Computer Associates, Compaq and Sybase.

I started my company twelve years ago to develop a product that is now widely known as Lotus Notes. Notes is in use by many major corporations worldwide as well as many branches of our government. Over twelve million people use it every day to communicate with one another and to collaborate using personal computers (PCs) and over networks such as the Internet.

Today, I would like to share with you my perspective on key recovery systems from the standpoint of the creator of Lotus Notes. Notes represents the world's largest commercial deployment to date of a cryptographically secured general purpose messaging and information system. It is also the world's largest deployment to date of a commercial key management infrastructure, which makes my company's experiences quite relevant in today's key management and key recovery debate.

Because my product uses cryptography and has been subject to U.S. export controls, and because I am a citizen and I am equally concerned about issues of law enforcement, national security, and personal privacy, I have spent a great deal of my time thinking about and focusing on encryption and its proper role in our society. Mr. Chairman, I am sure that you and the Committee are deluged with information and opinions on encryption and key recovery systems. I would, however, like to recommend that you give great weight to the National Research Council's CRISIS Report. My company's experiences only bear out the conclusions of this report, especially with regard to easy exportability of strong encryption and the need to go slowly on key recovery systems.

I also understand that your fellow Senators on the Senate Commerce Committee recently adopted S. 909, the Secure Public Networks Act, which does not align with the conclusions of the CRISIS Report. I believe that the debate on S. 909 was flawed as it did not take into account two critical points:

(1) Strong, secure encryption does not just aid criminals, it prevents crime.

It is obvious that encryption can be used by criminals. From rum-runners of old to drug-cartels of the present, criminals often are very clever in concealing their activities, and PCs and the Internet have become tools of their trade, alongside telephones, facsimile machines, and pagers. As you also know, virtually every major business and government worldwide now runs on—in fact now depends upon—computer networks that communicate with other computer networks. Strategic information flows through these networks, and all of their critical systems depend upon the integrity of these networks.

In this age of computer networks and widely dispersed information flow, corporations are demanding strong, secure information systems. Similar to the government, corporations "compartmentalize" their critical business information, and strictly control access to these compartments. Not everyone is trustworthy within a company, and it is this security, this compartmentalization, that prevents crimes such as insider trading, leakage of trade secrets, and corporate espionage.

In 1996 the Computer Security Institute/FBI Computer Crime Survey indicated that our worldwide corporations will be increasingly under siege: over half from within the corporation, and nearly half from outside of their internal networks. We will see many, many hundreds of millions in losses, and we may possibly see the destabilization of a company, the stock market or perhaps even a whole economy.

Information security is critical to the integrity, stability and health of both corporations and governments. While cryptography is but one element of security, it is the keystone of secure distributed systems. Frankly, there is no substitute for good, widespread, strong cryptography when attempting to prevent crime through these networks. For these reasons, corporations are now demanding 56-bit DES as a minimum, and much larger keylength, stronger encryption for financial applications as well as many other applications such as enterprise-wide messaging systems.

(2) Large scale key management and recovery systems are inherently imperfect and, if mandated, will cause an increase in crime.

All systems of cryptography, of keeping secrets, are based upon "keys". And the management of these keys—how you make them, where you keep them, how you hide them—is, always has been, and always will be the weakest link in secure systems.

Common claims about the unbreakability of various levels of cryptography, key recovery or non-key recovery, exportable or not, are vastly overstated in a practical sense; when implemented in actual products, cryptographic security ends up far less than one might imagine due to flaws in key management. Strong cryptography is exactly like a good safe. The best safe in the world cannot protect you if the combination is written on a scrap of paper and left lying around or is otherwise known to the safe-cracker.

For as long as there have been codes and ciphers, the weakest link has always been people. People choose bad or obvious passwords. People write passwords down or share them with others. Spies and diplomats have misused or re-used allegedly perfect one-time pads. People sometimes neglect to go secure on their STU phones. Often people are simply careless, make mistakes or are frequently too trusting of those willing to violate their trust.

We, in industry, after years of trying, have not been able to create completely secure information systems as we have not devised a system of managing keys that removes the human element from the equation. In the case of Lotus Notes we have tried for about 10 years. Our customers, especially our larger customers, have learned through trial and error that in order to manage the keys of hundreds of thousands of people, they must use a variety of techniques to keep their system's security in check.

These companies have found the need to compartmentalize not only information, but also the management of keys, so that if critical keys are compromised in one area, the entire organization's security is not compromised. They have found the need to keep diversity in their security systems, so that if a single technology fails or is compromised or is used improperly, the effect on the entire organization is limited. Finally, they have found the need to keep up-to-date with new key and certificate management technologies, such as key splitting, key escrow and recovery, smart cards, and biometrics devices.

Mr. Chairman, these companies are the best, smartest, and most advanced of our global multinational companies who are interested in securing electronic communications. These customers invest heavily and are willing to pay dearly for truly secure systems, but they have learned the hard way that theory does not always map to practice, mostly because of the frailties and unpredictable motivations of people. You should be aware that these companies are only dealing with employee populations of hundreds of thousands. Might I ask what would happen if one of them had to securely manage a user population of hundreds of millions? If we've learned one thing in our customer experiences, it is the fact that no single technology or technique has yet withstood the test of time in keeping information secure, and that relying upon a single technology or technique for anything creates a single point of failure, which entails too many risks for consumers—whether they are governments, businesses or individuals—to endure.

The problems created by designing a single point of failure into a system—a mandated infrastucture—is one of the reasons why the National Research Council recommended in its report that industry and government engage in controlled experimentation with key recovery and other key management techniques, rather than immediately mandating any single solution or set of solutions.

We should look to our past when examining our alternatives. In the early 1960's, the Interbank Card Association and National Bank Americard pioneered two very different networks for authorizing and settling purchase transactions. Yet today, Mastercard, Visa, American Express, Discover and others are all engaging in commerce without a single agreed-upon infrastructure to identify and authenticate cardholders. Key management is risk management, and this is something that major banks and corporations worldwide do quite well without a mandated universal key infrastructure or Universal Digital ID Card.

The NRC, industry, and the customers recommend a market-driven approach, an approach of natural selection and appropriateness-for-purpose, an approach of evolution and survival of the best methods, an approach of continuous learning and improvement. A diverse and market-driven approach is surely the most prudent course of action in attempting to prevent crime and protect our national economic security.

CONCLUSION

In summary, Mr. Chairman, I reiterate my two points. First, while encryption can indeed be used as a tool of crime, good encryption is absolutely necessary as a crime-fighting tool to prevent certain forms of crime. It is truly a double-edged sword, and it is needed by commercial enterprises today.

Second, while in theory mandated key management systems including key escrow and key recovery, can indeed be used as a tool to help law enforcement, all key management systems are inherently subject to failure of one form or another due to the nature of people and often due to errors in the technology. Mandated key management and key recovery methods remove diversity and centralize our vulnerabilities, dramatically magnifying the impact of real-world carelessness and abuse. This is likely to increase crime.

My thanks to you, Mr. Chairman, and to the Committee, for allowing me the time to voice my thoughts.

Senator KYL [presiding]. Mr. Neumann.

STATEMENT OF PETER G. NEUMANN

Mr. NEUMANN. I am Peter Neumann. I am here today primarily as one of the 11 cryptographers and computer scientists whose report you have before you and which I would like to be entered into the record, which discusses the technological and socio-economic risks associated with the use of key recovery. I am going to dwell primarily on the technological risks and not worry about the costs as much, which have been mentioned by the previous two speakers.

Incidentally, I was also a co-author of the NRC report and the earlier ACM report which included Scott Charney of Justice and Clint Brooks of NSA. I chair the ACM Committee on Computers and Public Policy, and I am on the EPIC advisory board. That is the Electronic Privacy Information Center. I work for a not-for-profit research institute, which I think is important.

You have before you, as well, which I don't think you want to put into the record, a list of thousands of cases that I have collected over the past many years of things that went wrong with computers relating to security, safety, reliability, and human well-being. That collection holds many lessons for us and I hope you will peruse that list very carefully.

It includes things like the fact that the U.S. Government has had real difficulties in developing large, complex computer systems. NCIC 2000, national crime; air traffic control, serious problems; IRS tax system modernization, which you are familiar with, all have had major stumbling blocks in their attempts to develop these complex systems.

There are also many cases of security vulnerabilities and if you will look through that list, you will see hundreds and hundreds of cases of systems that are vulnerable, flawed systems, penetrations, misuse by trusted insiders. You recall the break-ins to the World Wide Web sites of the Justice Department, the CIA, the Air Force, and NASA which have received a lot of publicity.

You recall, perhaps, the GAO report which documented in a very short period of time 62 cases of in some cases very serious abuses

44-452 - 97 - 4

of criminal history and law enforcement data by insiders, law enforcement employees. Several of those cases actually involved deaths of innocent people as a result of the misuse of the data. You may also recall some of the problems with the IRS agents selling off information, and Social Security folks selling off Social Security numbers.

Senator LEAHY. That, incidentally, is something that Senator Kyl and I tried to fix last year.

Mr. NEUMANN. Right, so I applaud your efforts to keep an eye on that one, and you certainly, Senator Leahy, have been very active in that one.

These problems, I think, could be child's play compared to the problems that result from the key recovery infrastructure. You have heard today that it is a piece of cake, it is not a problem, we know how to do it, from the previous panel. Yet every piece of indication that I have says that this is an extremely complicated thing.

Albert Einstein once said that everything should be made as simple as possible, but no simpler. I think key recovery being intrinsically complex, there are some very serious risks that need to be identified and examined. I think the Government experiments that are going on are, in fact, only trying to show that, hey, we can build a key recovery system. They are not worried about the costs, the risks, the security issues, the vulnerabilities of that system.

I think everything that I have seen in terms of computer systems suggests that computer systems frequently have lurking vulnerabilities and failure modes that are completely unanticipated. One of my co-authors, Matt Blaze, on the report was the one who discovered a very simple way to defeat the law enforcement access field of clipper. Another of my colleagues and co-authors, Ross Anderson, is one who has found very simple ways which don't involve cryptographic, exhaustive attacks on the 128 bits or 64 bits, or whatever it is. They find ways of forcing a master key that exists worldwide in every device made by that particular vendor to be spilled out of the device very simply.

Now, when we add key recovery, the notion that there is a universal trap door essentially in a device of that nature, you have suddenly introduced the possibility that malicious misuse either by insiders or possibly even by outsiders could lead to massive misuse of the system. So I think there are some enormous risks that must be considered, and I think we have got to listen to Einstein's message. In this case, key recovery is intrinsically complex and anybody who tells you that they know how to build something that has no risks and no hidden costs and provides meaningful assurances that this system will do what it is supposed to do simply is either lying to you or doesn't know what they are talking about. They have never been through the business of trying to create a very large and complex system.

Let me pick a couple of odd ends that have not been touched on and a couple that I have that I would like to reinforce. The notion of coupling key recovery with certificate keys and authentication keys is ludicrous. It opens up complete lack of integrity for the entire infrastructure that we are dealing with.

Digital commerce relies on good crypto. We cannot have digital commerce in any meaningful way without massive vulnerabilities in the presence of key recovery. Clearly, Commerce has tended to get waivers on things like that, but I think the key point here is that we could reduce the entire infrastructure to the notion of what you have been reading about, say, yesterday in the Post about the Russian lotteries where there is absolutely no integrity whatsoever in the system.

If you can believe that everybody is honest in the entire Government who has access to the keys, that the subpoena process is, in fact, adequate where warrants are currently required today, if you can believe that the computer systems were developed in ways that don't have any flaws, then maybe you can believe that the key recovery system would be impeccable. On the other hand, given all of the evidence, the chances are that it is not going to be.

So the bottom line is that we seriously need to bring in folks from the technical community to allow them to be involved in this process that you are going through. The idea of racing through legislation at this point seems to me to be a huge mistake and I would urge you to find some way around it. We can't in a 5-minute interval in a hearing give you the depth of the problems that we perceive. The risk issues are enormous. The cost issues are hidden and nobody really knows what they will amount to.

There are other points. For example, the drug cartels will have the resources to use their own crypto. They certainly will figure out that they are being scammed if they are, in fact, using key recovery schemes. There was a comment made earlier that even if the system is mandatory, it is still not fool-proof. It is much worse than that. Whether it is mandatory or not, criminals are not going to be encouraged to use it.

The final comments, then, are let us take the advice of the National Research Council, which says let the Government be its own guinea pig and try this stuff out on detailed experiments that look not only at whether you can build a thing like this. I can build something. That is easy. Can you build it safely, security, reliably, and with all of the cost factors from the infrastructure taken into account?

I have lots more to go and that is about it, but I would urge you to really slow down this process and look at it. We have a 1-minute demo just to show you that if Anne pokes at PGP on her Web browser, she discovers that there are 148 sites around the world where you can get PGP. And just picking one of them at random suggests that you can download it from anywhere in the world, not just in the United States. There are bulletin boards in 50 or 60 countries now from which you can get PGP, a free product which is becoming very easily embedded into E-mail products. It does not require any technical expertise to install.

Lo and behold, you can choose your key length and you can have a massive key length if you want to slow things down, or you can, in fact, have a very, very simple key length which could be breakable. But, in principle, PGP is very, very difficult to break. So we are left with a situation that cryptography is ubiquitous around the world. Good cryptography is becoming widely available in many, many different countries.

The comment that was made earlier that the Europeans love this stuff and they are going along with it is very misleading. Only 2 days ago, the European Union came out very strongly against many of the Administration requirements and many of the things that are in McCain-Kerrey, and I think it is an international problem that must be dealt with as an international problem. To legislate local solutions to something that is an international problem is going to cause us great grief. So the bottom line is very simply, let us analyze this a little bit more carefully.

We have various alternatives that the NSA is already pursuing that the FBI needs to pursue. They haven't gotten around to the point that they realize that they may have lost the battle already, and if that is the case, then they should follow the lead of the security agency in pursuing some of these alternatives.

Thank you very much for having me here.

[The prepared statement of Mr. Neumann follows:]

PREPARED STATEMENT OF PETER G. NEUMANN

I am very grateful for the opportunity to address you today on a matter that is one of our nation's most pressing sociotechnological issues. I speak to you as an individual, although I refer to several other efforts in which I have been involved jointly.

This written testimony begins with the executive summary of recent report on risks related to key recovery (Reference 1), of which I was a coauthor. It then discusses some of the potential risks related to key recover and draws some conclusions. At the end it provides various relevant references and some of my background. In particular, I draw your attention to the National Research Council crypto study (Reference 2) and the earlier ACM crypto report (Reference 3); I was a coauthor of both of these reports as well. Also of special relevance is my testimony for the Senate Permanent Subcommittee on Investigations from June 1996 (Reference 6).

For the record of this session, I have appended a copy of the cited report on risks related to key recovery (Reference 1). (On-line availability is noted in the reference.)

In addition, to provide further background for these hearings, I also have appended the most recent version of my summary of illustrative risks to the public (Reference 8), which contains numerous examples of security risks in our computer-communication environments, from which we can infer some of the many potential risks facing any would-be key-recovery infrastructures. (On-line availability is noted in the reference.)

INTRODUCTION

There are significant potential risks, costs, and implications that must be carefully considered prior to deployment of any key-management and key-recovery schemes. This testimony considers primarily the technological risks, and urges that legislation not be carried out hastily in the absence of detailed investigation of the long-term potential social and economic effects of those risks and the associated costs.

A self-constituted group of 11 cryptographers and computer scientists, Hal Abelson (MIT/HP), Ross Anderson (Cambridge University), Steven M. Bellovin (ATandT Research), Josh Benaloh (Microsoft Research), Matt Blaze (ATandT Research), Whitfield Diffie (Sun Microsystems), John Gilmore, Peter G. Neumann (SRI International), Ronald L. Rivest (MIT), Jeffery I. Schiller (MIT), and Bruce Schneier (Counterpane Systems), has issued a report (Reference 1) on the technical implications, risks, and costs of 'key recovery', 'key escrow', and 'trusted third-party' encryption systems. The report evolved via e-mail exchanges, achieving iterative consensus over a four-month period subsequent to one meeting in January 1997.

As a coauthor and someone who has studied computer-related risks for many years, I believe that the report addresses your closest study and further discussion. The next five paragraphs represent the executive summary taken from the appended full report.

A variety of 'key recovery,' 'key escrow,' and 'trusted third-party' encryption requirements have been suggested in recent years by government agencies seeking to conduct covert surveillance within the changing environments brought about by new technologies. This report examines the fundamental properties of these requirements and attempts to outline the technical risks, costs, and implications of widely deploying systems that provide government access to encryption keys.

The deployment of key-recovery-based encryption infrastructures to meet law enforcement's stated specifications will result in substantial sacrifices in security and greatly increased costs to the end-user. Building the secure computer-communication infrastructures necessary to provide adequate technological underpinnings demanded by these requirements would be enormously complex and is far beyond the experience and current competency of the field. Even if such infrastructures could be built, the risks and costs of such an operating environment may ultimately prove unacceptable. In addition, these infrastructures would generally require extraordinary levels of human trustworthiness.

These difficulties are a function of the basic government access requirements proposed for key-recovery encryption systems. They exist regardless of the design of the recovery systems—whether the systems use private-key cryptography or public-key cryptography; whether the databases are split with secret-sharing techniques or maintained in a single hardened secure facility; whether the recovery services provide private keys, session keys, or merely decrypt specific data as needed; and whether there is a single centralized infrastructure, many decentralized infrastructures, or a collection of different approaches.

All key-recovery systems require the existence of a highly sensitive and highly available secret key or collection of keys that must be maintained in a secure manner over an extended time period. These systems must make decryption information quickly accessible to law-enforcement agencies without notice to the key owners. These basic requirements make the problem of general key recovery difficult and expensive—and potentially too unsecure and too costly for many applications and many users.

Attempts to force the widespread adoption of key-recovery encryption through export controls, import or domestic use regulations, or international standards should be considered in light of these factors. The public must carefully consider the costs and benefits of embracing government-access key recovery before imposing the new security risks and spending the huge investment required (potentially many billions of dollars, in direct and indirect costs) to deploy a global key recovery infrastructure.

RISKS

This is an extremely complex subject, and requires discussion of technical issues as well as policy matters. I hope my presentation is understandable. If not, then please ask for clarifications or further details.

On one hand, cryptography is not a panacea for attaining security and privacy; it is just one technique among many. The cryptographic and system-security communities themselves must work harder to overcome some of the deficiencies in existing computer-communication environments (Reference 6)—hopefully with greater encouragement from the U.S. law-enforcement community (which as you know focuses primarily on prosecution, to the detriment of preventing computer misuse and related crime). This is a difficult problem, because essentially all systems have some potentially serious security risks.

On the other hand, the trapdoor access implicit in key recovery is not a panacea for law enforcement or fighting terrorism; at best, it provides peepholes into certain kinds of information. It would provide substantial administrative problems—for law enforcement and for everyone else.

The real costs that must underlie any extensive key-retrieval mechanisms and recovery infrastructures are a serious source of concern. To date, those costs have not been adequately considered by proponents of key-recovery, key-escrow, and key-management mechanisms and their supporting computer-commnunication environments. The costs in the large necessarily involve the entire key-recovery infrastructure itself, including its operational procedures, management, oversight, enforcement costs, legal liabilities, and costs of litigating misusers. There are also some hidden costs, namely, those necessary to ratchet up the security of the overall commercially available computer-communication systems and networks as well. Some of those cost issues are discussed at length in the key-recovery report.

We focus here more on the security and social risks, which to date have also not been adequately considered by the proponents of key-recovery and key-escrow infrastructures. There are numerous potential risks associated therewith:

- The key-hiding mechanism may itself contain a technological trapdoor that can be circumvented or otherwise compromised. Surprising attacks have been discovered on many security schemes thought to be virtually impenetrable.
- Testing and other analyses of components and indeed of an entire infrastructure cannot demonstrate the absence of flaws, vulnerabilities, and risks. They can demonstrate only the inherent incompleteness of the analyses.

• Failure modes tend to be very insidious. A system that appears to work perfectly on the surface may have deep faults. It may be not at all evident that security has been seriously undermined—for example, through bad design. bad implementation, sloppy operation, or even malicious activities. The recent history of flaws repeatedly being discovered in Netscape Navigator, Microsoft Internet Explorer, Java, JavaScript, Microsoft Word, etc., and an extensive series of system breakins (Rome Laboratory, Justice Department, CIA, Air Force, NASA) are barely suggestive of the extent of the difficulties involved. (For example, see References 5, 8, and 10.)

• If the administrative procedures surrounding key-recovery mechanisms are poorly conceived and poorly enforced, they could enable at least insiders and possibly outsiders to acquire keys and other information they should not have. Intrinsic flaws in those procedures and in their administration are likely, and could lead to compromise. The massive volume of keys that might have to be maintained could also greatly increase the risks of misuse and sloppy administration. The same keys are likely to be used for multiple purposes, to simplify administration.

• Retrieval of any key that is used for more than one purpose may yield access far beyond the expected purview. For example, acquisition of the key that is used to encrypt every file in a personal computer would immediately enable access to every file in that system. Acquisition of a file-encryption key unwisely used as an authentication key would compromise the corresponding authentication processes. Recovery or inadvertent release of master keys that are used worldwide by financial institutions could lead to actions that would doom those institutions forever to bankruptcy and ruin their customers. In addition, any smart-card purveyors and purveyors of digital commerce facilities who reuse keys or provide mechanisms for third-party key-recovery access may tend to destroy their own credibility. Such applications bear the risks of a system with intrinsic trap doors that may be openable surreptitiously and skeleton keys that may be copied or otherwise fabricated in ways that are not anticipated by the designers and purveyors—even if accompanied by restrictions on end-user products.

• The risks relating to certificate-authority infrastructures are even more insidious. Acquisition of the master key used by an authentication service or a digital-certificate service could be devastating; worse yet, access to anyone else's public key would then be sufficient to undermine the authentication infrastructure. As a result, the significance of the authentication would always be suspect, and the concept of nonrepudiation would effectively go out the window. That is, anyone could justifiably throw doubts on the legitimacy of a perfectly legitimate certificate. Furthermore, recovery access to certification keys would not be likely to provide any directly discernible benefits to law enforcement with respect to either storage keys or transmission keys, unless accompanied by further restrictions on all relevant end-user products worldwide.

• There is a serious risk of confusing encryption for communications and storage with cryptography used for authentication. Enforcing blanket key-recovery policies on the uses of crypto without recognizing the special risks of authentication would be extremely counterproductive, and could undermine the integrity of digital signatures and other authentication techniques that use cryptography (For example, the McCain-Kerrey Secure Public Network Act of 1997 may be making this mistake.)

• In addition, cryptography used for distribution of keys is also particularly vulnerable. Compromise of keys used for authentication as opposed to encryption may need to be treated differently.

• There are risks involving the proliferation of key-recovery infrastructures beyond any natural uses they might have. Whereas there is some legitimate commercial need for first- and second-party key preservation for stored information, there is basically no commercial need for key recovery in transmitting encrypted information. Once a transmission is complete, the key can be destroyed; if the transmission fails, it can be retried with a new key. Consequently, any key-recovery infrastructures that become available (or even mandated) for stored data might also be mandated for encrypted communications. The risks of misuse could be considerably increased thereby, rendering transmitted data subject to compromise by anyone able to misuse the key-recovery infrastructure.

• Even with specific legal restrictions on end-user products, it would be relatively easy to construct cryptographic implementations that totally circumvent, or possibly disable, the key recovery procedures. For stored data, you could simply use your own nonescrowed scheme, freely available elsewhere. For electronic mail and other transmitted data, you could simply use a Diffie-Hellman type of key exchange rather than RSA. (Such a scheme is part of the existing PCT and SSL protocols, and will be part of their successor, TLS.) There will be strong customer demand for hardware and software implementing such approaches, which if outlawed would represent an extraordinarily draconian measure.

• Supposedly trustworthy second or third parties who have the ability to enable surreptitious access could themselves be corrupt, or subjected to blackmail, extortion, and other threats. They could also be unreliable—intentionally or accidentally.

• In the future, well funded and well motivated high-tech criminals will find strong incentives not to us encryption that can be subjected to key recovery and to subvert systems that use key recovery. A world-wide ban on good unescrowed crypto does not seem to be a feasible alternative, because such crypto is already becoming widely available, and is becoming very easy to implement.

• Key-recovery infrastructures could greatly increase the opportunities for insider fraud, malice, and other misuse within governmental organizations. There are various reports of insider misuse of FBI and other law-enforcement databases. For example, House testimony from Laurie E. Ekstrand of the GAO (Reference 9) documents 62 cases of misuses of law-enforcement computer data. Similar misuse has been discovered in other Government offices, such as Social Security Administration employees selling information to enable the activation of 11,000 credit cards stolen from the mail, and IRS employees leaking tax information and altering records. It is clearly unwise to assume that our government is totally benevolent and incapable of illegal actions.

• The potential risks of misuse of key-recovery infrastructures extend far into our social structure. Loss of privacy can often result in serious consequences to individuals. (In addition, retrieval of incorrect data can have damaging results on the individuals involved, although that is true whether or not the information is encrypted). Constitutional issues are also at risk, such as protection against unreasonable search and seizure. If on-line infrastructures for key recovery are to use existing commercial systems, they may be seriously lacking in confidentiality, integrity, accountability, and assurance.

There are appalling weaknesses in the security of today's computer systems and networks—including operating systems, network software, Web browsers and servers, programming languages, cryptographic implementations, application software systems, and so on. Weak links exist at many points. Even strong cryptographic implementations can often be broken or completely circumvented by devious means.

Some of these security weaknesses could add considerably to the risks in key-recovery infrastructures. User and system authentication techniques in most commercially available systems represent enormous risks; typically, fixed reusable passwords are used, and transmitted unencrypted across unprotected communication media. In addition, systems are susceptible to penetration by other means. As a result, masquerading is often relatively simple to achieve. System accountability is often very poor, which makes it difficult to detect when, major misuse has occurred (particularly if it were to involve a critical component of the key-recovery infrastructure). In turn, the absence of meaningful authentication makes it even more difficult to identify the culprits—assuming their misuse can even be detected.

CONCLUSIONS

It is absolutely fundamental that security must be addressed as a systemic problem. Risks can certainly arise in the cryptographic algorithms and key lengths, as in the recent cracking of the RSA-challenge DES key (demonstrating that DES and 56-bit keys may be outliving their utility). However, even greater risks typically arise in how the cryptography is encapsulated in operating systems, networking software, and applications, and in other weaknesses in those components themselves. Key escrow and key recovery are sometimes (I believe, mistakenly) touted as inherently increasing security. They actually have the potential of seriously decreasing security overall. Even if they are very carefully conceived, implemented, and analyzed for security vulnerabilities, they will remain vulnerable to misuse, particularly by insiders. We must examine much more seriously all of the relevant security risks that can arise with key-escrow and key-recovery schemes. The third-party agents are themselves enormous potential sources of risks. Those people who seek to increase system and network security and those who believe that the inherent risks of key recovery are controllable all face similar problems. Because the infrastructure is weak, vulnerabilities are inevitable. If those vulnerabilities exist, they will be exploited.

Whereas legislation and strict administrative supervision of employees could help to reduce some of the risks, the fundamental weaknesses in the computer-communication infrastructure today are not likely to be overcome in the near future. Although there has been some improvement in recent years, many of the conclusions of the 1989 Computers at Risk study (Reference 4) are still valid today; furthermore, new security vulnerabilities are introduced with each new system. As a result, supposedly secure systems are penetrable (e.g., Reference 10). The risks are still ubiquitous, and are likely to remain so (Reference 5). Anyone who tells you they can develop an infrastructure that avoids or contains the risks—including but not limited to those that I have outlined here—is simply not familiar with the realities of computer-communication system security and the foibles of real human beings.

Consequently, the entire concept of key-recovery is riddled with potential risks. Because the underlying computer-communication infrastructure is so weak with respect to security, it would be extremely difficult to provide serious assurances that the key-recovery infrastructure is not substantially weaker. However, some recommendations for improving matters are included in my earlier Senate testimony from June 1996 (Reference 6) and in Computer-Related Risks (Reference 5), both of which I urge you to read.

Any meaningful assessment of the risks relating to key recovery must consider the costs and risks to the law enforcement community and to society associated with an inability to detect and prosecute crime. The notion of preventing computer-related crime (opportunities for which are likely to increase dramatically, even in the near future) should not be antithetical to prosecuting it. Arguments about costs and risks must be broadly based, not narrowly drawn just within the confines of law enforcement, and genuine tradeoffs must be clearly understood. The expected misuses of crypto would have to clearly dominate the benefits from the expected uses to justify a widespread key-recovery infrastructure. To date, there is little real evidence that crypto is becoming a significant problem for law enforcement, and considerable evidence at present that it is not—at least not yet—worldwide.

It must be recognized that the common goal is to reduce total crime, for which multiple approaches are undoubtedly necessary. However, whereas key-recovery schemes do not help the intelligence community (an probably hinder it), they might also backfire badly on the law-enforcement community—because of the risks outlined here. Law enforcement desperately needs to pursue other avenues. Among many other alternatives, database tracking facilities are already widespread, through telephone records, credit-card billing, airline reservations, etc. Intelligent programs for data fusion could be very effective—although perhaps risky from a privacy point of view. Additionally, use of biometric and other forms of less spoofable identification and authentication would add significantly to determining who is doing what to whom.

I conclude that the costs associated with implementing and administering something whose overall feasibility has so many unidentified risks (some of which are enumerated here) do not seem justifiable at this time, and certainly not until some thorough, objective detailed studies of the implications have been completed. To that end, detailed architectures and procedural definitions are required before the costs and risks can be realistically assessed. I note that this emphasis on understanding the costs and risks is completely consistent with the principles of the OECD Guidelines for Cryptography Policy, established 27 March 1997.

My primary observation here is that the nation is not ready for any widespread key-recovery infrastructures, especially those that might be mandated by the U.S. Government for nationwide use. Furthermore, this is an international issue, not just a national one—which may significantly complicate the search for adequate solutions. The complexities of legislation relating to the social implications of emerging technologies relating to the Internet are illustrated by the experiences surrounding the Communications Decency Act. Rushing into legislation without serious consideration (as appears to be happening with McCain-Kerrey, for example) runs the risk of prematurely establishing an unworkable and counterproductive policy. If there are genuine commercial demands for key-recovery for stored information, those needs will be satisfied naturally. However, there is no real need for key-recovery for communications apart from those of law enforcement, and the costs and risks are potentially too great to bear in the absence of further study. I fully believe the conclusion of our National Research Council study that recommends in essence that the U.S. Government itself as a guinea pig and explore the risks and costs and other factors before instituting any widespread key-recovery infrastructures.

REFERENCES

1. Hal Abelson, Ross Anderson, Steven M. Bellovin, Josh Benaloh, Matt Blaze, Whitfield Diffie, John Gilmore, Peter G. Neumann, Ronald L. Rivest, Jeffrey I. Schiller, Bruce Schneier, *The Risks of Key Recovery, Key Escrow, and Trusted Third-Party Encryption,* May 27, 1997 (ftp://research.att.com/dist/mab/key—study.txt or .ps; http://www.crypto.com/key—study). [Attached].

2. Kenneth W. Dam, W.Y. Smith, Lee Bollinger, Ann Caracristi, Benjamin R. Civiletti, Colin Crook, Samuel H. Fuller, Leslie H. Gelb, Ronald Graham, Martin Hellman, Julius L. Katz, Peter G. Neumann, Raymond Ozzie, Edward C. Schmults,

Elliot M. Stone, and Willis H. Ware, Cryptography's Role In Securing the Information Society (a.k.a. the CRISIS report), Final Report of the National Research Council Cryptographic Policy Study Committee, National Academy Press, 2101 Constitution Ave., Washington, D.C. 20418, 1996. The executive summary is available online. (http://www2.nas.edu/cstbweb).

3. Susan Landau, Stephen Kent, Clinton Brooks, Scott Charney, Dorothy Denning, Whitfield Diffie, Anthony Lauck, Douglas Miller, Peter G. Neumann, and David Sobel, *Codes, Keys, and Conflicts: Issues in U.S. Crypto Policy,* Report of a Special Panel of the ACM U.S. Public Policy Committee (USACM), June, 1994 (http://info.acm.org/reports/acm—crypto—study.html).

4. David D. Clark, W. Earl Boebert, Susan Gerhart, John V. Guttag, Richard A. Kemmerer, Stephen T. Kent, Sandra M. Mann Lambert, Butler W. Lampson, John J. Lane, M. Douglas McIlroy, Peter G. Neumann, Michael O. Rabin, Warren Schmitt, Harold F. Tipton, Stephen T. Walker, and Willis H. Ware, *Computers at Risk: Safe Computing in the Information Age,* National Research Council, National Academy Press, 1991, 2101 Constitution Ave., Washington, D.C. 20418, 1996.

5. Peter G. Neumann, *Computer-Related Risks,* Addison-Wesley, 1995.

6. Peter G. Neumann, Security Risks in the Emerging Infrastructure, written testimony for the U.S. Senate Permanent Subcommittee on Investigations of the Senate Committee on Govermnental Affairs, 25 June 1996. See *Security in Cyberspace,* Hearings, S. Hrg. 104–701, 1996, pages 350–363, with oral testimony included on pages 106–111. ISBN 0–16–053913–7 (http://www.csl.sri.com/neumannSenate.html).

7. Peter G. Neumann, *Security and Integrity Controls for Federal, State, and Local Computers accessing NCIC,* SRI Technical Report for the FBI, 29 June 1990.

8. Peter G. Neumann, *Illustrative Risks to the Public in the Use of Computer Systems and Related Technology* (ftp://www.csl.sri.com/pub/illustrative.PS). [Attached].

9. Laurie E. Ekstrand, *"National Crime Information Center: Legislation Needed to Deter Misuse of Criminal Justice Information,"* U.S. General Accounting Office testimony before the U.S. House of Representatives Subcommittee on Information, Justice, Agriculture, and Transportation, of the Committee on Government Operations, and the Subcommittee on Civil and Constitutional Rights, of the Committee on the Judiciary, 28 July 1993.

10. *Information Security: Computer Attacks at Department of Defense Pose Increasing Risks,* U.S. General Accounting Office, May 1996, GAO/AIMD–96–84.

11. Phillip A. Porras and Peter G. Neumann, *EMERALD: Event Monitoring Enabling Responses to Anomalous Live Disturbances,* Proceedings of the National Information System Security Conference, October 1997. A *preprint* is available on-line at http://www.csl.sri.com/intrusion.html, along with other information on current work and historical background.

PERSONAL BACKGROUND

I have been involved with the U.S. Government in different technological contexts for many years, including (among others) national security, law enforcement, air-traffic control, and NASA. My first computer-related job was for the Navy in the summer of 1953, 44 years ago next week.

I have long been concerned with security, reliability, human safety, system survivability, and privacy in computer-communication systems and networks, and with how to develop systems that can dependably do what is expected of them. For example, I have been involved in designing operating systems and networks, secure database-management systems, and monitoring systems that seek to identify abnormal patterns of behavior. I have also been seriously involved in identifying and preventing risks. Some of this experience is distilled into my book, *Computer-Related Risks* (Reference 5).

In activities directly related to cryptography and its applications, I was a member of the National Research Council committee (1994–96) study of U.S. cryptographic policy (Reference 2). I participated in an earlier study of the same subject sponsored by the ACM U.S. Policy Committee (USACM) (Reference 3). I was also a coauthor of the 1988–90 National Research Council study report, *Computers at Risk* (Reference 4).

Over the years, I have had several opportunities to consider the security needs of the FBI. From 1987 to 1989 I served on an expert panel for the House Judiciary Committee, Subcommittee on Civil and Constitutional Rights, addressing law-enforcement database systems at the request of then Congressman Don Edwards. In 1991, at the request of Al Bayse, then Deputy Director of the FBI, I wrote a report on security requirements in the use of the national (NCIC), state, and local databases (Reference 7). In addition, the SRI Computer Science Laboratory had an ongoing project to study the application of our technology for misuse and anomaly detection ("intrusion detection") to FBI internal applications. The most recent incarnation of that technology is summarized in Reference 11.

I am a Fellow of the American Association for the Advancement of Science, the Institute for Electrical and Electronics Engineers, and the Association for Computing (ACM). My present title is Principal Scientist in the Computer Science Laboratory at SRS International (not-for-profit, formerly Stanford Research Institute), where I have been since 1971—after ten years at Bell Telephone Laboratories in Murray Hill, New Jersey. I have doctorates from Harvard and the Technische Hochschule, Darmstadt, Germany (the latter obtained while I was on a Fulbright from 1958 to 1960). I am a member of the ACM USACM committee, chairman of the ACM Committee on Computers and Public Policy, and Moderator of its widely read Internet Risks Forum comp.risks).

Attachments for my Senate hearing written testimony:

1. Eleven-authored crypto report, May 1997 (http://www.crypto.com/key—study).
2. Latest edition of "Illustrative Risks" summary (ftp://www.csl.sri.com/pub/illustrative.PS).

The CHAIRMAN. Well, thank you. We appreciate the testimony. I am sorry I missed the——

Senator LEAHY. I have checked out a few of those sites myself. In fact, you had highlighted one in Korea and other places. It is amazing.

The CHAIRMAN. What does PGP stand for?

Mr. NEUMANN. Pretty Good Privacy. It is a relatively unbreakable E-mail concept that fits into your average E-mailer; for example, Ray's or anybody else's.

The CHAIRMAN. Well, we haven't put our Utah people on this yet, our teenagers on this yet. When we get them going on this, we will——

Senator LEAHY. That is what my signature looks like in PGP.

The CHAIRMAN. So you can take this right off the Internet right now for free? It is a 128-bit encryption?

Mr. NEUMANN. Sure, and it is free and it is only one product that is representatives of hundreds and hundreds of products that are available internationally. I might add that there are domestic systems that are using foreign crypto which is installed in other countries.

The CHAIRMAN. And these are the countries that can do this besides the United States?

Mr. NEUMANN. There are 67 countries.

The CHAIRMAN. There are many, many other countries, but at least those on there can do it right now?

Mr. NEUMANN. Those are just a few that Anne happened to have plucked out here for the demonstration.

The CHAIRMAN. This sure makes it tough on the law enforcement and security people, doesn't it?

Mr. NEUMANN. Yes, and this is why I say it is very important that they start looking at alternatives. They may have lost the battle completely as far as cryptography is concerned.

The CHAIRMAN. Well, let me just ask a few questions. I think this hearing has been very important and we have had a lot of information come out of this hearing that I think is going to benefit everybody.

Let me ask you, Ken, what are the affirmative steps of Government policy to help law enforcement and national security that your report recommended? I mean, how can we solve these problems?

Mr. DAM. Well, our report ranges over the entire area of security and there are many things that need to be done to make more secure our large public systems, like the air traffic control system, and so forth. That is not what this hearing has fundamentally been about.

The CHAIRMAN. No.

Mr. DAM. But that is one very important area, and frankly while certain steps have been taken, I don't think they have gotten very far within the executive branch yet. Also, we believe that, for example, the FBI should have greater research and development capability than they presently have, and this is without regard to cryptography. It is hard enough just to get the bits that are using packet switching, and so forth.

So that capability, I believe, the FBI should have, and they have asked for authority. I don't know where that stands. So there are lots of things that could be done unrelated to this particular cryptography problem which would give greater security to the Government, to our big systems, and to individuals.

The CHAIRMAN. What is your assessment of the draft administration bill which is largely embodied in S. 909, introduced last week by Senators McCain and Kerrey, particularly with respect to linkage of certificate authority to key recovery?

Mr. DAM. Well, I think there is a problem about using any kind of leverage to get people to do things where the thing you are asking them to do—i.e., key recovery—is not proven. You are not certain it is going to work, and my colleagues here have recently given a very articulate presentation on why you can't just expect this stuff to work right away and you could be creating enormous vulnerabilities.

With regard to the legislation more generally, I am somewhat concerned about things that I think could be fixed, and indeed it is partly just a question of how you read the legislation. Whether there would be the same kind of protection for individuals under McCain-Kerrey as there presently is under title III of the wiretapping authority, I think, is open to question. You can certainly read it the other way, particularly with regard to the subpoena power.

Remember, we are not just talking about the FBI. We are talking about thousands of State and local organizations. But beyond that, we are talking about subpoenas being available with regard to various organizations within the executive branch. So, that is something that I think when you look into it you can make the legislation say what I think Director Freeh read it as saying. I think those are some of the points to be borne in mind.

The CHAIRMAN. Mr. MacKay, what effect has current U.S. encryption policies had upon Novell's ability to effectively compete in the global software marketplace?

Mr. MACKAY. Well, you know, I think over the history of working with the evolving policy, I mean kind of the glib answer is at least that it has complicated our overall product development work, our overall design work, and delivery of product to the marketplace.

In a bit more detail, it is important to understand that, you know, as the other members of this panel have pointed out, designing security systems is, in fact, a very intellectually intensive and also engineering-intensive art to some level because there are a lot of considerations that go into designing a system that is truly robust.

In our field, in our industry, we are moving fast. We are moving as fast as, you know, the accelerating pace demands, but designing systems of this nature, designing, certainly, systems that begin to touch of this magnitude, I mean, takes considerable time. We, in fact, have put effort already in previous work into key recovery, key storage systems. Necessarily, we have to, and again motivated by commercial interests we have to look 18 to 24 months out on the development cycle.

So, you know, we try to interpret the policy. We try to interpret the intent. We try to, you know, put that into good technical designs that we believe will hold up and will pass muster with the policy as it evolves. As the policy evolves, sometimes this throws wrenches in the works. It causes us to have to change things. The evolving policy has been fairly problematic to deal with.

So I guess my best response to this in terms of how to actually improve the state of affairs is I think you need to put a legislative context—or it is desirable to have a legislative context in place that allows U.S. industry to be very, you know, competitive and be able to deal in the worldwide marketplace more effectively. Again, I point to some of the proposals in ECPA and Pro-CODE as being very good model legislation in that regard.

Beyond that, though, because it is important to address the public safety and law enforcement and security concerns, as well as the commercial interests, we do need, certainly, a way for industry and for Government to work together because putting in place a good key recovery system that would actually be comprehensive is something that is going to take additional work, you know. As Kenneth Dam and Peter Neumann have said, the desire to design these systems is going to take experience, it is going to take time.

Just to note briefly, I mean, you know, the interest of the commercial industry by participating in the Key Recovery Alliance—you know, there is evidence that the commercial sector, based on the motivations and requirements of the commercial business industry, is already moving to make some of the right steps happen here. But we need a legislative context that is favorable to competition, and then we also need to really work together and put in place a structure that allows Government and industry to collaborate.

The CHAIRMAN. Well, my time is up, but let me just ask this last question because I think I have to. Do you believe that the linking of Government-approved certificate authorities to a commitment to key recovery will have a negative impact upon the further development of electronic commerce, and if so, why?

Mr. MACKAY. Again, you know, going back to the—well, certainly for some of the technical reasons noted by Peter Neumann and Kenneth Dam, linking CAA's and key recovery agents is problematic and, in fact, not a good design approach in the first place to link these closely.

Beyond that, you know, in terms of the models that business is going to require in order to have a hierarchy certificate structure that also incorporates with it the appropriate liability models for the type of information which is being encrypted or signed with those generated certificates, I don't think you can mandate that. So I think that this would tend to have a chilling effect, putting legislation in place too early that preempts really more experience in developing and deploying these systems in the marketplace.

The CHAIRMAN. Senator Leahy.

Senator LEAHY. Thank you, Mr. Chairman.

I was intrigued by something you were saying earlier, Mr. Neumann. Incidentally, looking at the PGP sites, I remember when I first started checking those out, and I periodically go back now on the Net and just see what is there. That list has gotten longer and where you can get PGP. I talk with friends of mine in other countries and they just know they can click on very easily and pick it up.

You told us your concerns, your security concerns, with the Administration's key recovery infrastructure. You talk about both communications and stored files. You have also said that Government should try some of these things out themselves first. So tell us what you think about whether the sensitive communications and computer systems at the Department of Justice and Department of Defense should be reconfigured on what the Administration is proposing for industry.

Mr. NEUMANN. Not really, but I think what I am saying is that before a massive infrastructure is built, there should be some detailed experiments that carry it out. Now, who is concerned——

Senator LEAHY. Now, if you were the Secretary of Defense, would you be eager to just jump right in now as just a good soldier and take the Administration's proposal and say, here, a system that should be one of the most secure in our Nation—by golly, if it is good enough for good old industry, it is good enough for us, we will just slap it right on here? Would you be ready to do that, Mr. Secretary?

Mr. NEUMANN. Well, actually, if I were the Secretary, I would be very wary of using any of this stuff because the operating systems that you can get from the vendors these days are flawed. It is really not the fact that the crypto key is very long. It is the fact that the system in which it is embedded is almost trivial to break in some cases. You don't have to break the crypto. You break the system and you have access.

Senator LEAHY. It reminds me in a way, what you are saying about getting into the system—I recall once as a young prosecutor, we had this question of fraud in an election and the sheriff and I went out to this town where they stored the ballots. The town clerk was incensed that we would even suggest that anybody could have gotten a hold of the ballots.

They built at great cost in this small town a walk-in vault with this great combination lock, and this was where the ballots were stored, her point being to the sheriff and myself you couldn't possibly get into this. The sheriff happened to glance over and on the wall was a list of the telephone numbers of the town clerk, the telephone number of the chairman of the board of selectmen, and the combination to the vault, just in case somebody forgot it.

On this, I might ask Mr. Dam—you and I have worked in so many issues over the years, and I join with the chairman in welcoming you being here. To follow up on what Mr. Neumann said, the Administration is spending about $8 million on, 10 different key recovery pilot projects. That is what the National Research Council CRISIS report said; we ought to conduct these kinds of pilot projects before we adopt some overall program.

Do we have the results back from these key recovery pilot programs or are we pushing forward to make a proposal before we even get the facts in?

Mr. DAM. My understanding is that we don't have these results. At least we don't have them publicly so that we can take a look at them. Moreover, I don't understand—and I was not involved in these projects—that they really involve any attempt to break into them; that is to say, to red-team them, which I think is indispensable. They basically are demonstration projects that you can build a key recovery system. Well, I take that for granted that we can do so, but the question is can it meet these kinds of requirements.

Let me say in that respect with regard to Senator Hatch's questions of me that I did prepare—we did prepare some answers to some of the questions, one which you asked, and I would like to submit those also with my prepared testimony for your use in the future.

The CHAIRMAN. Without objection.

[The information referred to follows:]

COMPUTER SCIENCE AND TELECOMMUNICATIONS BOARD,
NATIONAL RESEARCH COUNCIL,
Washington, DC.

Hon. ORRIN G. HATCH,
Senate Judiciary Committee,
U.S. Senate, Washington, DC.

Dear Mr. Chairman: This letter responds to your offer to me to submit additional comments for the record of the hearing of the Senate Judiciary Committee on July 9, 1997, on key recovery and encryption.

In addition to addressing specific issues that might be of concern to you, I want to respond to the challenge you left us at the end of the hearing—to find a reasonable compromise among the various interests.

The NRC study on national cryptography policy that I chaired was formed in response to a Congressional request to study this topic. It came to a unanimous set of conclusions and recommendations that we collectively believed constitute a reasonable approach to national cryptography policy. The study involved a blue-ribbon committee, including a former Attorney General of the United States, a former deputy director of the National Security Agency, a former deputy commander-in-chief of the U.S. European Command in Germany, and several members with experience in the computer, software, and telecommunications industries. (The names of all committee members are appended to this letter.)

Among our primary recommendations were the following:

• No law should bar the manufacture, sale, or use of any form of encryption within the United States.

• National cryptography policy should be more closely aligned with market forces. Domestic users should be free to determine which kind of cryptography system best meets their needs.

• Export controls on cryptography should be relaxed progressively but not eliminated. Export controls on cryptography should be relaxed to help U.S. firms operating internationally protect vital information and to solidify the nation's leadership in the information technology field, which is critical to national security and economic competitiveness. Retention of some export controls would mitigate the loss to national security interests in the short term, allow the United States to evaluate the impact of further changes, and give authorities time to cope with a new technical reality. Relaxation would accommodate easier exports of 56-bit DES-based encryption products, without a time limit and without regard to key recovery; foreign consumers with needs for stronger encryption would be able to obtain stronger encryption if they agree to provide U.S. authorities with plaintext upon legally authorized requests.

• Because key recovery is a promising but unproven technology (a point acknowledged by the Administration), the U.S. government should experiment with key recovery for its own purposes to gain operational experience with it, rather than to aggressively promote it to the private sector as a proven technology.

• The U.S. government should take affirmative policy actions to help law enforcement and national security. For example, we recommended that government take an affirmative role in encouraging collateral uses of cryptography such as authentication. In addition, the government should promote better security for the public switched network through measures such as link encryption. (Link encryption is the application of encryption only to potentially vulnerable links (e.g., the wireless link of a cellular telephone call).) Such measures would not reduce the ability of law enforcement to obtain an authorized wiretap, but would reduce the demand for devices that encrypt communications from sender to receiver, making it more difficult for criminal users to obtain devices that could block lawfully authorized wiretaps. Most importantly, we strongly supported RandD to develop new technical capabilities that would ultimately be more useful than pushing key recovery onto a resistant market. For example, even without encryption, obtaining the relevant electronic data or signal from a complex communications channel will become much harder in the future, and law enforcement needs to be able to deal with that problem.

• The U.S. government needed to find a mechanism to promote information security in the private sector. No such mechanism existed in the United States at the time of the study, and though some steps have been taken since then (e.g., the formation of the President's Commission on Critical Infrastructure Protection), a comprehensive legislative and regulatory framework to support this need is still not in place.

Our assessment at the time was that the package of recommendations described above struck a good balance between the various interests, and I see no reason to change that assessment today.

DIFFICULTIES WITH ENCRYPTION ENCOUNTERED BY LAW ENFORCEMENT

At the hearing, Judge Freeh acknowledged that the use of encryption by criminals has been relatively minimal to date. In the course of the NRC study, we were not apprised of any Title III warrant for wiretapping that had been frustrated by encryption, and I have not learned of any example since then. Moreover, law enforcement officials have often (though not always) been able to cope with encryption when they have encountered it, whether by penetrating the security offered by encryption or by obtaining the necessary information through some other means.[1]

However, the major point is that no one knows the true extent of the problem with criminals using encryption, whether for communications or for stored files. Indeed, it was only last year that a law was passed mandating the collection and compilation of such data. (The Economic Espionage Act of 1996, Title V, Section 501.)

The magnitude of the future problem is unknown, and one of the reasons we adopted a wait-and-see attitude on the need for key recovery was that the nation needed real data on the extent of the problem and trends before it adopted policies based on the presumed existence of that problem.

WHAT NEEDS TO BE DONE BEFORE THE NATION ADOPTS A POLICY OF SUPPORTING KEY RECOVERY

The NRC report argued that too little was known about how key recovery might work before the government charges ahead with imposing key recovery on the marketplace. We believed that experience is needed in two major areas.

The first area is the actual business need for key recovery. Because we believe that a market-driven solution is the only stable long-term solution, experience is needed to know:

• how often business organizations need to recover keys to encrypted files and, especially, to encrypted communications;

• the extent to which users are willing to buy key recovery products domestically and overseas; and

• how these parties use key recovery products.

[1] Dorothy E. Denning and William E. Baugh, Jr., Encryption and Evolving Technologies as Tools of Organized Crime and Terrorism, National Strategy Information Center's US Working Group on Organized Crime, July 1997. Denning is professor of computer science at Georgetown University and an advisor to the FBI on encryption; William Baugh is former Assistant Director of the FBI's Information Resources Division.

The second area is vulnerability of key recovery products, where experience is needed for knowing:

- the frequency with which unauthorized parties are able to obtain keys improperly from key recovery agents;
- the extent of the financial losses suffered from such improper access to keys; and
- whether or not the inclusion of key recovery features introduces technical weaknesses into products.

Again, as noted above, the actual extent and nature of the encryption problem for law enforcement is unknown. We don't know how often encryption is encountered, the forms in which encryption is encountered (files or communications), and how often investigations or prosecutions are thwarted by encryption.

THE McCAIN/KERREY LEGISLATION: THE SECURE PUBLIC NETWORKS ACT OF 1997

For the most part, the McCain/Kerrey bill (S. 909, The Secure Public Networks Act (SPNA)) is inconsistent with the general thrust of the NRC report. The SPNA is a highly aggressive promotion of key recovery for the private sector, establishing that technology as a pillar of national cryptography policy.

Nothing has happened since May 1996 to alter our basic position that the nation lacks the experience to make legislation that would govern the behavior or deployment of key recovery agents. In addition, the bill attempts to use something that all parties agree is needed for electronic commerce, namely a public key infrastructure (PKI), as leverage for obtaining approval for something fundamentally unrelated, namely key recovery for domestic use. Our committee opposed the use of export controls as a lever to force industry to produce and sell key recovery products, and it is also dubious public policy to use the leverage of electronic commerce (e.g., a public key infrastructure) to promote key recovery.

Furthermore, the Administration has said on one hand that it believes there is a strong market for key recovery products. On the other hand, it feels the need to use the leverage of export controls and the need for a PKI to promote key recovery. Because government intervention is necessary only when the market fails, the Administration's actions raise the question of why intervention is necessary if market forces are in fact working.

Finally, while I have not undertaken a detailed analysis of the bill, some elements of the SPNA are inconsistent with the NRC report, while a few are consistent with it.

Inconsistencies between McCain/Kerry and the NRC report

- The bill attempts to draw a distinction between public keys that may be used for "authentication and digital signatures" (Section 402, (b)(1)) and public keys that may be used for "encryption" (Section 402, (b)(2)). However, such a distinction is artificial in the context of the bill: once a certificate is issued, the use of the associated public key cannot be limited to any single purpose. Thus, the bill would allow one of two things.
    - A recipient of a public key certificate intended for use in authentication and digital signatures could in practice use it for encryption purposes, thus circumventing the intent of the bill.
    - To close this loophole, the government might interpret the law so as to obtain access to the private key associated with a given public key certificate. However, anyone in possession of such a private key would be able to impersonate the true owner of the public key certificate. In particular, possession of the private key would give government authorities the technical capability to forge documents that were ostensibly created by the true owner, and to do so in an undetectable manner. While government employees are generally trustworthy, any such access creates risks, and the bill would grant many state and local authorities and even foreign governments access to keys under certain circumstances. Because of such potentially broad disclosure, the validity of any electronic contract based on the security of this key could thus be called into question. In turn, doubt and uncertainty in this area could have a major negative impact on the development of electronic commerce.
- Section 306 prohibits the export of encryption upon the showing of evidence that the product would be used in acts harmful to certain U.S. national interests. Since foreign terrorists and criminals have access to commercially available products and are likely to use these products to further their goals, this section as drafted could be construed so as to prohibit the export of essentially all encryption products even to legitimate overseas customers (which would be contrary to the bill's stated objective of improving information security).

• Section 901 ("Waiver Authority") allows the President to waive any provision of the act for reasons of national security or domestic safety. Even if this provision is not exercised. Its mere presence will create considerable market uncertainty and thus act as an inhibitor to broad commercial development and use of cryptographic products.

• Section 106 allows the government to obtain the plaintext of encrypted messages using a subpoena rather than a search warrant. Further, Section 110 prohibits informing the owner of an encrypted text that his information has been made accessible to government authorities. Subpoenas generally require a lesser showing than that required for search warrants. We felt that the plaintext of encrypted information require strong protection, and we regarded the protection afforded by Title III for the privacy of telephone conversations as a good balance between the needs of law enforcement and the privacy rights of citizens, especially as it imposed further showings by law enforcement for the granting of a court order because of the surreptitious nature of electronic surveillance.

We are aware that the FBI does not accept this interpretation of the SPNA. During the hearing, I understood Director Freeh to say that a court order analogous to a Title III warrant for wiretapping would be required for access to encryption keys and that the surreptitious subpoena power would be used only to implement the earlier court order. Of course, the issuance of a Title III warrant is subject to a number of mandated protections for the subject of the wiretap, such as the wiretap being the investigative technique of last resort. Perhaps it is the FBI's intent to require safeguards that parallel those required by Title III for wiretaps, but the bill as written certainly does not so state. This is a sufficiently important matter, not only substantively but also in terms of public acceptance, that it should not be left for legislative history but should be carefully spelled out in the legislative text.

Further, the issuance of a Title III warrant is subject to a requirement for minimization (only conversations relevant to the subject of the investigation may be recorded and used). By contrast, the legislation as written (Section 105, Privacy Protection) is not drafted in such a way as to clearly preclude the possibility that once the decryption key to one relevant message is obtained, it will not be used to decrypt other non-relevant messages associated with that decryption key.

• The SNPA is primarily a law enforcement bill that is intended to facilitate law enforcement access to encrypted data and communications; as such it does not deal with the larger—and in our view more significant—dimensions of the information security problems facing the nation. Moreover, by focusing so strongly on the law enforcement desire for encryption keys, it distorts the nature of the overall problem. A comprehensive approach to information security will still be needed, and that comprehensive approach may well be inconsistent with key portions of the SNPA.

As one example, the NRC report noted that key recovery entailed a number of risks to users. For example, key recovery necessarily involves the possibility that technical vulnerabilities or human weaknesses in the key recovery system may result in the compromise of keys. The current key recovery experiments being undertaken by the Federal government are intended to demonstrate the feasibility of key recovery, but not its strength against unauthorized penetration or compromise. The SNPA presents an opportunity to require such testing (often called "red-teaming"), but fails to do so.

Consistencies between McCain/Kerry and the NRC report

• Section 302 requires that encryption products using 56-bit DES be exportable under a license exception after a one-time review. Depending on the nature of this review, this provision could well be consistent with our recommendation that restrictions on the export of DES-based encryption products be relaxed.

• Title VI directs the President to negotiate with other nations on mutual recognition of key recovery agents and certificate authorities. This title is in general consistent with our recommendation that the U.S. should work with other nations on harmonization of cryptography policy.

THE BURNS, LEAHY, AND GOODLATTE BILLS

Essentially, these bills all relax export controls on encryption to the standard of "foreign availability"—they would allow the export of U.S. encryption products whose strength was comparable to that of products available from foreign vendors. Our report made a recommendation to relax export controls on encryption to the level of 56-bit DES, rather than the current 40-bit limit, and we made no reference to foreign availability.

We chose not to rely on a "foreign availability" criterion because of our desire to avoid arguments about what was or was not really available from foreign vendors. Anyone knows that simply labeling a box is not a guarantee of the performance of

44–452 - 97 - 5

a product inside that box. Thus, the use of "foreign availability" as a criterion entails a complex inquiry requiring hearings and bureaucratic fact-finding. History demonstrates that a foreign availability requirement almost always entails delay (or worse, the excuse for delay) in an industry in which the time scale of decision-making makes delay one of the most objectionable aspects of the export control process. By contrast, the U.S. has a well-established procedure for determining the exportability of products using 40-bit RC–2 and RC–4 algorithms, and it would be a simple matter to adapt that existing procedure to 56-bit DES.

In addition, the Leahy and Goodlatte bills provide sanctions for the use of encryption for criminal purposes. We believed that such a provision—if drawn narrowly-was worth examining by the U.S. Congress, but that many issues had to be resolved before such a provision was actually legislated. To the best of our knowledge, no hearings have explored issues such as what it means to "use" encrypted communications when communications are automatically encrypted without user intervention. I therefore believe not only that such hearings are desirable but also that the subject of the definition of such a crime (which is bound to be controversial and which perhaps might raise constitutional problems in view of the potential absence of intent where the user does not consciously choose encryption) is well within the jurisdiction and the long-established competence of the Senate Judiciary Committee.

THE ADEQUACY OF 56-BIT DES

While the recent cracking of a single DES message is impressive, I do not think it fundamentally changes our view on 56-bit DES. Is DES good enough for everyone? No, and we said so in the report. We understood the limitations of DES given modern computing technology, but we still concluded that DES provided "good enough" security for most commercial requirements. The cracking of DES was based on the simultaneous use of 14,000 computers connected through the Internet, and even so it took months to undertake. That is a lot of effort to crack one message, and in general, an adversary may not know which encrypted message is worth that effort.

On the other hand, this effort does demonstrate two points made in our report—that a determined adversary, such as a well-funded foreign government, would be required to mount a successful challenge to DES on a large scale, and that a replacement for DES will be needed in the not-too-distant future. Note that today, NIST is coordinating an effort to designate a suitable replacement.

CONCLUSION

I continue to believe that the recommendations of the NRC study would lead to enhanced confidentiality and protection of information for individuals and companies, thereby reducing economic and financial crimes and economic espionage from both domestic and foreign sources. In addition, they would result in improved security and assurance for the information systems and networks used by the nation—a more secure national information infrastructure. While the recommendations of the committee would thus contribute to the prevention of crime and enhance national security, the spread of encryption would also increase the burden of those in government charged with carrying out certain specific law enforcement and intelligence activities. In order to reduce the impact of this burden, the government should take certain steps (outlined in the report) to help law enforcement and national security authorities to cope with the new technical realities of the information age. The NRC report concluded that widespread commercial and private use of cryptography in the United States and abroad is inevitable in the long run and that its advantages, on balance, outweigh its disadvantages. Thus, the overall interests of the government and the nation would best be served by a policy that fosters a judicious transition toward the broad use of cryptography.

I commend your attention to this vital though often confusing and obscure issue. If I can be of further assistance to you on this matter, please contact me. The relevant staff contact is Dr. Herb Lin, National Research Council, who can be reached by phone at 202-334-3191 or by email at hlin@nas.edu.

Sincerely,

KENNETH W. DAM.

MEMBERS OF THE NRC COMMITTEE TO STUDY NATIONAL CRYPTOGRAPHY POLICY

(AFFILIATIONS ARE THOSE OF MAY 1996, THE DATE THE STUDY WAS RELEASED)

Kenneth W. Dam, Chair, is the Max Pam Professor of American and Foreign Law at the University of Chicago Law School. Mr. Dam served as deputy secretary of state (1982–1985), as provost of the University of Chicago (1980–1982), and as corporate vice president for law and external relations at IBM (1985–1992).

W.Y. Smith, Vice Chair, is president emeritus of the Institute for Defense Analyses, and served as its president (1985–1991). His military posts include deputy commander in chief of the European Command in Germany (1981–1983) and chief of staff of SHAPE, Belgium (1979–1981).

Lee Bollinger is provost of Dartmouth College. He was also dean of the Michigan law school (1987–1994).

Ann Caracristi was deputy director of the National Security Agency (1980–1982). She is also a member of President Clinton's Foreign Intelligence Advisory Board.

Benjamin R. Civiletti practices law with Venable, Baetjer, Howard and Civiletti in Baltimore and Washington, D.C. He served as attorney general of the United States (1979–1981).

Colin Crook is the senior technology officer of Citicorp.

Samuel H. Fuller is vice president and the chief scientist of Digital Equipment Corporation. He is also a member of the National Academy of Engineering.

Leslie H. Gelb is president of the Council on Foreign Relations. He also served as director of the Bureau of Politico-Military Affairs in the Department of State (1977–1979).

Ronald Graham is director of Information Sciences Research at ATandT Laboratories. He is also a member of the National Academy of Sciences.

Martin Hellman is professor of electrical engineering at Stanford University, and a co-inventor of public-key cryptography.

Julius Katz is president of Hills and Company, International Consultants. Ambassador Katz held the position of deputy U.S. trade representative (1989–1993) and was the U.S. chief negotiator for the North American Free Trade Agreement.

Peter G. Neumann is principal scientist in the Computer Science Laboratory at SRI.

Raymond Ozzie is the founder and president of Iris Associates, the developer of Lotus Notes. Iris is a wholly-owned subsidiary of Lotus Development Corporation and IBM Corporation.

Edward C. Schmults was senior vice president for external affairs and general counsel of GTE Corporation (1984–1995). Previously he served as deputy attorney general of the United States (1981–1984).

Elliot M. Stone is executive director of the Massachusetts Health Data Consortium.

Willis H. Ware is a member (emeritus) of the Corporate Research Staff at the RAND Corporation. He is also a member of the National Academy of Engineering.

Senator LEAHY. If I could also follow with another one on this, S. 909, the McCain-Kerrey bill, allows law enforcement to use a subpoena if they want to obtain key recovery information. Now, issuing a subpoena is fairly simple. You don't even have to go to a judge in most instances. You just have relevance and you issue the subpoena. But getting the subpoena for this encryption key, aren't you sort of opening up an awful lot more?

I mean, the subpoena is to find out if somebody had filed something at 10 o'clock the night before, but once you open it up you also find everything that has been filed there for the last 6 months. Couldn't such a subpoena for a key decryption open up far, far more than the targeted information that law enforcement seeks, without a hearing of probable cause and a search warrant, and so forth?

Mr. NEUMANN. This is very true.

Mr. DAM. Absolutely, absolutely. Now, I think what the FBI has had in mind from what the Director said and other conversations I have had is that the subpoena would only be used as a follow-up to a title III court order for wiretapping. It would be used as simply an implementation of a wiretapping order, but that is not what the statute as drafted says.

Senator LEAHY. That is what I was afraid of.

Mr. DAM. I think that is where there are lots of issues and which I think is important to resolve, not only to quiet legitimate concerns, but also to avoid constitutional tests, for example.

Mr. NEUMANN. I gave the example, Senator Leahy, of the master key that is used worldwide. Compromise of that key would be devastating. The idea of subpoenaing the key for a very narrow purpose gives the impression that, oh, yes, it would only be used for that very narrow purpose. But unless there are very strict controls on how it can be used, the fact that many keys are used multiply or for many different purposes or, in fact, unlock other things—typically, in the case of the master key, you have possession of this one key which then unlocks all sorts of other things and, in fact, is generate keys and is used to decrypt other things.

The fundamental thought here is that the key recovery infrastructure is like having not only the neighbor to whom you give your key when you go away, but that there is a master key, universal key, that can be used for every house in the Nation, basically, covertly, surreptitiously, without any knowledge. I think the really important point here is the one you made, which was the distinction between communication and storage. There is a business need for some sort of key recovery for stored information. There is essentially no business need for communications.

Senator LEAHY. That would be a very, very costly one, the communications.

Mr. Chairman, I think these have been extremely important hearings. I commend you again for holding them. I suspect that we will probably have both on the Government side and others some who have either testified or have been available in these hearings who may have differing views, but I would encourage them to write to you and write to me if they do.

The CHAIRMAN. Well, I would encourage them, also, because we need to find some sort of solution here. You all admit that we need to solve some of these problems, but that every solution seems to create more problems, and that is one of the worries that I have. I commend Senator McCain and Kerrey for trying to do what they have done, but I have real qualms about what they have done and I would like to have your best views on that to the extent that you can continue to give us additional information.

There is no question we need to do something about law enforcement and national security. The question is what and how, and we would sure like to have the best advice you can give us on that. I just don't know what else to do, other than to keep plodding ahead and doing the best we can, but I am worried about Congress really messing this up. We have that tendency, they tell me.

Senator LEAHY. Before you and I got here, Orrin.

The CHAIRMAN. "They" includes a pretty wide group of people.

But in any event, I want to thank each of you for the work you have done in this area and for the time that you have given to us. It has been helpful to us and I think this hearing has been particularly gratifying to everybody concerned who is really concerned about this. So thank you for your time. We appreciate it.

We will adjourn until further notice.

[Whereupon, at 1:07 p.m., the committee was adjourned.]

APPENDIX

QUESTIONS AND ANSWERS

RESPONSES OF PETER NEUMANN TO QUESTIONS FROM SENATOR THURMOND

Question 1. Mr. Neumann, you state in your prepared testimony that there is little evidence that encryption is becoming a significant problem for law enforcement. Is it your view that the concerns of the Director of the FBI are misplaced, and that encryption should not be a priority for him?

Answer 1. Senator Thurmond, your question cannot be answered with a single yes or no. In the following response, my answer to the first part—are his concerns misplaced?—indicates that his concerns need rebalancing. My answer to the second part—should encryption not be a priority for him?—is that encryption should not be his top priority; I think that putting all of his eggs in the key-recovery basket could prove to be self-defeating for the FBI. But this greatly simplified summary requires some careful explanation.

I believe that the expressed concerns of the Director of the FBI relating to cryptography are indeed seriously misplaced—they overemphasize one element of the big picture (key recovery as a would-be magic bullet), and essentially ignore everything else. If the security of our computer-communication infrastructure is not radically improved in the very near future, through the use of vastly improved system security and cryptography that is much more impervious to misuse than the proposed key-recovery schemes are likely to be, then our entire nation will be seriously at risk regarding computer-related crimes. The FBI Director apparently has little interest in improving the infrastructure, only in achieving the establishment of an unproven key-recovery infrastructure that could be very badly misused. In the absence of a dramatically improved general security infrastructure, the desired key-recovery infrastructure is likely to be riddled with security vulnerabilities and subject to undetected compromises. Yes, I believe his emphasis is badly misplaced, and that he is almost completely ignoring some very important issues—and their potential consequences.

First of all, a recent report by Professor Dorothy E. Denning of the Computer Science Department at Georgetown University and William E. Baugh Jr., vice president of Science Applications International Corporation suggests that the concerns of Judge Freeh may be overstated at this time. Their report says, "Most of the investigators we talked to did not find that encryption was obstructing a large number of investigations. When encryption has been encountered, investigators have usually been able to get the keys from the subject, crack the codes or use other evidence." Professor Denning for many years has been an outspoken supporter of the FBI's needs, and William Baugh is a recently retired FBI employee.

Second, the following direct quote from my written testimony is relevant: "It must be recognized that the common goal is to reduce total crime, for which multiple approaches are undoubtedly necessary. However, whereas key-recovery schemes do not help the intelligence community (and probably hinder it), they might also backfire badly on the law-enforcement community—because of the risks outlined here. Law enforcement desperately needs to pursue other avenues. Among many other alternatives, database tracking facilities are already widespread, through telephone records, credit-card billing, airline reservations, etc. Intelligent programs for data fusion could be very effective—although perhaps risky from a privacy point of view. Additionally, use of biometric and other forms of less spoofable identification and authentication would add significantly to determining who is doing what to whom."

I reiterated that point in my oral testimony on 9 July 1997, and added that the National Security Agency has already realized that it can no longer succeed in attempting to stop the worldwide spread of good unrestricted cryptography (that is, without key recovery), let alone the use of such cryptography within the United States. I also mentioned that NSA is already actively pursuing most of these alternatives, and that the FBI would be wise to follow NSA's lead. I might add here that DARPA has an extensive ongoing program in anomaly and misuse detection that can be used to detect unusual potential misuse of computer-communication facilities and penetrations, and that this technology could also be used to identify situations suggestive of criminal activities. Also, as a further example, police in various countries have had considerable success in extracting history logs from confiscated smart cards and cellular telephones, even when those logs are encrypted although such access may not always need to be surreptitious.

Furthermore, our National Research Council study recognizes that the FBI is seriously lagging behind NSA in expertise related to computer security, and recommends that the FBI undertake a major effort to improve its technical expertise relating to computer and communication technologies. Please read that report for background if you have not already done so (Kenneth W. Dam, W.Y. Smith, Lee Bollinger, Ann Caracristi, Benjamin R. Civiletti, Colin Crook, Samuel H. Fuller, Leslie H. Gelb, Ronald Graham, Martin Hellman, Julius L. Katz, Peter G. Neumann, Raymond Ozzie, Edward C. Schmults, Elliot M. Stone, and Willis H. Ware, Cryptography's Role In Securing the Information Society, a.k.a. the CRISIS report, Final Report of the National Research Council Cryptographic Policy Study Committee, National Academy Press, 2101 Constitution Ave., Washington, D.C. 20418, 1996).

I have absolutely no doubt that the presence of cryptography will in the future make the FBI's task more difficult. This is inevitable, because excellent cryptography without key recovery will be available throughout the world irrespective of U.S. actions; criminals can always use nonrecoverable keys even in the presence of key-recovery systems (for example, by superencrypting, or by disabling the key recovery, or by using a system without key recovery), and because security has become an international problem, not just a national one. Consequently, it is clear that the FBI should be pursuing alternatives.

Incidentally, I have worked directly with various U.S. Government (including NSA and FBI) people over the past 24 years, and have a considerable appreciation of their needs and their technological strengths and weaknesses. I believe that the FBI will have difficulties with increased uses of cryptography, but I also believe that the nation is not ready for any key-recovery scheme that can be foreseen today. Too many unidentified risks have yet to be evaluated, only a few of which are outlined in my prepared testimony and in its attached jointly authored report (Hal Abelson, Ross Anderson, Steven M. Bellovin, Josh Benaloh, Matt Blaze, Whitfield Diffie, John Gilmore, Peter G. Neumann, Ronald L. Rivest, Jeffrey I. Schiller, Bruce Schneier, "The Risks of Key Recovery, Key Escrow, and Trusted Third-Party Encryption," 27 May 1997).

RESPONSE OF PETER NEUMANN TO QUESTIONS FROM SENATOR GRASSLEY

Question 1. [Let us assume that the Grassley Amendment is adopted, relating to reporting whether wiretaps were impeded by encryption.] "If the results of these information-gathering procedures show that criminals are using encryption to commit crimes and frustrate legitimate law-enforcement investigations, how would you suggest Congress address the problem of criminals misusing encryption?"

Answer 1. Senator Grassley, efforts to increase the amount and quality of information available regarding the use of encryption by criminals are very worthy of Senate action. Congress urgently needs accurate information. Unfortunately, the case made by the FBI thus far has been largely based on very emotional arguments rather than on factual analyses.

The U.S. Government has been running escrow centers at Treasury and NIST for some time. Congress would do well to have the relevant Government escrow agents testify on how frequently their services have been used, by whom, and in what connection. Also, Congress would do well to request similar information from the FBI.

Cryptographic hardware and software without key recovery are already becoming widely available worldwide, and are going to be increasingly available in the future. Congress cannot stop that. Nor should it. High-quality cryptography has many beneficial effects on society, including increased privacy, freedom of association, and integrity of the physical infrastructure. Cryptography researchers have First Amendment rights to pursue and spread knowledge of cryptography, and it is not a long stretch to say that the right of an individual citizen to protect his or her own privacy with cryptography may be protected by the freedom of expression and the "right to be let alone" inherent in our Constitution.

Congress must recognize these realities, rather than assuming that key recovery will solve the problem. Criminals will soon have at their disposal cryptographic techniques from numerous countries throughout the world. Consequently, crime should be treated as crime, whether or not the use of cryptography is involved. The use of cryptography, in the absence of crime, should not be made into a crime; and the use of cryptography in furthering a criminal scheme should not be any more illegal than the use of a pen or a computer in furthering an illegal scheme. The evil is in the crime itself, not in the tools used to pursue it.

Whether or not there is a dramatic increase in the use of encryption in the process of committing crimes, Congress should encourage the FBI to urgently explore other avenues that could facilitate its efforts to detect and prosecute crimes. In addition, Congress should urgently act to encourage much greater security in the entire computer-communication infrastructure. Today's systems and networks are simply riddled with security vulnerabilities, and apparently the FBI has very little interest in seeing that situation improved. However, a greatly improved computer-communication infrastructure is absolutely essential for the well-being of our nation, the soundness of our commerce, and the international competitiveness of our computer industry. A sound infrastructure with adequate attention to authentication and accountability would also greatly help to reduce computer-related crime and would at the same time facilitate the FBI's role in preventing, detecting, and prosecuting crime.

My response to the [preceding] direct question from Senator Thurmond notes that law enforcement urgently needs to pursue other avenues besides key recovery. My prepared testimony outlines a few such alternatives, and is reinforced by my oral testimony on 9 July 1997—where I noted that the National Security Agency is already actively pursuing many of these alternatives.

Question 2. Many of your written statements assert that key-escrow systems should not be pursued because such systems have too many technical flaws or weaknesses. Assuming that these flaws or weaknesses could be resolved, would you still oppose key escrow? In other words, if we could get a technologically acceptable key-escrow system, would you support an escrow system?

Answer 2. Senator Grassley, your question implies a possible misperception of what my prepared testimony says, and of what our National Research Council report says. Therefore, I have taken the liberty of modifying your first sentence slightly to represent properly what I do believe I can address more reasonably:

"Many of your written statements assert that key-escrow systems should not be pursued because such systems *would very likely* have too many technical flaws or weaknesses."

First of all, no such systems exist in the full measure of technological implementation and administrative procedures necessary to evaluate whether there is any hope that the potential risks of misuse can be controlled. Thus, it is impossible to assess the technical flaws and weaknesses based on what is known today. But I do believe there is a strong likelihood that serious vulnerabilities will exist in every key-recovery system. Essentially every system I have ever studied has been compromisible, and years of experience in the field suggests that will remain true in the future.

However, I do not agree that key-recovery systems should not be pursued. In particular, our National Research Council report explicitly recommends that, in the absence of detailed understanding of the risks that might result, the Government should actively pursue such techniques for its own internal use and should seriously evaluate the efficacies and risks of key-recovery systems. The problems experienced with the Clipper effort to establish a key-escrow infrastructure for telecommunications suggest that key recovery may be even more difficult, because NSA had complete control over Clipper, which would certainly not be the case in the anticipated distributed collection of key-recovery infrastructures. This suggests that Congress should ask the Government to elaborate on its experiences to date with key escrow and key recovery, including an evaluation of the potential risks. [The cited NRC report is: Kenneth W. Dam, W.Y. Smith, Lee Bollinger, Ann Caracristi, Benjamin R. Civiletti, Colin Crook, Samuel H. Fuller, Leslie H. Gelb, Ronald Graham, Martin Hellman, Julius L. Katz, Peter G. Neumann, Raymond Ozzie, Edward C. Schmults, Elliot M. Stone, and Willis H. Ware, Cryptography's Role In Securing the Information Society (a.k.a. the CRISIS report), Final Report of the National Research Council Cryptographic Policy Study Committee, National Academy Press, 2101 Constitution Ave., Washington, D.C. 20418, 1996.]

It is very important to realize that key-recovery mechanisms imply a dramatic centralization of trust and power, even if the key-recovery facilities are distributed among different entities, and even if the keys are fragmented as is the case in Clipper. Compromise of a single key-recovery authority could have enormous consequences. I wonder whether Senators and Representatives would be willing to trust every President, Attorney General, FBI Director, down to local law-enforcement officers who might easily gain access to their keys, with all the concomitant risks.

I strongly believe that as a nation we are not ready for key-recovery infrastructures with surreptitious access in the absence of detailed procedures for the administration of the process of controlled government access, together with detailed evaluations of the risks involved and the overall implications on our constitutional wellbeing.

It is intriguing to me that you have chosen to use the term "key escrow"—a concept that has apparently been totally abandoned by NSA and the FBI as unworkable, and replaced by the alternative term "key recovery" that is claimed to be totally workable—presumably because of the public trashing that key escrow underwent. The Government is attempting to make a distinction between the two concepts; however, they are both inherently surreptitious access in one form or another, irrespective of how the keys are handled, whether there are single individuals or groups that must be responsible, etc. There are no significant conceptual differences between key escrow and key recovery, despite what you may be told; there are of course operational differences. Key recovery has most of the same potential risks as key escrow, although no one in the Administration seems to be admitting that.

There are two ways for me to properly answer your question. The first way is to say that all of my professional experience tells me that you are presupposing the impossible. It is highly likely that we will never be able to resolve some of the most serious flaws or weaknesses in a key-recovery system, because many of them are based on human nature and many others are based on the impossibility of guaranteed security. Your hypothesis is unrealizable to the satisfaction of people who truly understand the flaky nature of our existing computer-communication infrastructure and its necessary dependence on people who may not be sufficiently trustworthy. Even with advanced algorithms for secret sharing, vulnerabilities are likely to exist in the underlying infrastructure. As I note in my written testimony, "Surprising attacks have been discovered in many security schemes thought to be virtually impenetrable." Worse yet, it is truly impossible to create a system with no vulnerabilities, and also impossible to demonstrate the absence of security flaws and vulnerabilities—even if there were none (which is itself impossible). Although some flaws can certainly be tolerated or controlled, or at least monitored for misuse, the robustness of proposed key-recovery infrastructures is unknown today, but historical evidence suggests that we approach this conservatively.

The situation reminds me of the statement that "if we had ham, we could have ham and eggs—if we had eggs"—but in a world in which there are no hens. In theory, truly secure systems are impossible. In practice, experience has shown that essentially every system has vulnerabilities that can be exploited. As a consequence, I am unable to give you the positive answer that you are seeking. Whereas the best minds in the country could design significantly better systems than we have today, those systems might very likely be implemented by developers whose bottom-line concerns would stumble on unsecure simplifications, those systems would be operated by people with inadequate awareness of the risks, the opportunities for internal fraud and abuse would exist where significant financial benefits might result, and there might even be opportunities for outsiders to penetrate the security. If you could demonstrate that all of those risks can be overcome, then you would have solved a problem that no one else has come close to solving in our entire history and that most sensible people believe cannot be solved without encountering serious risks. Certainly, there is no perfect security and neither the Government nor the nation is expecting perfect security. However, until the risks have been properly addressed—objectively, openly, and honestly—you are dealing with a powder keg. Risk-management professionals may claim that they can limit the risks to what is acceptable, but in an electronic era in which one discovered vulnerability can suddenly become amplified and massively misused, much of the would-be assurance provided by risk managers can become rapidly invalidated.

The second way to answer your question is for me to assume that my judgment is wrong, that brilliant people could succeed in designing and building a system that would provide keys only to authorized Government parties. Would I support or oppose such a system? Personally, I would still oppose it, because there is as much danger to society from the Government officially "authorizing" itself access to everyone's keys as there is from some teenager or private investigator stealing them. Attorney General John Mitchell regularly signed entire blank pads of wiretap-authorization forms, whose details were later filled in as desired by the FBI. I would not be surprised if some current Senators and Representatives have had personal experiences of being wiretapped, blackmailed, or otherwise harassed by J. Edgar Hoover. If such power is created and centralized, it will attract those who desire to abuse it. Just as Kim Philby, the Soviet spy, naturally steered his career toward high secret positions in the British government, someone who seeks to accumulate power in the U.S. would be drawn to a position where that power over others can be obtained, and where potential opponents (defenders of democratic rule) could be watched and neutralized.

REPSONSES OF PETER NEUMANN TO QUESTIONS FROM SENATOR LEAHY

Senator Leahy, your very perspicacious questions suggest that it would be helpful for me to preface my answers with a little background.

It is very important to make a careful distinction between key recovery in data storage and key recovery in communications such as telephony. It is also necessary to make a careful distinction between key recovery for decrypted information and key recovery for authentication (identity verification, integrity, digital signatures, certificates, etc.) and other purposes. I believe your questions show that you clearly understand these distinctions, but I mention this for other readers of my responses to your questions.

Question 1. Are businesses now using key-recovery encryption and, if so, for what purposes?

Answer 1. There are certainly applications in which a corporation wants to retain access to keys used by its employees for encrypting stored information—for example, to protect against death, absence, or the disgruntled-employee syndrome. Some businesses do this at present, or are considering it.

Question a. Are you aware of any businesses using key-recovery encryption for communications, including e-mail?

Answer a. For pure communications, as in computer network transmissions, faxes, and telecommunications, there has been little or no reason to retain communications keys after transmitted information has been decrypted, and no reason to provide key recovery for the transmission itself because, if the transmission is botched, it can simply be sent again—perhaps with a new set of keys. Whereas there are some businesses who have their own internal key-recovery procedures for stored data, there are few such reasons for key-recovery in communications—apart from the needs of law enforcement. The potential breaches of security resulting from having duplicate sets of one-time keys floating around create significant risks, and thus this practice entails some inherent risks. It is important to note that, whereas some companies will wish to have access to their employees' communication content, if those companies use trusted network servers that provide the encryption automatically, then the unencrypted information would be available without the need for key recovery—because that information would be available at the server in unencrypted form.

Incidentally, very few individuals and only some businesses record their own communications (phone calls, faxes, etc.). Those who do (e.g., to maintain a log of all customer transactions) would almost always be able to do so at an endpoint, where unencrypted text is available.

Encrypted e-mail blurs that distinction somewhat, in that encrypted e-mail in transit through the Internet acts as communications data, but becomes stored information when it is received. However, in various schemes such as PGP, the keys for authentication are embedded in the message itself and in the user's private keys. Having user private keys escrowed or otherwise recoverable by second or third parties is inherently dangerous, because it can completely undermine all security everywhere. Furthermore, the demand for surreptitious key access implies that perfectly innocent users might never know that their keys had been compromised—at least not until they were arrested for a masquerader's illegal actions through identity theft, or until their life savings had been stolen.

There is a corporate message recovery version of the commercial version of PGP that automatically adds a corporate key that can be used to decrypt the message. It is not intended primarily for surreptitious key access, because the installer has local control over who may be granted access—without revealing private keys. However, I have no idea who if anyone is using it, and how.

First-party key recovery: There is no need for first-party key-recovery schemes in communications (where a user holds his or her own keys), because a user could quickly rekey in the event of a lost key or a garbled transmission. However, note that first-party key recovery or key escrow tends to defeat law-enforcement desires for surreptitious access. Nevertheless, holders of their own keys could be asked to reveal their keys under court order.

Second-party key recovery: There is a possible desire for a second-party (in-house) key recovery in communications on the part of an employer who wants to be able to find out what is being transmitted. But that desire may be typically irrelevant, because the employer typically already has a right and an ability to see unencrypted messages and e-mail and can do so by gaining direct access to the computer systems involved; then, law enforcement could simply gain access to that information in its unencrypted form, with the help of the second party. So, there may not be much of a need for second-party key recovery in communications. Some companies have indicated that they might want to have this capability, although apparently most organizations have said they do not want it.

Third-party key recovery: Only a very weak case can be made for third-party key recovery for transmitted information. No sensible highly competitive business should trust a third party to hold sensitive keys that can control the survival of the company, irrespective of whether surreptitious law-enforcement access is possible. Whether or not the third party is of identifiable trustworthiness, it could be subject to bribes, coercion, and other deviations from expected behavior.

Question b. Have customers * * * expressed interest in such a key-recovery encryption product for communications?

Answer b. Although some interest has been expressed by system purveyors seeking to justify key recovery for communications (perhaps with the goal of improving the exportability of their products), there seems to be considerable conflict even within those purveyors as to the ultimate desirability and marketability—particularly in the absence of knowledge about the possible risks. On the other hand, the real customers—system users and businesses—seem not to have been particularly interested in such applications, although a few examples have been mentioned, such as uses of key recovery to enable recording of telephone conversations to detect fraud or defend against lawsuits. However, in almost all of those cases, the employer already has more convenient access to unencrypted content. In any case, the needs of such an extremely small set of hypothetical applications should not impose the large expected costs and potentially massive security risks on everyone else.

Royal Dutch Shell is the only company I can think of that has expressed such a need. In a different "customer" context, you might say that the FBI has expressed an interest in key recovery for internal communications, in its desire to use Clipper phones for its own employees. But that effort has apparently been put into deep freeze—at least for the time being.

Question c. Do you believe there will be a market for, and consumer interest in using, key-recovery encryption for communications, including for telephone communications or fax machine transmissions?

Answer. Only if no other encryption options would be available—for example, if the Government were to mandate the use of key recovery in all products with encryption. There may eventually be a viable market for encrypted telephones and fax transmissions. If products without key recovery are available, they will clearly be preferable. However, above and beyond the desires of law enforcement to restrict the marketplace to only products with key recovery, the risks of misuse such as inadvertent or malicious interception may be too great for corporations as well—which could result in the use of off-shore encryption facilities without key recovery. I do not believe that mandating inherently vulnerable cryptography is a wise approach.

Incidentally, another distinction is important, particularly with respect to communications—between communication privacy and communication integrity. The various types of mobile telephones—cellular, portable, etc.—suffer from some serious integrity problems, such as the lack of customer authentication and device authentication. Criminals can take considerable advantages of those integrity vulnerabilities as well as the privacy vulnerabilities. Both require nonsubvertible cryptography, but in different ways. Neither can afford to be subverted by key recovery.

Question 2. Do you have any estimate on how much it will cost to deploy key-recovery systems of the type that will meet law enforcement's stated specifications for access to encrypted data and communications?

Question a. How much will it cost consumers?

Question b. How much will it cost the government to oversee?

Answers 2 a and b. One of the biggest problems is that no one has any realistic estimates on either the costs to deploy or the costs to operate and administer such key-recovery systems in such a way that undesirable misuse can be controlled. Indeed, no one has succeeded in the past in developing systems that could not be misused, and there is strong evidence to suggest that will remain true in the future. However, the situation is even worse with respect to the projected future of key recovery because there are no detailed fully fledged designs for how such a key-recovery system could be soundly implemented and operated. Perhaps even more critical, however, is that no one has conducted any evaluations of the risks that might occur as a result of the misuse of such key-recovery infrastructures. That would also be very difficult today, because the risks have yet to be enumerated and analyzed. (You might wish to skim through my book, Computer-Related Risks, which gives some of the flavor of the incredible breadth of risks that must be considered and the lengths to which we must go in trying to avoid those risks.)

Question c. Have you heard about any plans by the Administration to subsidize the key-recovery system?

Answer c. I have heard some statements to that effect. It is an interesting question, particularly because William Crowell, NSA Deputy Director, and others have repeatedly stated that there won't be a single big system, that the playing field will be level, and that the Government will find a way to help the key-recovery technology along, presumably through subsidies. Because of the expected distributed nature of any key-recovery infrastructures across many corporations and governments, the coordination required, and the defensive measures that would have to be taken in attempts to defend against the risks I have outlined in my prepared statement and in our attached report (Hal Abelson, Ross Anderson, Steven M. Bellovin, Josh Benaloh, Matt Blaze, Whitfield Dime, John Gilmore, Peter G. Neumann, Ronald L. Rivest, Jeffrey I. Schiller, Bruce Schneier, "The Risks of Key Recovery, Key Escrow, and Trusted Third-Party Encryption," 27 May 1997), the Administration would have to do a lot of subsidizing.

Question 3. The Commerce Department has announced new rules to allow banks and other financial institutions to use encryption of any key length including for direct home banking software for their customers worldwide. Do customers have the same need as banks and financial institutions to protect their global communications with strong encryption?

Answer 3. Certainly. Any high-stakes commerce using the Internet will have to rely on the strongest encryption available that is not subject to compromise, subversion, and other misuse. Privacy of very sensitive databases will be very difficult to ensure in any case, but even more difficult if users cannot trust the encryption used in accessing those databases.

On the other hand, the banking community has always had special treatment, for example in its international use of the Digital Encryption Standard, DES. The big difference is that citizens and unregulated businesses have constitutional rights, whereas banking institutions do not; they are ready to disclose sensitive information at Government request—without your knowledge.

Question 4. The Administration's draft bill and now the McCain-Kerrey bill, S. 909, both tie the use of certificate authorities for digital signatures to use of key recovery for confidentiality. Under the bill, a person who gets a public-key certificate from a licensed certification authority for a digital signature and who decides to use the same public-private key pair for confidentiality, would have to store his private key with a government-licensed key-recovery agent." Is there any technical reason to tie these two uses together?

Answer 4. No. The only reason is a misguided belief that it would help law enforcement, whereas in fact it could greatly impede law enforcement and considerably increase the amount of computer-related crime using the Internet and related technologies that depend on robust authentication.

On the contrary, my prepared testimony states that any linkage of a key-recovery infrastructure with a certificate infrastructure would be a true disaster, undermining the credibility of all authentication and destroying the legal validity and operational importance of nonrepudiation. The idea of escrowing or otherwise providing surreptitious trapdoor access to authentication keys is utterly ridiculous, because it throws out the baby with the bathwater. The idea of compromising the key-management process itself by including any key-recovery mechanisms could completely undermine the integrity of every authentication and every cryptographic use—exposing them not only to authorized Government access, but to worldwide misuse by anyone from any country anywhere in the world. This is an unbelievably dangerous risk, and has not even been mentioned by any of the proponents of key recovery.

In particular, my prepared testimony from 9 July 1997 has this paragraph: "Acquisition of the master key used by an authentication service or a digital-certificate service could be devastating; worse yet, access to anyone else's public key would then be sufficient to undermine the authentication infrastructure. As a result, the significance of the authentication would *always* be suspect, and the concept of nonrepudiation would effectively go out the window. That is, anyone could justifiably throw doubts on the legitimacy of a perfectly legitimate certificate. Furthermore, recovery access to certification keys would not be likely to provide any directly discernible benefits to law enforcement with respect to either storage keys or transmission keys, unless accompanied by further restrictions on all relevant end-user products worldwide."

Question a. Could the federal government create a certification authority system that did not require the use of key recovery?

Answer a. Of course. Key recovery is not essential to certificate authorities, and indeed is completely contrary to the notion of a high-integrity certificate authority. In fact, there are already very serious intrinsic risks to the integrity of any certificate authority, and those risks would be drastically amplified by the presence of key recovery.

Question b. In your view, why is the Administration tying the two uses together?

Answer b. I can believe only that the Administration has not adequately studied the associated problems, and has followed the lead of the FBI—which has clearly not adequately studied the associated problems because it has rather simplistically decided that key recovery is its last hope in the war against cryptography, regardless of its costs and risks on the nation in every other respect. I believe that the FBI has very legitimate concerns about its future role in the presence of more widespread cryptography, but I also believe that there are many other approaches that should be considered before key recovery is perceived as the last hope. I believe it is a false hope with very serious side effects on the nation, and that it will not even achieve the FBI's desired goals. There are too many ways to avoid key recovery in the commission of a crime, or in civil disobedience by totally honest people. This approach simply will not work as hoped unless it is made mandatory—which I strongly oppose, for many reasons. (However, the Director of the FBI has said on various occasions that he would attempt to make it mandatory if that is what it takes to fulfill his mission, and the Administration and McCain-Kerrey both seem to want to jawbone the country in that direction.)

Question 5. Deputy Director Crowell states in his testimony that "the Administration has engaged various industry and international groups to further define the infrastructure concept. All agree that the emergence of KMIs [Key-Management Infrastructures] is necessary." This implies that industry groups support the Administration's vision of a linked certificate authority and key-recovery infrastructure. Is that correct?

Answer 5. You must note the distinction between (i) a key-management infrastructure, which is realistically necessary for sound electronic commerce, authentication, and any sensible use of crypto, and (ii) key recovery or key escrow, which requires some sort of exceptional key-access facility. A sensible KMI does *not* require any exceptional key access, and in fact would be potentially undermined by such a mechanism. You should also note a distinction between NSA/DoD-style key management (with absolutely no key escrow or key recovery) and a KMI that is likely to be used in electronic commerce.

It is certainly true that industry groups and foreign governments all want a sensible KMI. (For example, the Organization for Economic Cooperation and Development Cryptography Guidelines define a key management system as "a system for generation, storage, distribution, revocation, deletion, archiving, certification or application of cryptographic keys.") Encryption systems rely on reliable ways to generate keys, to publish the "public" keys so they can be used to communicate with the owner, and to store the private" keys securely. But ordinary KMIs never require users to disclose their private keys; whenever this feature" is mentioned, it is because of law enforcement demands.

Ordinary KMIs would easily out-compete escrowed KMIs that provide less security, and promise to act against the interests of their clients. Only a government-enforced requirement that users *must not* use an ordinary KMI would make these escrowed KMIs viable. Some draft British legislation on key recovery, which was widely seen as a "feeler" preceding a similar attempt in America, was one such attempt (but was opposed by the citizenry, and repudiated by the Labour party, which won the election by a considerable margin). In the United States, if the government attempts to restrict the publication of unescrowed public keys, it will likely run afoul of the First Amendment. Public keys should be published; private keys should remain private, under the full control of their owner.

However, returning directly to your question, it is *not* true that such agreement exists relating to key recovery or to any form of key management that facilitates law-enforcement access to private keys. In particular, many foreign governments (see below) have expressed strong opposition to the Administration policy for key recovery, and in particular to the requirement for linking certificate authorities and key-recovery infrastructures. This is another example of an intentionally oversimplified lumping together of concepts that are in fact quite distinct—a tendency that also occurs in the Government claim that there is a business need for key recovery (ignoring the reality that there is no real need in communications, even if there is one for storage).

As I noted in my oral testimony on 9 July 1997, the European Union released a statement on 7 July 1997 in which it disagreed strongly with the U.S. policy relating to key recovery. The EU statement followed earlier recommendations of the OECD in Paris, which earlier this year issued its own guidelines on cryptography policy. The OECD rejected endorsement of the key-escrow proposal even after extensive lobbying by Administration officials and recommended instead a policy based on voluntary, market-driven development of crypto products.

Indeed, several nations that appeared to be supportive earlier have backed off. This is the case, for example, in the U.K.—where in addition to the new government having taken an explicit anti-escrow stand in its election platform, strong opposition was more recently expressed in a Department of Trade and Industry consultation exercise; the new government has put the issue on hold. Denmark is about to announce that it will not tolerate key escrow whatever. Belgium passed an escrow law apparently to mollify the U.S., but has explicitly failed to issue the regulations necessary to put it into effect. Switzerland, Singapore, and Japan appear to be moving in a direction counter to key recovery. I suggest that your staff double-check on the truth of such statements by Deputy Director Crowell, who has said that key recovery is being received warmly abroad.

Incidentally, the systems that are favored by those supporting escrow facilities worldwide are assuming the use of identity certificates (that is, electronic identity cards) rather than the authorization certificates that electronic commerce really needs. This links in another issue that is usually considered to be very unwise, namely imposing identity cards on the citizenry—which in turn could create a massive new underground industry for forged cards and identity theft. Much greater care is necessary in understanding the deeper issues before any legislation is enacted, whether it is to support law enforcement or to protect lawful citizens.

Irrespective of who might currently support it (and I believe the U.S. Government may be fighting a losing battle on that one), the vision of linking key recovery with certificate authorities could be a true disaster for electronic commerce and more generally the integrity of everything done electronically, whether on the Internet or not.

Question 6. S. 909 would permit law enforcement to use a subpoena to obtain key-recovery information. Issuing a subpoena is a fairly simple process: no appearance before a judge is required and only a low standard of "mere relevance" need be shown to sustain the subpoena. When law-enforcement agencies obtain a decryption key, are they potentially gaining access to far more than the plain text of the targeted item? Could the key provide access to a large portion of a company's or individual's files, and the ability to decrypt past and future information?

Answer 6. It is very important to realize that key-recovery mechanisms imply a dramatic centralization of trust, even if the key-recovery facilities are distributed among different entities, and even if the keys are fragmented as is the case in Clipper. Compromise of one key-recovery authority could have enormous consequences. Compromise of a single decryption key in a single key-recovery authority might have less serious consequences—unless that key were used to unlock other systems, as is the case with worldwide master keys that are used in certain systems for electronic commerce—in which case such compromises could have truly devastating consequences worldwide.

In the context of wiretaps, something on the order of half of the taps are done at state and local levels. The signoff authority can be as low as a local prosecuting attorney or the state Attorney General's office. If this were the case in key recovery or key escrow, the requirement of merely a subpoena would further weaken the accountability of the process. There is also the pocket subpoena that has been so much trouble in the past. The subpoena process is clearly not stringent enough for key recovery and key escrow.

Question a. Do you have privacy concerns about authorizing law-enforcement access to keys on a mere subpoena?

Answer a. Absolutely. The idea that information that, under the Fifth Amendment, could not even be compelled from a defendant on the witness stand but can be easily obtained by law enforcement without even seeing a judge, is anathema to our system of civil rights. The subpoena process is so much weaker that there could be fewer qualms about key-recovery agents ignoring the authorization process altogether. But the subpoena process is vastly too weak in any event.

One of many civil-rights objections to key recovery is that it attempts to subvert the Fifth Amendment by forcing users to create second-or third-party records of their keys. The defendant (or the suspect, in a wiretapping case) would have the right under current Constitutional law to keep his or her private key private—but only if it is kept in their heads instead of on paper or in another party's control, such as a safe-deposit box. Copies on papers or computers can be obtained under a search warrant issued by a judge. Because second and third parties have no Fifth Amendment right to keep these keys private, these parties can easily be coerced into handing them over. For example, copies of your telephone bills are available to any policeman upon request, without a judge's approval. Hundreds of thousands of phone bills are obtained every year in police "fishing expeditions". Only about a thousand wiretap orders are legally conducted each year, because this requires probable cause and a judge's approval. If private keys were as easily available as phone bills, hundreds of thousands of people would have their privacy violated annually.

Question 7. Do you know whether all Department of Justice information and communication systems that use encryption meet the key-recovery requirements currently spelled out in the Commerce Department regulations for export of 56-bit DES?

Answer 7. I believe that very few if any of those systems meet those requirements. The exceptions are likely to be restricted to those developed in recent months. However, in many of the less secure systems, keys or unencrypted content can often be obtained because of software flaws in the operating systems and networking.

Question a. If so, do you know how the government is protecting the keys to the the Department's encrypted communications and files?

Answer a. The Fortezza approach keeps keys on a separate chip, so that they never appear in the operating systems. Unfortunately, even in that expensive design, the PINs go into the chip in the clear, which represents a security vulnerability. Furthermore, the keys were to be escrowed in order to enable authorized law-enforcement access. Apparently the entire Fortezza program with escrowed keys has been decommissioned.

Question b. Can you estimate the cost of bringing the Justice Department alone into compliance with these regulations?

Answer b. No, I could not begin to do that. But because of what I believe are inherent potential vulnerabilities in the key-recovery process, I also believe that it would be an enormous mistake for the Justice Department to rush into key-recovery schemes prematurely. On the other hand, the Justice Department is certainly a natural guinea pig for experimental use.

Question 8. About 24 states have already passed legislation on digital signatures, including the pioneering legislation reflected in Utah's Digital Signature Act. Vermont has similar digital signature legislation pending. Would passage of S. 909, or similar legislation establishing Federal certificate authorities preempt much of this work done on the state level, where we have traditionally left matters of commercial and contract law?

Answer 8. Yes. Even among supporters of digital signatures, there are differing opinions on how the laws should be changed to reflect this technology and supporting administrative procedures. Some people believe that legally limiting or eliminating the liability for compromised signatures will also limit or eliminate the market for such signatures. Others feel that the potential liability for compromises is so great that nobody would enter the business; consider the signature on a ten-million-dollar check, purchase order, or contract. If such a signature could be forged by subverting a low-paid employee in a certificate authority, who should bear the cost? Federalizing the response to issues such as this will prevent the natural experimentation that would occur in the fifty states, showing us the best answer as opposed to the first one to come to mind.

Question 9. The encryption bill voted on by the Commerce Committee, S. 909, creates a number of new crimes. Some of the new crimes go to the heart of the controversial linkage between the use of certificate authorities and key-recovery agents. For example, a user who gets a public-key certificate from a licensed certificate authority may use that key only as a digital signature to verify his identity even though the same key might be used to protect the privacy of encrypted personal messages. If the user uses this public-private key pair to protect privacy—for example, to encrypt his e-mail messages—under this bill, the user would be committing a crime and subject to 5 years in jail, or subject to a civil penalty of $100,000. Do you find these penalties excessive, particularly since for users the simplest way to encrypt their electronic communications is using the same encryption key they use for their digital signatures?

Answer 9. These proposed penalties are absurd, for several reasons.

First of all, and perhaps most important, any linkage between certificate infrastructures and key-recovery infrastructures is itself most unwise. See my response to your Question 4.

It is also unwise for anyone to use the same key for authentication and for encryption. In recommended usage, a private-public key pair (e.g., RSA) is used for authentication of identity, whereas different keys should be used for encrypting communications. Ideally, a different private-public key pair should be used to reach key agreement on a one-time conventional key (e.g., a symmetric encryption system such as DES) or keys (e.g., triple-DES). For example, the Diffie-Hellman algorithm can be used for the establishment of a one-time key for end-to-end conventional encryption without the actual session key ever being transmitted.

Because there are already significant risks of using the same keys for multiple purposes, stupidity and ignorance should not be punished with long jail terms and civil penalties.

Question a. What, in your view, is the purpose of stopping users—with the threat of a jail term—from using the same public-private key for which they have a public key certificate for both digital signatures and for encryption?

Answer a. Given my response to (a), there is no purpose whatsoever in stopping the rather unwise practice of multiple ("polymorphic") use of keys. It would provide law enforcement with further cryptographic attacks! However, if the intent of the would-be legislation is to stop the use of all cryptographic algorithms that do not use key recovery, then Diffie-Hellman, PGP, and many other algorithms would have to be outlawed worldwide, which is in itself absurd.

Question 10. Sections 405 and 702 of S. 909 would punish with 5 years in jail, and civil penalties of up to $100,000, violations of regulations to be issued some time in the future by the Secretary of Commerce. That is an enormous grant of power to give an appointed Executive Branch official to define what is illegal conduct in this country. Do you agree?

Answer 10. Yes.

Question a. Is there any provision in S. 909 that would bar the Secretary of Commerce from issuing regulations requiring all licensed certificate authorities to employ NSA's Digital Signature Standard (DSS) or all licensed key-recovery agents to employ the Clipper chip?

Answer a. I know of no such provision in S. 909. Generally, S. 909 is in need of considerable modifications in this and other respects noted here.

Question b. Is there any provision in S. 909 that would bar the Secretary of Commerce from requiring certificate authorities or key-recovery agents from using only those encryption algorithms or systems that have been adopted as "Federal Information Processing Standards" (FIPS)?

Answer b. I know of no such provision in S. 909. My response to 10(b) applies here as well.

Question 11. The Administration contemplates negotiating multilateral agreements to provide foreign governments with keys to the encrypted files and communications of Americans. Do you think there should be clearly defined legal standards governing the terms of these multilateral agreements so that buyers and users of key-recovery products are confident their rights will be protected?

Answer 11. This is equivalent to the classic question, "Am I still beating my wife?" First, I do not believe that such multilateral agreements can meaningfully be agreed upon worldwide that will prohibit the use of products that do not support key recovery. To do that worldwide would require enforced *mandatory* worldwide key recovery and total outlawing of all other products. Even if such agreements were reached among the democratic countries of the world, massive off-shore cryptographic centers would appear. In addition, software and hardware development might tend to migrate to other countries.

Question a. What protections, in terms of procedures and release of keys to foreign governments, should be in place in these multilateral agreements so that U.S. buyers and users of key-recovery products are [could be confident their rights will be protected?

Answer a. There are in all likelihood *no* such protections that could ensure that the rights of U.S. citizens could be protected. There can be no such protections even within the United States, even without any involvement of foreign governments. However, the intrinsic foreign governments would greatly exacerbate the problem. I will not even begin to suggest that I can come up with a because I believe that task is essentially in the presence of untrustworthy individuals and untrustable governments.

It is senseless for rapists and burglars to be put in jail for short terms, while innocent citizens, who harm no-one and who are merely protecting their own privacy, would for political reasons spend five years behind bars, or lose their life's savings. In no sense does the punishment fit the crime.

However, in addition to the philosophical objections to this provision, there is a practical objection. Modern key-agreement protocols never use the citizen's long-term keys for encryption, only for signature. Yet these protocols still produce an encrypted connection that cannot be compromised. The user would be using signature keys for their intended purpose—to verify his or her identity, but the result would be the full protection of privacy. An example of such a key-agreement protocol is the Station-to-Station protocol invented at Northern Telecom by Whitfield Diffie and others.

In order to prevent such uses of signature keys, the Government would have to outlaw the use of entire branches of cryptography. This would have a serious impact on First Amendment protected cryptographic research, as well as being realistically unenforceable. I believe that the worldwide research and civil-rights communities would furthermore work hard to undermine such a ban—for example, by writing and releasing free software that gets around it, and by researching alternative ways to provide privacy even under the imposed restrictions. PGP itself was written and given away free for exactly this purpose, while the Senate was considering a bill that would have required that the plaintext of encrypted communications be made available to law enforcement. Several papers at the Crypto '97 conference in August 1997 were presented by researchers inspired by Government attempts to subvert the cryptographic infrastructure, such as the Clipper and Fortezza initiatives. A Congress alarmed by the decline in respect for law would do well to avoid passing laws that would get no respect.

Question 12. Do you believe that certificate authorities, merely because they are registered with the [U.S.] government, should receive total immunity from all noncontractual liability, as provided in S. 909?

Answer 12. The immunity clause is presumably included in S. 909 primarily as a jawboning mechanism in an attempt to coerce all would-be certificate authorities to go along with key recovery. I think the granting of total immunity would lead to enormous opportunities for fraud and misuse on the part of people associated with the certificate authorities, which must be even further beyond reproach than most existing financial institutions.

Granting any party immunity from liability is an immense gift. Would Congress grant me immunity from all noncontractual civil suits? Could I violate patents and copyrights with impunity? Could I slander and libel at will? Do I just have to give the Government copies of all my customers' private keys in order to get these privileges? In many ways it sounds like commissioning a privateer, a Government-sanctioned pirate on the high seas.

Although not directly relevant to the question of immunity, the mere creation of domestic certificate authorities whose key holding may not be completely trustworthy could encourage the existence of untrustworthy off-shore certificate services, whose identities might appear to be totally equivalent to any approved authority, because of the inherent flakiness of the existing computer-communication infrastructure and its likely successors—even in the presence of apparently legitimate certificate authorities.

Question 13. Should certificate authorities [that] are not registered with the government, and their customers, be denied the same protections from federal law-enforcement abuse offered in S. 909 only to those who use registered certificate authorities?

Answer 13. This is another "Are you still beating your wife?" question. I believe that S. 909 is totally misconceived in trying to jawbone certificate authorities into enabling key recovery. I have already stated that the linkage is in and of itself enormously risky; see my response to your Question 4. Therefore, I do not believe that anyone should be granted blanket immunity.

Question 14. Is the STU–III classified telephone system based on a key-recovery system? If S. 909 becomes law, and all government communication systems, and equipment purchased with government funds, are required to use key-recovery systems, will the STU–III classified telephone system have to be replaced? Could you explain?

Answer 14. It is my understanding that the STU–III and other NSA-developed high-security encryption devices intentionally do *not* use any key-recovery schemes, precisely because the risks of compromise by untrustworthy persons and untrustworthy computer systems would be vastly increased. Indeed, technical measures are taken to ensure that no copy of any key is *ever* accessible outside of the phones, precisely to avoid the danger of compromise by such persons. The risks of key compromise are already great enough—as seen by various past breaches of classified security—without introducing the enormously greater potential risks of key recovery.

The Department of Defense already uses a variety of highly classified encryption devices (e.g., KG boxes) whose key-generation algorithms are vastly more secure than anything that is possible in the presence of key-recovery mechanisms. If the key is lost, the systems are rekeyed. The presence of a key-recovery facility in those systems that are intended to be as secure as possible would totally undermine their security. Thus, NSA and the Department of Defense must laugh in the face of S. 909 and ignore key-recovery mechanisms altogether for such devices. Key access to KG boxes and STU–III systems could totally undermine their intended security. However, note that new-key generation (rekeying) is always possible. Please realize that the mere existence of a trapdoor necessary for key recovery suggests that such a trapdoor may be exploitable by people other than those who are supposedly authorized to use it.

This suggests how absurd things are becoming. The U.S. Government can certainly use any key-recovery, key-escrow, or key-management scheme it wants, for its own purposes. However, in my opinion it would be very foolish to do have a trapdoored key-recovery system whenever secrecy is really critical.

RESPONSE OF PETER NEUMANN TO QUESTION FROM SENATOR FEINSTEIN

Question 1. There have been some very legitimate privacy concerns expressed by speakers today. What additional privacy could be lost by providing law-enforcement access to encrypted phone calls and electronic mail?

Answer 1. Senator Feinstein, Thank you for your recognition of the privacy concerns expressed by the second panel. They are indeed very profound and quite insidious. It was unfortunate that you were not able to attend the second panel in person, but from the nature of your question, I trust that your staffers did an excellent job of briefing you afterwards.

One of the most serious potential risks with covert and surreptitious law-enforcement access to arbitrary communications and stored information involves the risks of misuse of that access. The existing process of judicial warrants does impose some restraints, but the relatively unencumbered use of subpoenas as proposed by McCain-Kerrey is an open invitation to misuse. However, even if legal law-enforcement access could be rigidly controlled (for example, with warrants equivalent to those required in wiretaps), essentially all computer-communication systems can be subverted by means that lie outside of normally expected access—for example, exploiting trapdoors and planting Trojan horses that guarantee unmonitored access, or simply misuse by authorized insiders. In all my years of analyzing system security, I have never found a system whose security could not be broken—and often broken in ways that would not be detected or traced to the culprit. Key recovery is in essence a monster potential trapdoor. Passing laws that make misuse illegal do not stop the exploitation of fundamentally weak systems, especially across foreign boundaries.

The notion of privacy in the context of your question is usually considered in a way that is significantly too narrow. We must also consider the very serious implications of the consequences of (i) reuse of information beyond its intended use, (ii) the propagating effects of incorrect or intentionally false information, and (iii) the risks of identity theft. My book, Computer-Related Risks (Senators Hatch and Leahy both have copies), is full of examples of these serious threats to human well-being. For example, (i) a master key might be used far beyond the intended purpose of one-time surveillance; (ii) there are numerous cases of false arrest resulting from incorrect data or misidentifications; (iii) in quite a few cases, actions of masqueraders have actually caused their victims to be arrested, in some cases after their life savings and pensions had been stolen.

To illustrate the point that government databases have been abused and government employees have been guilty of serious misuses of computer systems, here are just a few examples involving motor vehicle bureaus, the IRS, and the Social Security Administration. Employees of the Virginia DMV created and sold thousands of fraudulent drivers' licenses. Actress Rebecca Schaeffer was murdered by someone who had acquired her address from DMV records. A former Arizona law-enforcement officer tracked down and killed his ex-girifriend based on information friends that some of his friends extracted from government databases. Employees of the Social Security Administration sold internal database information (including Social Security Numbers and mothers' maiden names) of more than 11,000 people to a credit-card fraud ring, which then used the information to activate newly issued Citibank credit cards that had been stolen. An IRS employee was accused of giving tax data on judges and jurors to a defendant. Various IRS employees have been indicted for fraud. These are just a few of the cases documented in the archives of the Risks Forum and in my RISKS book.

Perhaps most threatening of all is that the FBI's demand for easily misused surreptitious key access implies that perfectly innocent users might never know that their keys had been compromised, with many possible adverse consequences.

One other issue deserves your consideration. Privacy is an international problem; each nation has its own notions of what must be protected and what penalties might be incurred for violators. Similarly, computer-communication security is an international problem, and cannot be solved nationally. Significant international cooperation must be involved. Creating a national key-recovery infrastructure in the absence of consideration of the international issues is itself a risky business—for a wide variety of reasons. Attempting to create an international key-recovery infrastructure is a truly imposing task, and raises the issue of having to trust potentially untrustworthy agents and governments with keys.

The following two paragraphs are taken directly from my prepared testimony (with the inclusion of the reference to the GAO report).

"Key-recovery infrastructures could greatly increase the opportunities for insider fraud, malice, and other misuse within governmental organizations. There are various reports of insider misuse of FBI and other law-enforcement databases. For example, House testimony from Laurie E. Ekstrand of the GAO documents 62 cases of misuses of law-enforcement computer data. Similar misuse has been discovered in other Government offices, such as Social Security Administration employees selling information to enable the activation of 11,000 credit cards stolen from the mail, and IRS employees leaking tax information and altering records. It is clearly unwise to assume that our Government is totally benevolent and incapable of illegal actions." [The cited GAO report is: National Crime Information Center—Legislation Needed to Deter Misuse of Criminal Justice Information, U.S. General Accounting Office testimony before the U.S. House of Representatives Subcommittee on Information, Justice, Agriculture, and Transportation, of the Committee on Government Operations, and the Subcommittee on Civil and Constitutional Rights, of the Committee on the Judiciary, 28 July 1993.]

The potential risks of misuse of key-recovery infrastructures extend far into our social structure. Loss of privacy can often result in serious consequences to individuals. (In addition, retrieval of incorrect data can have damaging results on the individuals involved, although that is true whether or not the information is encrypted.) Constitutional issues are also at risk, such as protection against unreasonable search and seizure. If on-line infrastructures for key recovery are to use existing commercial systems, they may be seriously lacking in confidentiality, integrity, accountability, and assurance."

It is very important to realize that key-recovery mechanisms imply a dramatic centralization of trust, even if the key-recovery facilities are distributed among different entities, and even if the keys are fragmented as is the case in Clipper. Compromise of one key-recovery authority could have enormous consequences. Compromise of a single decryption key in a single key-recovery authority might have less serious consequences—unless that key were used to unlock other systems, as is the case with worldwide master keys that are used in certain systems for electronic commerce—in which case such compromises could have truly devastating consequences worldwide.

By the way, you must be aware of the importance of electronic commerce to the computer industry. The bottom-line reason for good security and nonsubvertible crypto is economics. The vast sums of money that will be protected by such systems are sufficient to entice and induce corruption. A key purchased illegally from a recovery site could be very inexpensive relative to the profits that could be gained.

Forged warrants, bogus subpoenas, dishonest insiders, criminals impersonating law-enforcement officials, and many other modes of misuse have occurred and will continue to occur. However, the existence of single points of vulnerability greatly compounds the problems—and greatly increases the likelihood of misuse. A German lawyer involved in the opposition to key recovery in Germany has stated that "trust structures in the electronic world should as far as possible mirror relationships in existing practice." The opportunity to gain electronic access to massive numbers of keys and massive amounts of sensitive information without proper authorization is truly a disaster waiting to happen.

The existence of a trapdoor that can be used surreptitiously in widespread computer-communication systems is an open invitation to an enormous range of potential misuses. Hopes of avoiding those misuses would have to rely in part on the security of the key-recovery infrastructure, which is very likely to be flawed—despite anything you may hear to the contrary. (Surprising attacks have been discovered in many security schemes thought to be virtually impenetrable. Indeed, serious system security flaws are common in all computer systems, and have plagued essentially every computer system I have ever had the pleasure to analyze.) But more importantly, those hopes of avoiding misuses would have to rely on the impeccable trustworthiness of an unfortunately large number of people who might either misuse their legitimate access or find a way to acquire clandestine unauthorized access to the keys (for example, because of inherent flaws in the system security). In essence, what is advertised as law-enforcement access could easily become subject to extensive misuse, even in the presence of supposedly restrictive administrative procedures.

RESPONSES OF THE NATIONAL SECURITY AGENCY TO QUESTIONS FROM SENATOR THURMOND

Question 1. Isn't it the duty of the Congress to balance the interests of business against the interests of national security in many areas, and shouldn't we do the same thing regarding encryption?

Answer 1. Congress and the Executive Branch should work together with substantial input from affected industry and users to develop a balanced national encryption policy that promotes electronic commerce. The widespread use of strong encryption, while continuing to protect public safety and national security, is essential to U.S. success.

Question 2. What specific steps should the Congress take to encourage the development of key management infrastructure (KMI), such as through limiting liability of registered certificate authorities?

Answer 2. Congress should pass legislation that provides a variety of incentives that promote the development of trustworthy KMIs. Such legislation should, at a minimum, address issues of liability limitations, privacy, and promote the intangible but pivotal aspect of "trust."

RESPONSES OF THE NATIONAL SECURITY AGENCY TO QUESTIONS FROM SENATOR GRASSLEY

Question 1. How would you suggest Congress address the problem of criminals misusing encryption?

Answer 1. NSA defers to the Department of Justice and the FBI on the issue of criminal activity.

Question 2. In terms of analyzing how difficult it is to unscramble text which has been encrypted with strong encryption, why should we look to the "brute force" method? Are there other, more sophisticated ways of cracking encryption other than "brute force" attacks which are perhaps quicker and more efficient? If so, why don't we use those measures to determine at what level encryption becomes so strong that law enforcement concerns are implicated?

Answer 2. When properly implemented (i.e., the encryption is based on a mathematically sound algorithm and care is taken to achieve a high-quality implementation), encryption can only be exploited by brute force attacks or by those who hold the key. In the absence of a weak implementation (either in design or construction) there is no "silver bullet." It should be noted as well that a continuous part of the cryptologic effort is to search for flaws in encryption systems, including those systems that are generally presumed to be without exploitable flaws. As a consequence, many of the techniques available to attack powerful encryption systems are especially sensitive and may only be discussed in a classified setting.

Question 3. Why doesn't law enforcement just let NSA break encryption for law enforcement purposes when necessary?

Answer 3. It is not feasible for NSA to "break encryption" on demand because it takes too long to be able to meet the timeliness requirements of law enforcement and the measures needed to protect NSA sources and methods often complicate criminal investigations and prosecutions.

For example, when law enforcement encounters an encrypted phone call, they often need to know the content immediately. Brute force attacks against strong encryption can take months (e.g., a recent publicized brute force attack against 56 bit encryption took 96 days to break one message using ~78,000 computers on the Internet) or be impossible (a brute force attack against 128-bit encryption would require ~8.6 trillion times the age of the universe for one message). Attacks using other-than-brute-force methods can take months to develop against a typical target.

Question 4. If encryption becomes commonplace in criminal cases, is NSA realistically in a position to lend assistance in all those cases without being distracted from its primary mission?

Answer 4. NSA is not funded/staffed to provide a substantially increased level of support to law enforcement. Furthermore, if widespread, unregulated, and highly sophisticated encryption is used world-wide, NSA's challenges will be significantly increased in all respects, not just the law enforcement support component.

Question 5. My understanding of your concern is that for the unscrambled text to be admissible in evidence in a trial, the government has to provide the jury with an explanation of how the puzzle was solved. This would involve revealing some of the most sensitive secrets that this government has in a public trial. That being the case, is it fair to say that even though you would like to help law enforcement, the national security concerns severely limit what you can do for them?

Answer 5. The measures needed to protect them in court often complicate criminal investigations and prosecutions. It is correct, then, that national security concerns may severely limit the assistance we may provide to law enforcement.

Question 6. Can't people already buy 128-bit encryption right now? Doesn't that mean that the "genie is out of the bottle" as the proponents of strong encryption like to say? Is it the case that it's too late for the government to act?

Answer 6. Although high grade encryption is becoming more readily available, at this point is not very widely used. This provides us the imperative as well as opportunity to influence the coming use in a way that is favorable to the needs of all concerned, including the U.S. business community, law enforcement, and the national security community.

Further, it is important to distinguish between the advertised capabilities of a given product, and the quality of the implementation. It is extremely difficult to achieve a high quality implementation of a given encryption scheme. As a consequence, there are few genuinely strong encryption products available for use outside of those regulated by governments around the world.

Responses of the National Security Agency to Questions From Senator Feinstein

Question 1. I know that our national security requires that our intelligence gathering agencies have access to or possess the keys to many foreign encryption systems. Potentially, what would have to happen in your agency to respond to a world filled with inexpensive, easily available, highly complex encryption systems?

Answer 1. NSA's strategy for some time has included addressing the potential situation of what has been called "ubiquitous encryption." NSA expects very high-grade encryption programs to eventually be used world-wide. We are trying hard to meet this challenge and we are doing our best to develop new methods to meet this serious threat to our nation's security.

Question 2. U.S. companies may export 64-bit technology only if they have pledged to develop key recovery products for export within two years. (1) What good is developing the technology to decode encrypted messages when you already have a non-key recovery system in use? (2) Why would I want to, as a user, voluntarily allow for the decoding of my encrypted data?

Answer 2. The Administration's export policy enables commercial key recovery products of any strength to immediately be licensed for export. In recognition of the fact that industry would like to export 56-bit DES, 56-bit or equivalent strength encryption can be licensed for export during 1997–98 so long as the exporter has a valid business plan to produce key recovery products.

The two-year interim policy that allows companies to export non-key recovery technology is appropriate because it allows the export of stronger encryption immediately and gives industry the time it needs to develop key recovery products.

The interim export of 56-bit products is not expected to seriously undermine the long-term key recovery initiative since it is expected that consumers will soon demand higher-strength products that will displace the 56-bit exports. Those higher-strength products will be required to support key recovery. In addition, there is a growing market demand for key recovery encryption products which will displace non-key recovery products.

Both private and corporate users will likely want a means of decoding their encrypted data in circumstances when they have lost their encryption key. This will create a market demand for key recovery-based encryption products. For a user, key recovery is like an insurance policy. If you lose your key, you can recover easily from the loss. Without key recovery, you cannot recover the information. This insurance policy is invaluable to an individual or company who loses the key to a critical file that was encrypted. It is valuable for a corporation that wants to preserve its access to company data created, manipulated by its employees. For example, with key recovery encryption corporations could not be held hostage to by a disgruntled employee who sabotages company files by encrypting valuable company information. without key recovery, encryption can become an electronic shredder.

RESPONSES OF THE NATIONAL SECURITY AGENCY TO QUESTIONS FROM SENATOR LEAHY

Question 1. What are the results, if any, of any of the ten key recovery pilot projects that the government is sponsoring? (i) When do you expect to get results about how well key recovery systems work and how much they cost, at least at the pilot program scale? (ii) If we were to pass the sweeping key recovery legislation, such as the bill, S. 909, reported by the Commerce Committee would we be moving ahead precipitously when we do not even have in hand the results of pilot projects on whether these systems will work?

Answer 1. The ten key management pilot projects sponsored by the government in conjunction with private sector participants are still being conducted, but initial results suggest that key recovery is a useful and workable approach for a variety of applications. We expect more detailed information to be available in about 60 days.

No, we would not be moving ahead precipitously. Several companies are already selling secure key recovery products. 80+ companies have already built products that support key recovery or are members in the Key Recovery Alliance who are also working on this technique.

Question 2. Is there any technical reason to tie together the use of a digital signature and confidentiality protection to one public key certificate?

Answer 2. There is no reason to tie digital signatures and confidentiality to a single public key certificate. The administration does not propose to do this, does NOT have a requirement to escrow signature keys, and continues to actively advocate against this type of escrow.

Question 3. Could the federal government create a Certification Authority system that did not require the use of key recovery?

Answer 3. Yes. The administration position does not require the use of key recovery. Moreover, the administration is relying on the private sector to develop a public key infrastructure that includes certificate authorities. Certificate Authority services are an integral part of a key management infrastructure. They would not necessarily perform key recovery. Certificate Authorities certify the authenticity of keys used for encryption and keys used for digital signature.

Question 4. Why is the administration tying the two uses together?

Answer 4. The administration is not tying the use of digital signatures and confidentiality with key recovery. This is a misunderstanding since the government does NOT have a requirement to escrow signature keys, and we continue to actively advocate against this type of escrow.

Question 5. Is the Administration tying the use of encryption for digital signature purposes to the use for confidential purposes in order to encourage the domestic uses of key recovery systems?

Answer 5. The administration is not tying the use of digital signatures to the use of cryptography confidentiality purposes. Neither does Title IV, Section 402 of S. 909, which states that registration with a Certificate Authority does not require the storage with a third party, information used solely for purpose of digital signature.

Question 6. Which industry groups or companies support the Administration's proposal to link key recovery and certification authority functions in one infrastructure?

Answer 6. We cannot state authoritatively the positions of outside groups. However, some major companies have formed business ventures to thrive within the new climate of the KMI initiative. In October 1996, IBM formed the Key Recovery Alliance and that alliance has grown to over 50 domestic and international companies. Alliance members include Apple, Mitsubishi, Boeing, DEC, Hewlett Packard, Motorola, Novell, SUN, America Online, Unisys, and RSA.

Question 7. How do you respond to the critique that the key recovery system envisioned by the Administration will not work because it assumes that we can handle millions of public-private key pairs and billions of recoverable session keys across thousands of different products?

Answer 7. The key recovery service that individuals will want—and that nation's public safety officials will need—will evolve in a decentralized, scalable manner. There are over 30 different methods to perform key recovery; vendors and users can select from any of these methods depending on their applications or needs. A key management infrastructure with key recovery will enable encryption to be used widely, securely, and with confidence.

Question 8. Can the Administration's key recovery system scale to hundreds of millions of users generating billions of keys?

Answer 8. We are relying on the private sector to develop decentralized, scalable KMI and key recovery services. The true potential of encryption will not be realized without KMIs such as that proposed by the Administration.

Question 9. How is DOMESTIC electronic commerce (which includes DOMESTIC public key infrastructure and certificate authorities) an NSA issue?

Answer 9. NSA's role is that of a technical advisor. For decades, NSA has been the nation's center of cryptographic expertise. NSA plays an important role in using cryptography to produce the safeguards that control our nuclear arsenal, enable our military commanders and policy makers to communicate securely anywhere in the world, and provide our intelligence customers with vital information to support U.S. interests. It is important for the nation's encryption policy makers to base their decisions on the best possible technical advise from the nation's experts, NSA.

Question 10. (a) Is the STU–III classified telephone system based on a key recovery system? (b) Under the provisions of S. 909, would the STU–III system have to replaced?

Answer 10. No. The STU–III telephone system is not based on a key recovery system.

There are already plans in effect to stop production on the STU–III phones to be replaced with the STE, the next version of the STU–III. The STE phones are currently being tested with different algorithms to successfully allow key recovery in the STEs. Commercial solutions for key recovery in the STE phones is also being researched.

RESPONSES OF THE COMMERCE DEPARTMENT TO QUESTIONS FROM SENATOR LEAHY

Question 14. Sections 405 and 702 of S. 909, would punish with 5 years in jail, and civil penalties of up to $100,000, violations of regulations to be issued sometime in the future by the Secretary of Commerce. That is an enormous grant of power to give an appointed executive branch official to define what is illegal conduct in this country. (i) Do you agree?

Answer 14. No. The grant of rulemaking authority, such as that in S. 909, is not unusual in U.S. law. Moreover, such rulemaking authority is not unfettered. It is circumscribed by the provisions and purposes of the law being implemented and, of course, is subject to oversight and challenge through various means. In addition, the imposition of criminal penalties requires a criminal trial with the attendant constitutional and legal protections.

The pertinent provisions of S. 909 are similar to those contained in the Export Administration Act of 1979 (EAA) which, with its predecessor laws, has been the basis for export controls on dual-use items for close to 50 years. As in S. 909, the EAA authorizes the Secretary of Commerce to issue regulations to implement the objectives of the EAA to protect the national security and further U.S. foreign policy interests, subject to the provisions and purposes of the law. The Export Administration Regulations (EAR) implement the EAA and set forth all the requirements that are imposed on the exporting community, including licensing, recordkeeping, and other requirements. The EAA provides criminal penalties for violations of the law and the EAR of up to 10 years imprisonment and a $250,000 fine for individuals, and up to $1,000,000 for corporations. The EAA also authorizes administrative penalties of up to $100,000 per violation.

Question (ii). Has the Administration drafted any of these regulations to give Congress some idea of what conduct the Secretary of Commerce might criminalize?

Answer (ii). No. Should S. 909 become law, the Department would start the process of drafting regulations consistent with the provisions and objectives of the law. This process normally includes one or more opportunities for public comment before the regulations become effective.

Question (iii). Is there any provision in S. 909 that would bar the Secretary of Commerce from issuing regulations requiring all licensed certificate authorities to employ NSA's digital signature standard (DSS) or all licensed key recovery agents to employ clipper chip?

Answer (iii). Section 207 of S. 909 bars the United States Government from mandating the use of encryption standards for the private sector other than for systems and networks of United States Government, or systems created using Federal funds. Moreover, we are not aware of any provision in S. 909 that would authorize the Secretary of Commerce to compel licensed key recovery agents to use specific technology, Including the clipper chip, by regulation or otherwise. A regulation that required the use of any specific standard or technology by private persons would be inconsistent with the provisions and purposes of S. 909.

Question (iv). Is there any provision in S. 909 that would bar the Secretary of Commerce from requiring certificate authorities or Key Recovery Agents from using only those encryption algorithms or systems that have been adopted as "Federal Information Processing Standards" or FIPS?

Answer (iv). See response to (iii), above.

ADDITIONAL SUBMISSION FOR THE RECORD

PREPARED STATEMENT OF STEPHEN T. WALKER

Trusted Information Systems, Inc. (TIS), headquartered in Glenwood, Maryland, specializes in research, product development, and consulting in the fields of computer and communications security. We hereby submit these comments for the record to assist the committee during the consideration of S. 909, The Secure Public Networks Act of 1997.

Cryptography is an enabling technology that is absolutely essential in order to realize the promise of electronic commerce. However, this extraordinarily useful tool has the capability to deprive information owners of access to their own information (in the event an encryption key is lost or damaged), and to seriously impact the law enforcement and national security missions of governments around the world. We as a nation have been struggling to find a solution to this dilemma that meets users' needs to protect sensitive information and governments' needs to have lawful access to encrypted data.

TIS believes that a resolution to this issue could be achieved through the use of user controlled key recovery techniques. To that end, TIS developed RecoverKey™ Key Recovery Technology: a scaleable, flexible method forusers to obtain emergency access to their own encryption keys.

RecoverKey™ implementations using Triple-DES and 128-bit encryption keys where users control all access to their keys have already been approved for export. TIS is currently the only company to have received approval to export general purpose cryptographic products using a qualified system of key recovery.

Since the early 1990's, TIS has advocated an encryption policy that balances the needs of users, businesses and governments. S. 909, The Secure Public Networks Act of 1997, attempts to achieve this objective. While there are many necessary and useful provisions in S. 909, the bill seeks to link the use of encryption key recovery technology to a Government licensed key management infrastructure. TIS believes that this linkage is both unnecessary and ill-advised.

User-controlled key recovery can and does work with any public key infrastructure. However, the use of key recovery should not be a pre-condition to participation in such an infrastructure. Accordingly, the provisions of S. 909, which either create a de-facto domestic requirement for key recovery, or which otherwise require or encourage the linkage between key recovery and certification authorities should be removed.

Removal of these provisions will enable the bill to address only those issues that permit and encourage a robust market for encryption products and technologies with user-controlled key recovery features.

TIS believes that this linkage between key recovery and certification authorities is the most significant issue before the Committee with respect to S. 909. However, there are additional issues that should also be addressed in the context of the Committee's consideration of the bill. Should the Committee desire any additional information from TIS regarding these issues, TIS would be pleased to provide it.

TIS hereby offers the attached specific modifications to S. 909 that reflect the above considerations.

SUGGESTED MODIFICATIONS TO
S. 909: THE SECURE PUBLIC NETWORKS ACT OF 1997

TITLE I -DOMESTIC USES OF ENCRYPTION

SEC. 101. LAWFUL USE OF ENCRYPTION.

Except as otherwise provided by this Act or otherwise provided by law, it shall be lawful for any person within ~~any State~~ **THE UNITED STATES** to use, **MAKE OR SELL** any encryption, regardless of encryption algorithm selected, encryption key length chosen, or implementation technique or medium used.

SEC. 103. VOLUNTARY PRIVATE SECTOR PARTICIPATION IN KEY MANAGEMENT STRUCTURE.

The participation of ~~the~~ private persons in ~~the~~ **ANY** key management infrastructure ~~enabled by this Act~~ is voluntary.

SEC. 104. UNLAWFUL USE OF ENCRYPTION

Whoever knowingly encrypts data or communications in furtherance of the commission of a criminal offense for which the person may be prosecuted in a court of competent jurisdiction and may be sentenced to a term of imprisonment of more than one year **MAY**, in addition to any penalties for the underlying criminal offense, be fined under title 18, United States Code, or imprisoned not more than five years, or both, for a first conviction or fined under title 18, United States Code, or imprisoned not more than ten years, or both, for a second or subsequent conviction. The mere use of encryption shall not constitute probable cause to believe that a crime is being or has been committed.

SEC. 105. PRIVACY PROTECTION.

(a) In General. It shall be unlawful for any person to intentionally --

....

(5) impersonate, **OR OTHERWISE ASSUME THE IDENTITY OF** another person for the purpose of obtaining recovery information of that person without lawful authority;

SEC. 106. ACCESS TO ENCRYPTED ~~MESSAGES~~ INFORMATION BY GOVERNMENT ENTITIES

(2) LAWFUL PURPOSES - A key recovery agent, whether or not registered by the Secretary under this Act, shall disclose recovery information:

(a) To a government entity ~~if~~ **PROVIDED** that entity is authorized to use the recovery information **AND USES THE RECOVERY INFORMATION ONLY** to determine the plaintext of **THAT** information it has obtained or is obtaining pursuant to a duly-authorized warrant or court order, a subpoena authorized by Federal or State statute or rule, a certification issued by the Attorney General under the Foreign Intelligence Surveillance Act, or other lawful authority; or

SEC. 107. CIVIL RECOVERY.

(a) IN GENERAL. -- Except as otherwise provided in this Act, any person described in subsection (b) may in a civil action recover from the United States Government the actual damages suffered by the person as result of a violation described in that subsection, a reasonable attorney's fee, and other litigation costs reasonably incurred.

ACTUAL DAMAGES ARE DIFFICULT TO QUANTIFY IN THE INVASION OF PRIVACY CONTEXT. A PUNITIVE DAMAGE PROVISION MUST BE INCLUDED FOR THIS SECTION TO BE MEANINGFUL.

b) COVERED PERSONS. Subsection (a) applies to any person --

(1) whose recovery information is knowingly obtained without lawful authority by an agent of the United States Government from a key recovery agent ~~or certificate authority registered under this Act~~;

(2) whose recovery information is obtained by an agent of the United States Government with lawful authority from a key recovery agent ~~or certificate authority registered under this Act~~ and is knowingly used or disclosed without lawful authority; or

(3) whose recovery information is obtained by an agent of the United States Government with lawful authority from a key recovery agent ~~or certificate authority registered under this Act~~ and is used to publicly disclose decrypted information without lawful authority.

TITLE II -- GOVERNMENT PROCUREMENT

–THIS TITLE SHOULD BE DELETED ALTOGETHER, AS IT IS QUITE CONTROVERSIAL, AND ITS IMPLEMENTATION WILL BE QUITE PROBLEMATIC. HOWEVER, IF IT MUST REMAIN, NOTE CLARIFYING MODIFICATIONS BELOW:

SEC. 202. FEDERAL PURCHASES OF ENCRYPTION PRODUCTS.

Any encryption product purchased or otherwise procured by the United States Government for use in secure government networks shall ~~be based on~~ **INCORPORATE** a qualified system of key recovery.

SEC. 203. ENCRYPTION PRODUCT PURCHASED WITH FEDERAL FUNDS.

Any encryption product purchased directly with Federal funds for use in secure public networks shall ~~be based on~~ **INCORPORATE** a qualified system of key recovery.

SEC. 204. UNITED STATES GOVERNMENT NETWORKS.

Any communications network established by the United States Government after the date of enactment of this Act which uses encryption products as part of the network shall use encryption products ~~based on~~ **WHICH INCORPORATE** a qualified system of key recovery.

SEC. 205. NETWORKS ESTABLISHED WITH FEDERAL FUNDS.

Any encrypted communications network established after the date of enactment of this Act with the use of Federal funds shall use encryption products ~~based on~~ **WHICH INCORPORATE** a qualified system of key recovery.

OR SIMILAR LANGUAGE TO INCORORATE THIS CONCEPT INTO THE FRIST AMENDMENT TO SECTION 205.

SEC. 206. PRODUCT LABELS.

DELETE THIS SECTION IN ITS ENTIRETY.

TITLE III -- EXPORT OF ENCRYPTION

SEC. 301. THE DEPARTMENT OF COMMERCE.

The Secretary of Commerce in consultation with other relevant executive branch agencies shall have jurisdiction over the export **AND REEXPORT** of commercial encryption products. The Secretary shall have the sole duty to issue export licenses on**, AND LICENSE EXCEPTIONS FOR** commercial encryption products.

SEC. 302. LICENSE EXCEPTION NON-KEY RECOVERY.

Exports **AND REEXPORTS** of encryption products up to and including 56 bit DES or equivalent strength shall be exportable under a license exception, following a one time review, provided the encryption product being exported –

(1) is otherwise qualified for export;

. . .

(b) the country to which the encryption product is to be exported OR **REEXPORTED** is otherwise qualified to receive the encryption product.

SEC. 303. PRESIDENTIAL ORDER.

The President may by executive order increase the encryption strength for encryption products which may be exported **AND REEXPORTED** under section 302 of this Act. The encryption strength for encryption products which may be exported **AND REEXPORTED** under section 302 of this Act shall be reviewed by the President on an annual basis. Consistent with other provisions of this Title and Section 901 of this Act, the President shall take such action as necessary to increase the encryption strength for encryption products which may be exported **AND REEXPORTED** if similar products are determined by the President to be widely available for export from other Nations.

SEC. 304. LICENSE EXCEPTION FOR KEY RECOVERY.

Encryption products may be exported **AND REEXPORTED** under a license exception, following a one time review without regard to the encryption algorithm selected or encryption key length chosen when such encryption product is based on, **INCORPORATES, OR FACILITATES** a qualified system of key recovery, provided, the encryption product being exported **OR REEXPORTED** –

(1) is otherwise qualified for export;

. . .

(b) the country to which the encryption product is to be exported OR **REEXPORTED** is otherwise qualified to receive the encryption product.

SEC. 308. CRIMINAL PENALTIES.

DELETE SECTION. IT IS ALREADY A CRIME TO EXPORT IN VIOLATION OF THE LAW.

TITLE IV -- VOLUNTARY REGISTRATION SYSTEM

LINKING KEY RECOVERY PROVISIONS TO CERTIFICATE AUTHORITY PROVISIONS IS UNNECESSARY AND ILL-ADVISED. ACCORDINGLY ALL REFERENCES TO CERTIFICATE AUTHORITY REGISTRATION (SEC. 401, 402, 404, 405 AND 407) SHOULD BE DELETED. THE CONSUMER PROTECTION PROVISIONS OF SEC. 406 SHOULD BE PRESERVED.

IN ADDITION, REGISTRATION OF KEY RECOVERY AGENTS (SEC. 403) SHOULD BE VOLUNTARY AND OPTIONAL.

TITLE V – LIABILITY LIMITATIONS

THE "SAFE HARBOR" PROVISIONS SHOULD NOT EXTEND ONLY TO THOSE KEY RECOVERY AGENTS THAT REGISTER. ANY KEY RECOVERY AGENT SHOULD BE ENTITLED TO THE SAME PROTECTIONS.

SEC. 502. COMPLIANCE DEFENSE.

Compliance with the provisions of this Act and the regulations thereunder is a complete defense for ~~certificate authorities and~~ key recovery agents ~~registered under this Act~~ to any noncontractual civil action for damages based upon activities regulated by this Act.

SEC. 503. REASONABLE CARE DEFENSE.

The use by any person of a ~~certificate authority or~~ key recovery agent ~~registered under this Act~~ shall be treated as evidence of reasonable care or due diligence in any judicial or administrative proceeding where the reasonableness of the selection of the ~~authority or~~ agent~~, as the case may be~~, or of encryption products, is a material issue.

SEC. 506. CIVIL ACTION

Civil action may be brought against a key recovery agent~~, a certificate authority~~ or other person who violates or acts in a manner which is inconsistent with this Act.

TITLE VI -- INTERNATIONAL AGREEMENTS

The President shall conduct negotiations with other countries for the purpose of mutual recognition of key recovery agents ~~and certificate authorities~~; and to safeguard privacy and prevent commercial espionage. The President shall consider a country's refusal to negotiate such mutual recognition agreements when considering the participation of the United States in any cooperation or assistance program with that country. The President shall report to the Congress if negotiations are not complete by the end of 1999.

TITLE VIII -- RESEARCH AND MONITORING

SECTION 801 OF THIS TITLE SHOULD BE DELETED. IT IS UNNECESSARY TO CREATE A NEW BOARD. SOME SUBSET OF THIS AUTHORITY SHOULD BE GIVEN TO THE EXISTING COMPUTER SYSTEM SECURITY AND PRIVACY ADVISORY BOARD. THERE IS NO NEED TO CREATE A NEW LAYER OF BUREAUCRACY.

TITLE IX – WAIVER AUTHORITY

THIS TITLE SHOULD BE DELETED ALTOGETHER, AS IT UNDERMINES THE MARKETPLACE CERTAINTY PROVIDED BY THE REMAINDER OF THE BILL.